FEEDING THE DRAGON

FEEDING THE DRAGON

a culinary travelogue through china with recipes

东食西读

MARY KATE TATE & NATE TATE

Andrews McMeel
Publishing, LLC

Kansas City • Sydney • London

Andrews McMeel Publishing, LLC
an Andrews McMeel Universal company
1130 Walnut Street, Kansas City, Missouri 64106

www.andrewsmcmeel.com
www.feedingthedragon.com

11 12 13 14 15 TEN 10 9 8 7 6 5 4 3 2 1

Library of Congress Control Number: 2010937874

ISBN: 978-1-4494-0111-5

Design: Kate Basart/Union Pageworks
Photography: Nate Tate and Mary Kate Tate, except for page ii by Jonathan Leijonhufvud

Attention: Schools and Businesses
Andrews McMeel books are available at quantity discounts with bulk purchase for educational, business, or sales promotional use. For information, please e-mail the Andrews McMeel Publishing Special Sales Department:
specialsales@amuniversal.com

For Mom & Dad

CONTENTS (THE ITINERARY)

RECIPES BY CATEGORY

The recipes in this book are arranged in the order of our travel itinerary. If you are looking for a specific category of food, browse this list and then refer to the index on page 281 for recipe page numbers.

APPETIZERS AND SALADS

Beijing Summer Salad
Spicy Stir-Fry Peanuts
Tea Eggs
Radish and Baby Corn Quick Pickles
Ham and Cheese Bundles with Honey-Pear Sauce
Potato Balls with Spicy Dipping Sauce
Cool Cucumber-Pear Salad
Tsampa with Tomato Chutney Sauce
Jiaozi Dumplings
Guotie Pot Stickers
Shanghai Soup Dumplings
Char Siu Pork Buns
Macau Table Salad
Vegetable Momo Dumplings with Cilantro-Yogurt Dipping Sauce
Dai Tomato-Mint Salad
Wild Mushroom Salad
Kashgar Onion Salad
Tangy Chickpea Salad

SOUPS

Hot and Sour Soup
Comfort Beef Noodle Soup
Wonton Soup
Peanut–Pork Chop Soup
Cheater's Roast Duck Soup
Macanese Caldo Verde Soup
Tamarind Pork Stew
Barley Beer Beef Soup
Tibetan Noodle Soup

POULTRY

Peking Duck
Jian Bing Crêpes
Soy Sauce Chicken
Farmhouse Omelet
Chicken Spring Rolls
Chicken Lettuce Cups
Coca-Cola Chicken Wings
African Chicken
Lemongrass Chicken Wings

Bang Bang Chicken
Kung Pao Chicken
Nepalese Chicken Tarkari
Uighur Roast Chicken
Big Plate o' Chicken

MEAT

Mao's Favorite Pork (Hong Shao Pork)
Mongolian Hot Pot
Sesame Dipping Sauce
Char Siu Roast Pork
Black Bean Spareribs
Pork Chop Buns with Chili-Soy Mayonnaise
Hei Sanduo Pork and Greens Stir-Fry
Tangerine Beef
Grilled Lamb Kebabs with Yogurt
Sichuan Hot Pot

SEAFOOD AND FISH

Ma La Crawfish (aka Spicy Little Dragon Shrimp)
Popiah Rolls
Ginger-Steamed Fish
Mussels with Black Bean Sauce
Peel 'em and Eat 'em Shrimp with Chile-Soy Dipping Sauce
Sweet and Sour Shrimp
Macanese Crab Curry
Dai Banana Leaf Fish
Sichuan Spicy Fish

VEGETABLES AND TOFU

Stir-Fry Spinach with Oyster Sauce
Stir-Fry Potatoes and Peppers
Buddha's Delight
Corn and Pine Nut Stir-Fry
Stir-Fry Sugar Snap Peas
Stir-Fry Baby Bok Choy
Spicy Sichuan Green Beans
Mapo Tofu
Fish Fragrant Eggplant
Stir-Fry Bean Sprouts

Tibetan Curry Potatoes

NOODLES, RICE AND BREAD

Shanghai Fried Noodles
Yangzhou Fried Rice
Sha Cha Noodles
Chicken and Mushroom Congee
Macanese Fried Rice
Crossing the Bridge Noodles
Pineapple Rice
Dan Dan Noodles
Polo Carrot Rice
Laghman Noodles with Tomato Sauce
Naan Flatbread

DESSERTS

Bread Bun Dessert
Chocolate-Sesame Balls
Youtiao Fried Dough Sticks
Mango Pudding
Danta Vanilla Custard Tarts
Macanese Almond Cookies
Fried Bananas
Green Tea Shortbread Cookies
Raisin-Walnut Pastries

DRINKS AND COCKTAILS

Lychee Martini
The Shanghai Lil Cocktail
Hong Kong Milk Tea
Hot Ginger-Lemon Coke
Dragon Fruit Sangria
Jungle Passion Fruit Smoothie
Strawberry-Chile Cocktail
Tibetan Butter Tea
Cinnamon Spice Tea

O f his travels and observations in China, the travel writer Colin Thubron wrote that it was "the land of a billion uncomprehended people." Watching the foreign landscape whiz by through the window of the train—a land of rural farming villages and factory cooling towers connected by unkempt roads and scattered with unfamiliar trees—I can't help but feel just as overwhelmed. A history stretching back to the Xia Dynasty and prehistoric times, China is a world comprised of varied peoples with their own subcultures, variations of Mandarin, and unique foods to dish up. Even a lifetime seems too short for the greatest of sinologists to explore and comprehend. I look over at my brother, his head bouncing with the train, eyes still fighting jet lag, and I wonder what we're doing here. Who do we think we are? Two twentysomethings, packs on our back, meager belongings, and an ambition bigger than both of our résumés combined. How could we possibly record each person's story, taste every dish? Have we bitten off more than we can chew?

—MARY KATE, *travelogue day 1, May 23, 2005*

INTRODUCTION

I unfolded the map and spread it out on the restaurant table, moving a plate of dumplings and our two half-empty glasses of Tsingtao beer to the side. A long hand-drawn black line traced what would be our itinerary over the summer, starting from Beijing, the capital city of China, and then running down China's east coast, looping through the southern jungles of Yunnan Province, over the Tibetan Plateau in the west, through the Taklimakan Desert in the north near Afghanistan, and then back to the capital.

When I had drawn this line—a 9,700-mile line across eighteen provinces and territories—months ago with a Sharpie marker in my apartment back in New York City, it had seemed like the trip would be easy enough. My younger sister, Mary Kate, and I would meet in Beijing over our college summer breaks and then travel around the country collecting photos, travel stories, and traditional Chinese recipes to compile what I called a "culinary travelogue." By my estimate we would only need a few weeks to test all of the recipes once we were back in the United States. Sure, we didn't have a book deal with a publisher, but I had convinced myself that would be a minor detail; the whole effort—the research, the travel, studying regional foods, testing the recipes, getting a literary agent and a publisher—would be finished by the end of the summer. "It will be in bookstores in time for Christmas!" I assured my skeptical parents. Now, having arrived jetlagged in Beijing with two backpacks (weighing forty

and sixty pounds respectively) stuffed full of books, new camera equipment, blank journals, two laptop computers, a Chinese dictionary, and three very maxed-out credit cards, the line on the map looked at best overly ambitious and at worst like the scribblings of a crazy man.

"So we're going to just walk into restaurants and ask the chef if we can go into the kitchen and watch him cook?" Mary Kate asked.

"Yeeeah. That's our plan," I said, a little unsure.

"And I'm going to write down our travel stories while you write down how to cook the food, right?" she asked.

"Yes, and at the same time we're both going to be taking photos," I said.

"Okay. But I don't know how to take amazing photos and neither do you," she said.

"Well, we're going to have to figure it out," I replied.

"Figuring it out" proved to be the theme of our summer. Mary Kate was studying film at the University of Texas at Austin and I was majoring in graphic design at the School of Visual Arts in New York City, but travel photography was a whole new beast for us. As we learned to work our cameras, photography became a way for us to connect with the people we met and an opportunity for us to document the beauty of rarely visited parts of China. We also figured out how to travel on a very tight budget by taking any mode of transportation we could find and afford. This mostly came down to trains (some legs lasting

more than thirty hours), but we also rode on rickshaws, motorcycles, bikes, taxis, buses, horses, camels, boats, rafts, ferries, planes, and even a donkey cart. We stayed in more than forty different accommodations (none exactly luxurious), including a monastery in Tibet, a tarp propped up by sticks in the jungle, and a park bench in Hong Kong's Kowloon district.

The most important thing we figured out was how to collect recipes. Asking a chef to share his secrets with us or making friends with someone only to invite ourselves back to his or her home to cook a meal together was awkward at first, but we were rarely turned away; Chinese people are incredibly hospitable, especially when they realize you are a foreigner who has made the effort to learn to speak their language. I can only imagine trying something like this in a restaurant in New York City by approaching the waitress: "The meal was excellent! Do you mind if we go back in the kitchen to observe the chef and write down his recipes?" I picture a Gordon Ramsay–like character bursting forth from the kitchen wielding a large ladle and screaming at us to leave his restaurant at once. In China, we were often greeted as friends or even as family and ushered into home and restaurant kitchens alike. A family in Fujian Province invited us to stay for the weekend and cook stir-fry after stir-fry with vegetables picked straight from the backyard garden and to learn to prepare steamed fish that was caught in the nearby river. A chef from Xinjiang Province outfitted us in chef's whites and put us to work in his restaurant making hand-pulled noodles and *samsa* pies alongside fifty other line cooks. Food is central to Chinese culture and a source of national pride. Most cooks were so happy to share their knowledge with us in hopes that we could enjoy the food of China too and share it with others.

By the end of the summer, we had followed the black line on our map to its end, and it seemed we'd lived enough adventures and eaten enough for a lifetime. We had played soccer on the grasslands of Inner Mongolia, discovered what were, in our opinion, the best soup dumplings in the world, ridden more than 180 miles on bicycles through mountains while at one point being chased by a pack of feral dogs, toured a soy sauce factory, witnessed a massive protest for democracy

in Hong Kong, and learned to make *tsampa* from monks in Tibet. We had notebooks and journals filled with handwritten recipes, travel notes, and interviews, and two computer hard drives full of photos, but we certainly didn't have a completed book. What we had instead was a strong friendship rooted in our joint solidarity for the project. This would propel us to cook and test our recipes stateside for years to come and eventually to move back to China to complete the book.

Feeding the Dragon is the story of our gastronomic adventure crisscrossing China, and its chapters are arranged according to our travel itinerary to highlight the cultural and culinary uniqueness of the nine specific regions in China we find most inspiring. In addition to our intense culinary tour that we chronicle in this book, Mary Kate and I have been traveling back to China over the past ten years: living, working, traveling, and studying. Our goal for this book from the beginning was to bring accessible yet traditional Chinese recipes

to novice cooks in the West. Beyond observing cooks at work in China and tasting every dish we found, Mary Kate and I have streamlined our recipes by testing them in our tiny New York City apartment kitchens while using ingredients readily found in the West. We include step-by-step preparation techniques but also time-saving work-around options. The Glossary includes descriptions and equivalent substitutions for unfamiliar ingredients as well as their Chinese names to help you navigate the daunting shelves at local Asian grocery stores.

Our unlikely obsession with all things China and Chinese food has changed our lives, but the fact that we ever got interested in the country at all was almost a fluke. I started college studying business at Baylor University in Texas and I needed a language credit. My dad insisted that I study Mandarin Chinese. "China is the future of business, son. Mark my words," he said, and so after a few semesters of Chinese classes, I headed to Beijing's prestigious Tsinghua University in early

2001 as the first student to take advantage of Baylor's study-abroad program in China.

My first few weeks in China were difficult. The little Chinese I had learned in Texas could barely get me anywhere, and I had to come up with elaborate charades to communicate with people. I bought a shiny new bicycle to get around town, which was promptly stolen. To make matters worse, most restaurant menus were written only in Chinese characters. I didn't see anything that looked like egg rolls, General Tso's chicken, or the Chinese food I had eaten in America at mall food courts. Instead I ate food from street vendors, which I could easily order by pointing and grunting. Things started looking up, however, after surviving the initial culture shock and a bout of typhoid fever. I started learning how to get around Beijing on my own. I bought a rusty old bike that no one would ever want to steal and a better lock. I gathered very little from classes that I did not regularly attend, but I discovered Chinese culture and food by exploring the city and befriending the people I met.

During the middle of that school year abroad, Mary Kate came to visit me for a few months. She was still in high school back in Ohio, and it was thrilling for me to show her China. She was shocked to find out that sushi was not Chinese but actually from Japan, an entirely different country, and that Chinese characters were not just decorations and tattoos, but that people actually read them. Traveling together around the country, we found our definition of Chinese food changing with each

new place we visited. Sure, we found stir-fries and *kung pao* chicken, but we also ate mouth-numbingly spicy food in Sichuan Province, tropical food from the southern province of Yunnan, Portuguese fusion dishes in Macau, Muslim food in Xinjiang Province (lamb kebabs and flatbreads), *dim sum* dishes in Hong Kong, Tibetan vegetarian dishes, Mongolian hot pot from Inner Mongolia, and home-style northern Beijing food. This eye-opening culinary excursion triggered a fascination in us, and after we shared an adrenaline-filled near-death experience while lost in China's southern jungles, we both knew we'd be back again someday to write a book about these amazing foods that can't be found in the West. We had found a new frontier in China and a people with whom we readily connected despite the culture gap. Back in Beijing, I immersed myself in the Chinese culture and language and began experimenting with Asian cooking techniques, starting from scratch. I got hooked on cooking Chinese food through watching and learning from Xiao Zhang, my extremely patient *ayi*, or housekeeper. Stateside, Mary Kate learned Mandarin in college classes that she regularly attended, and she ended up having her own study-abroad experience at Nanjing Normal University.

Our joint interest in adventurous eating began early. Our dad was in the United States Air Force, and we had the opportunity to experience the food of other cultures while living and traveling around the world. Our mom is an incredible cook, and she was constantly trying out new

recipes with us from her cookbook collection, which seemed to grow exponentially each time we traveled to a new place. By high school we had eaten grilled pigeon at the foot of the Great Pyramids and ceviche served on a banana leaf in Central America, but having never traveled anywhere in Asia meant that the little we learned about Asian culture and food was picked up from Jackie Chan movies and Chinese take-out restaurants. We now know that there's a whole lot more to the East. Chinese cuisine is a world of food and is by far our favorite to cook and eat.

We are honored to have the opportunity to share with you our passion for cooking Chinese food and to bring you along on our adventures of traveling and eating in this fascinating country. Chinese food is meant to be eaten and enjoyed with friends and family, and we hope you have as much fun cooking the recipes in this book as we do.

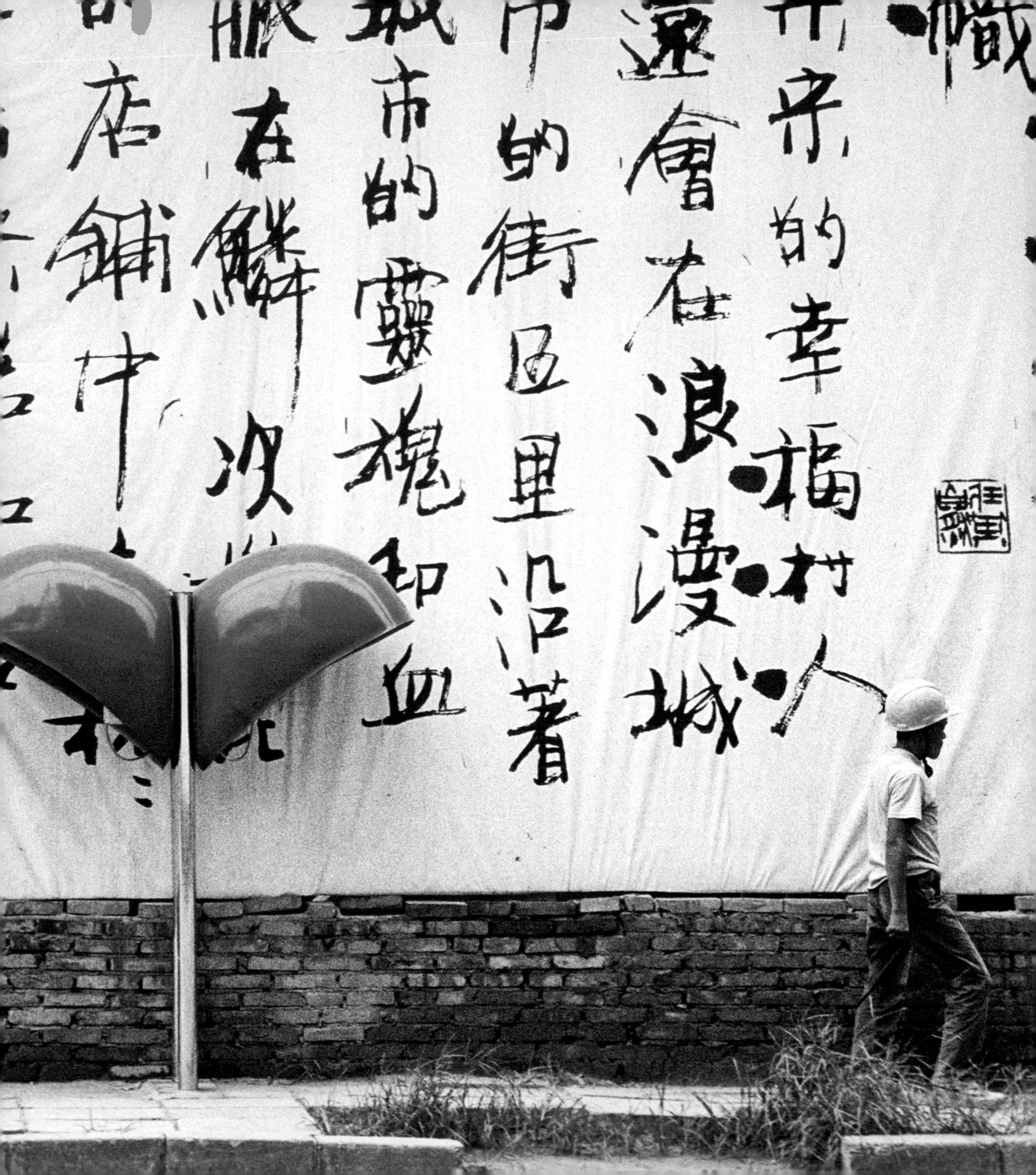
的幸福村人
還會在浪漫城
市的街
城市的靈魂和血
在鱗次
的店鋪中

BEIJING

北京

BEIJING 北京

My bike hums along the crowded streets of Beijing, the capital of the People's Republic of China, where rickety rickshaws and Mercedes-Benz cars compete for the road. Poplar trees, tall as buildings, sing in the November winds high above my head, and by moonlight I see the city's skyline—a vast field of sprouting skyscrapers coloring the night and illuminating the numerous construction cranes that stretch ever higher below. In the shadows, Beijing's ancient stone structures that baffle the Western mind and hint at a 3,000-year history—the Forbidden City, the Temple of Heaven, the ten-meter-high Beijing wall remnants—are swallowed by the night.

Exploring Beijing is a favorite pastime of mine. It is never anything fancy or planned, but just me and a bike on a road that never ends; Beijing is 100 miles across, with new adventures around every bend. Tonight I veer down a back alley and follow a narrow path that smells of gritty, smoldering coals. During Beijing winters, families use coal furnaces to heat their homes—I am far from mine and in the cold air I can see my breath.

I lean my bike against a graffitied wall and venture into the darkness on foot. Down the road, a fruit-cart vendor sells fresh-carved pineapple on sticks to a group of older men. For five *mao* (four cents), I buy my own. "Hello! Hello!" one of the men hollers at me. A few others chime in, in what surely is to be their only English word, "Hello!" I wave back and flash them the international thumbs-up sign. Standing, sitting, squatting—they crowd around a wooden Chinese chessboard lying on the ground. Shuffling aside, they gesture for me to join. Above the chessboard, an exposed lightbulb dangles by twine and covers us in a warm yellow glow. The bright lights of the city seem ages away.

A salt-and-pepper-haired man points to me and says, "These chess pieces are older than you!" I answer back timidly in Mandarin, wishing I had paid more attention in Chinese class, "But not older than you." The night erupts in laughter—I must be a sight. Not only am I a foreigner wandering their neighborhood at night in the dead of winter, I am also one who speaks Chinese. Forgetting the cold and the long ride

home still ahead of me, I sit through the night and practice my Chinese with a most forgiving audience.

I fell in love with China as a study-abroad student at Tsinghua University in Beijing, and this is now my seventh return. China's food, its art, its history and culture have captivated my imagination, but it is the people who keep me coming back. With the many wondrous landmarks to visit in Beijing, its über-modern architecture to gawk at, and all the pomp surrounding the 2008 Summer Olympic Games, travelers can easily miss the best that Beijing has to offer. But slip down a back alley and join a game of Chinese chess, journey through a *hutong* (ancient neighborhood of alleyways), or wander into a noodle shop that is not in any tourist book, and there you will come face to face with the heart of the city—its enigmatic, openhearted residents, or *Beijingren* (Beijingers), as they have titled themselves.

Beijingren are a proud people, and rightly so; Beijing is the political and cultural center of China. If residents of the rest of the country start to forget this, they need only look as far as a clock. Despite covering three traditional time zones, all of China runs on Beijing time. The government in Beijing is also

responsible for writing all of the country's laws and for the standard Mandarin dialect.

In 3,000 years of history, Beijing has seen Imperial rule, Mongolian domination, and Communist revolution, and has recently become the site of one of the biggest construction booms in history. In an effort to exceed the expectations of the world, Beijing spent more than 40 billion U.S. dollars hosting the 2008 Summer Olympics.

Culturally, Beijing could hardly be more diverse, and nowhere is this diversity more apparent than on the city's menus. International expatriates and all fifty-six official ethnic minorities of China are represented in the city, each group of people bringing with them their own ideas of food. Lamb kebabs, Mongolian hot pots, and steamed breads are but a few of the foods that compose the city's culinary identity. Traditional Beijing food is a northern home-style cuisine with a mix of hearty Shandong Province food and spicy dishes from Sichuan Province. With so many dishes available, Mary Kate and I are back in Beijing on the start of our travelogue adventure to find the recipes that we feel best highlight the personality of the city and the people we have come to know and love.

HOT AND SOUR SOUP · 酸辣汤

Whenever I feel under the weather, I like to curl up on the couch with a bowl of Hot and Sour Soup and watch bad TV. This soup's list of ingredients reads like a Chinese-medicine doctor's prescription for the common cold. Chinese healing remedies like black tree ear fungus, ginger, black Chinese mushrooms, and lily buds all make an appearance. Although I cannot vouch for the actual healing properties of the ingredients, I always feel better after finishing a bowl.

There is some debate over the origins of hot and sour soup. Most people, however, agree that it came out of Sichuan Province, an area known for its spicy food, because its broth has the bold flavors of hot chili oil, spicy white pepper, and sour black vinegar. Regardless, Beijing chefs have wholeheartedly embraced the soup as their own creation. You can find it on many home-style (*jia chang cai*) restaurant menus around the city.

After several attempts (and watching a *Baywatch* marathon on TV), we were able to re-create this soup back in my New York City apartment. We think our recipe achieves the perfect balance between hot and sour. It is based on the hot and sour soups we tasted in Beijing, but we replaced the traditional ground pork with protein-rich tofu.

SERVES 4

Soak the lily buds, mushrooms, and tree ear fungus in separate bowls of hot water for 20 minutes. In a small bowl, toss the tofu strips with the soy sauce and let marinate. Drain the lily buds and cut off their tips, slice lengthwise, and then cut each in half. Drain the mushrooms and reserve 1 cup of the mushroom soaking water. Cut off and discard the mushroom stems. Drain the tree ear fungus and then slice the mushroom caps and tree ear fungus into thin strips. Whisk the egg and sesame oil together in a small bowl.

In a large saucepan or wok, combine the stock, lily buds, mushrooms, mushroom soaking water, tree ear fungus, tofu and marinade, bamboo shoots, ginger, black rice vinegar, chili oil, salt, and white pepper. Bring to a boil over medium heat, and then decrease the heat and simmer for 6 minutes. Stir in the cornstarch slurry and simmer for 1 minute. Slowly pour the egg mixture into the soup, stirring continuously so that the egg forms little threads.

Before serving, sprinkle each bowl of soup with the chopped green onions and cilantro leaves.

10 dried lily buds

5 dried Chinese black mushrooms

1 (2-inch-square) dried black tree ear fungus

8 ounces firm tofu, cut into strips

1 tablespoon light soy sauce

1 large egg, beaten

2 teaspoons toasted sesame oil

4 cups Chicken Stock (page 262) or low-sodium chicken broth

½ cup bamboo shoots, slivered

1 teaspoon minced fresh ginger

½ cup Chinese black rice vinegar

1 tablespoon Chili Oil (page 257)

½ teaspoon salt

1 teaspoon freshly ground white pepper

2 tablespoons cornstarch, dissolved in 1/3 cup cold water

2 green onions, green parts only, chopped

Handful of fresh cilantro leaves, coarsely chopped

STIR-FRY SPINACH WITH OYSTER SAUCE · 蚝油炒菠菜

Stir-frying, called *chao* (炒), is a Chinese cooking technique used to preserve textures and lock in flavors and essential antioxidants. Using little oil, cooks quickly fry vegetables over high heat to retain their crunchy goodness. This stir-fry recipe uses spinach but will work with virtually any leafy green.

SERVES 4

Combine the soy sauce, oyster sauce, sugar, and cornstarch in a small bowl and mix well.

Heat the vegetable oil in a wok over high heat. Add the garlic and stir-fry for 10 seconds. Add the spinach and stir-fry for about 1 minute, or until the leaves are slightly wilted. Add the soy sauce mixture to the wok and stir-fry for 20 seconds. Drizzle a little sesame oil over the spinach and serve.

1 teaspoon light soy sauce
1 tablespoon oyster sauce
½ teaspoon sugar
1 teaspoon cornstarch
2 tablespoons vegetable oil
3 cloves garlic, sliced
12 ounces spinach, tough stems
    removed
Toasted sesame oil, for drizzling

BREAD BUN DESSERT · 炸馒头

Kitchens in China do not have ovens. Consequently there are no baked goods in traditional Chinese cooking, not even baked breads or baked cakes. Rather, flour products are steamed in bamboo steamers. Steamed bread, or *man tou* (馒头), is a staple carbohydrate of the northern Chinese diet.

Bread Bun Dessert is steamed bread buns fried and dipped in sweetened condensed milk. When you take a bite, their crispy shells give way to a soft and fluffy center unique to steamed bread. The gooey dipping sauce complements the dessert's texture and adds a well-placed sweetness. These fried buns are a quick dessert to prepare for a large party and are best served while their golden crusts are still hot from the wok. You can buy packages of frozen steamed bread buns at most Asian markets or at specialty grocery stores.

SERVES 4

Heat 2 inches of oil in a wok over medium heat until a small piece of bread added to it turns golden brown in 30 seconds. Place 4 or 5 bread buns in the wok and fry, turning frequently in the oil, for about 1 minute, or until they turn golden brown. Remove the buns with a perforated strainer and place on paper towels to drain. Fry the remaining buns.

Sprinkle the cinnamon, if using, over the fried buns and pour the condensed milk into a small bowl for dipping. Serve piping hot.

Oil, for deep-frying
12 (3-inch-long) frozen Chinese
    steamed bread buns, thawed
1 teaspoon ground cinnamon
    (optional)
1 (8-ounce) can sweetened
    condensed milk

IMPERIAL CUISINE: A SLICE OF HEAVEN

One grande macchiato with skim milk!" yelled the barista from behind the counter. I grabbed my coffee and shuffle out the door, past hordes of tourists. I couldn't believe they had put a Starbucks there in the middle of the Forbidden City, the ancient Imperial Palace in Beijing; times sure have changed. From the Xia Dynasty in the twenty-first century B.C. until the collapse of the Qing Dynasty in 1911, China thrived under Imperial rule. The Emperor, or "Son of Heaven," enjoyed ultimate authority on earth. In the fifteenth century, the Forbidden City was built to accommodate the Emperor's excessive lifestyle and to provide a home for him, his royal family, his concubines, and his Imperial court. The palace is said to have 9,999 rooms and cover 200 acres. In the twenty-first century A.D., it was updated with a Starbucks though the coffee shop has since been removed.

Imperial chefs had a lot on their plate. Not only did they have to serve the Emperor a spread of 150 to 300 dishes per day but the meals also had to be a slice of heaven. The recipes were so involved and the craftsmanship so intricate that some Imperial chefs spent their entire lives perfecting one dish. Vegetables were ornately cut to resemble orchids. Elaborate designs were carved on melon rinds. Shark fins, snakes, camel hooves, and other exotic ingredients were creatively incorporated into dishes. A particularly special delicacy for the Emperor was an edible bird's nest made from the saliva of the rare swiftlet bird. The nests were dangerously extracted from the high ceilings of caves in southern Asia. Before the Emperor would partake of his meal, an attending eunuch was required to taste the food, testing for poison with each bite. They would also insert a silver plate into the food, believing that it would change color if fatal toxins were present.

"Imperial cuisine" is the school of cooking that developed out of this extravagant culinary culture, and its influence lingers today. It is said that each Imperial cuisine dish should be a work of art; color and presentation are paramount. Today, many Beijing restaurants still prepare meals in this spectacular style of cooking, and rare ingredients like snakes and shark fins continue to be delicacies in Chinese restaurants worldwide. Peking duck (or Beijing duck), appropriately named after its city of origin, is a popular and world-renowned Imperial cuisine dish.

Swiftlet bird's nest, though a decidedly scarce commodity, is also still available to purchase. However, if you are set on making bird's nest soup, be ready to fork out some dough. Six ounces of cave swiftlet bird's nests cost upward of $1,500 on the streets of New York's Chinatown.

PEKING DUCK · 北京烤鸭

Peking Duck (Beijing Duck) is probably the most well-known dish from Beijing, and it is a favorite of locals and foreigners alike. We think of it as the Chinese fajita: crispy skin, juicy and succulent duck meat, wedges of sliced cucumber, slivers of green onion, and tangy sauce, all wrapped up in a thin tortilla-like pancake.

If you have never made it yourself, keep reading! It is not as difficult as it looks. There are only four main ingredients. We often make Peking Duck at dinner parties when we really want to impress our guests but do not feel like cooking for hours in the kitchen.

The key to cooking great Peking Duck is getting the skin crispy while keeping the meat inside moist. Beijing chefs do this by first pumping the ducks with air so that the skin separates from the fatty meat. Then they blanch the birds, coat them with sugary syrup, and hang them in a windy space to dry for up to twenty-four hours. When the skin is dry and stiff, the ducks are roasted in a special oven where they hang for hours over coals and fragrant smoking wood chips until their skin turns that bright orange color.

Obviously, you are not going to be able to cook Peking Duck at home using this elaborate process, but we have devised an easy method that works just as well. You don't have to pump the duck with air, and you can use your regular oven. When you serve the dish, instruct your guests on how to assemble a duck "fajita." To add a final bit of theatrics, carve the duck tableside.

SERVES 4 TO 6

Bring a large pot of water to a boil. Use a knife to scrape any rough patches off the duck's skin. Remove the innards if necessary, cut off the wing tips, and remove excess fat around the cavity opening. Rinse the duck and blanch in the boiling water for 4 minutes. Remove and pat dry with paper towels.

Combine the honey, rice wine, and warm water in a small bowl. Liberally brush several coats of the honey mixture all over the duck. Place the duck upright in a refrigerator and let dry for 6 hours, uncovered—or speed up this step by drying the duck with a hair dryer (on the cool setting) for 20 minutes. (We developed this shortcut one night when we were running way behind schedule. The results are comparable. However, try to complete this special step before your guests arrive, as you will look silly blow-drying dinner in the kitchen!)

Preheat the oven to 400°F. Place the duck breast side up on a broiling pan and cover loosely with foil to prevent burning. Roast the duck for 1 hour and 20 minutes. Remove the foil and roast for an additional 10 minutes, or until the skin turns a deep orange-brown.

Place the green onions and cucumber slivers on a serving plate. Warm the individual pancakes in a dry skillet over high heat for a few seconds and place them on a separate serving plate. Carve the duck with a sharp knife into thin strips and arrange the meat on a platter. Now you are ready to make Chinese fajitas: Roll some of the duck meat, green onions, cucumber, and a smear of Chinese sweet noodle sauce up in a Mandarin pancake, eat, and repeat.

1 (5-pound) duck
3 tablespoons honey
1 tablespoon Shaoxing rice wine or dry sherry
1 tablespoon warm water
8 green onions, white parts only, slivered into 3-inch lengths
1 medium English cucumber, peeled and slivered into 3-inch lengths
20 Mandarin Pancakes (purchased frozen, or see page 260)
½ cup Chinese sweet noodle sauce

JIAOZI DUMPLINGS ▪ 饺子

It is no coincidence that in Chinese, the word for "family" (*jia*, 家) is the same as the word for "home"; home is a central part of family life in China. Parents, children, mothers-in-law, grandparents, and other family members often all live together for generations, taking care of one another. *Jiaozi*, or classic Chinese dumplings, is a dish that celebrates this supportive community. Often made at holidays, these labor-intensive dumplings are prepared in an assembly line, with the greatest to the least in the family all having a hand in their production.

The process starts when wheat dough is kneaded, rolled flat into teacup-size circles, and stacked as dumpling wrappers. The next person in the line spoons a pork or vegetable filling (depending on the recipe) in the center of each wrap before passing them on to the "crimper." My first experience making *jiaozi* was at the house of one of my professors, Mr. Zhang. Having been invited to dinner, I was surprised when Mr. Zhang put me to work in the kitchen. I was the "crimper," charged with folding and crimping the edges of the dumpling wrappers to form plump, sealed pockets of goodness ready to be thrown into a boiling pot. That night, in that room full of brothers, sisters, cousins, and grandparents who were not my own, all of us working together to make *jiaozi*, I felt more like family than simply a guest in the Zhang home. Invite your friends and family over and put them to work. We like to make more dumplings than we can eat and freeze the extra for later (see Dumpling Freezing Tips on page 256).

MAKES ABOUT 60 DUMPLINGS

To make the filling, toss the cabbage and salt together in a large bowl and let sit for 15 minutes. Drain the cabbage in a colander over a sink and use your hands to squeeze out excess moisture.

In a large mixing bowl, combine the cabbage, pork, soy sauce, rice wine, sesame oil, ginger, green onions, and pepper. Stir in one direction with a chopstick until just mixed.

To form the dumplings, rest a wrapper in the palm of your hand and place a heaping teaspoon of filling in the center. Dip your finger in a bowl of water and run it around the edge to help make a good seal. Lightly fold the wrapper over on itself but don't touch the edges together. Starting at one end, use your fingers to make a small pleat on the side of the wrapper closest to you, then press the pleat into the other side and pinch together firmly. Keep making pleats down the dumpling opening in this way until completely sealed (see Dumpling Folding Tips on page 255). Repeat this process with the remaining filling and wrappers.

Bring a large pot of water to a boil. Drop half of the dumplings into the water and stir once so they don't stick together. When the water boils again, add 1 cup of cold water to the pot. Then when it boils again, add 3 cups of cold water. The third time the water boils, the dumplings are cooked. Remove them with a slotted spoon and repeat with the remaining dumplings. Serve immediately with small bowls of Chinese black rice vinegar for dipping.

FILLING
2½ cups minced napa cabbage
½ teaspoon salt
11 ounces ground pork
2 tablespoons light soy sauce
2 teaspoons Shaoxing rice wine or dry sherry
2 teaspoons toasted sesame oil
1 teaspoon minced fresh ginger
½ cup minced green onions, green and white parts
1/8 teaspoon freshly ground black pepper

▪

About 60 round Dumpling Wrappers (purchased premade, or see page 258)
Chinese black rice vinegar, for dipping

Just south of Beijing's Houhai Lake, past the record shop and left around the corner, you will find a man called "Eagle Kite Wang." When he is not flying a kite alone (usually his giant eagle kite) or entertaining tourists with acrobatic kite-flying stunts, he is sitting in his workshop in a courtyard home in Nanguanfang Hutong, making kites by hand.

Hutong neighborhoods in Beijing, like Nanguan-fang Hutong, are a motley of ancient alleyways with houses, restaurants, and shops. Once covering the entire city in a radial pattern that converged on the central Imperial Palace (the Forbidden City), *hutongs* now account for only a small fraction of the city. Still, an ancient, close-knit community way of life lives on in the courtyards and conversations within the brick walls of the remaining *hutongs*.

Wandering these neighborhoods is like journey-ing back in time to Old Beijing. In the alleyways, you can overhear old-timers swap stories, their caged pet birds singing nearby, and listen in on women gossiping about their neighbors over a pot of jasmine tea and a game of mah-jongg. The typi-cal residences of *hutongs* are *siheyuan*, or courtyards shared by four adjoining homes, leaving little room for secrets: Everybody knows everybody's business. Peek inside an open gate, through a circular door-way, and curiosity will get the best of you. Entering, you will venture into a beautiful courtyard of brick and stone, potted chrysanthemums and roses, bikes, and birdcages. You will linger under the cypress tree

but will soon be shooed away by a woman cooling herself with a large bamboo fan. You are, after all, standing in her yard. These might not be your exact experiences roaming the *hutong* alleyways, but you will almost certainly encounter fascinating residents and discover one-of-a-kind curio shops. In fact, this is how we found Eagle Kite Wang and his Hand-made Chinese Kite Shop.

Nate and I were lost in the winding *hutongs* near Houhai Lake, getting nowhere but angrier, when Wang Chi Feng, a kindly man in his fifties, invited us into his workshop. The room took my breath away. A menagerie of exotic animals surrounded us, kites so intricate and colorful they looked real: dragons, but-terflies, parrots, and frogs. He paints them ten times to color them perfect. We asked Chi Feng if we could take a picture of him with his favorite kite. He smiled and without hesitation reached for an eagle with a broad wingspan, gingerly lifting it from its place on the wall to perch on his shoulder.

" 'Eagle Kite Wang' they call me," Wang said as we followed him and his bird outside. "I did not always make kites for a living, but kites have always been a part of my life." Kite-making is a 2,000-year-old art, and for Wang it has been a fifty-year love affair. Six years old, under the tutelage of his grandfather, Chi Feng made his first kite, a soaring eagle.

We watched Eagle Kite Wang's bird take to the summer sky, its silk feathers ruffling in the breeze, dart-ing and diving as if on its own accord.

北京 *15*

COMFORT BEEF NOODLE SOUP · 牛肉面

When I was a foreign exchange student new to China, I often wandered the maze of *hutong* alleyways in search of comfort food. I missed my family, and something about beef noodle soup—a dish you cannot go wrong with—brought back memories of Grandma's chicken and dumplings and Mom's homemade chicken soup. Mary Kate and I went back to visit my favorite noodle shop— really just a kiosk that sells *niu rou mian*, beef noodle soup. The shop was crowded with hungry schoolchildren on their way home from school, so I stepped outside into the *hutong* alley. I found an ancient marble block to sit on and pay attention to my favorite noodles: braised and tender beef chunks in a savory and fragrant broth. I greedily slurped up the chewy wheat noodles, drained the bowl, and then leaned back against the *hutong* wall. This soup brings new meaning to the term "comfort food"; it is my favorite home-style (*jia chang cai*) dish.

SERVES 4

1½ pounds beef brisket, cut across the grain into ¼-inch-thick slices
8 cups beef stock or low-sodium beef broth
3 cups water
2 tablespoons Shaoxing rice wine or dry sherry
1 (1-inch) piece ginger, sliced
1 star anise
½ teaspoon sugar
Salt
1 pound fresh or 11 ounces dried Chinese egg noodles
3 cups lightly packed spinach leaves
2 green onions, green parts only, chopped
Toasted sesame oil, for drizzling
Asian chili sauce, such as sriracha sauce, for serving

In a large pot, combine the beef, stock, water, rice wine, ginger, star anise, and sugar. Bring to a boil, then decrease the heat and simmer for 1½ hours. Season to taste with salt.

Prepare the noodles according to their package instructions or boil until al dente. Drain and pile them in 4 large serving bowls.

Add the spinach to the soup pot and let simmer for 1 minute, or until the spinach leaves are bright green and wilted.

Top each bowl of noodles with beef slices and spinach leaves, and ladle the broth into each bowl over the noodles and beef. Sprinkle with the green onions and drizzle with sesame oil. Serve with a side of fiery hot sauce.

JIAN BING CRÊPES ▪ 煎饼

Jian bing street crêpes come with a soundtrack: the continual click of bicycle wheels, the layered sounds of footsteps, sporadic car honks—the sounds of a city morning. They are such a common breakfast in Beijing that local expats have nicknamed them Egg McMaos. During the early morning hours, they are sold from glass-enclosed pull carts parked on sidewalks to some of the 20 million Beijing residents. "Two for one dollar" competes with "three for two" down the congested street.

I go to my favorite *jian bing* cart—kind of like a bagel cart on any street in New York, but not really—on Dongzhimen Wai Street. The woman behind the glass, Yuan Yuan, knows just how I like mine. She drops a spoonful of batter in the center of a hot, circular griddle. Then she uses a wooden squeegee-like tool to spread the batter into a flat crêpe. Brushing whipped egg and sauces onto the surface, scattering spices and fresh green onions, and adding a crunchy wafer to the mix, Yuan Yuan creates a breakfast-to-go masterpiece in less than five minutes. I'm giddy as I wait. *Sizzle . . . pop . . .* and the best sound they make: *crunch.*

I like to fry a bunch of the crunchy wafers and save the extra to crumble on soups or use as funky salsa chips. *Jian bing* uses a couple of sauces (leek flower sauce and red fermented bean curd) that you will have to find in an Asian grocery store. The Glossary (page 264) has the Chinese names for these ingredients so that you can point and shop.

SERVES 4

To make the crunchy wafers, heat ½ inch of oil in a wok over medium heat until a small piece of wonton wrapper added to it turns golden brown in 20 seconds. Drop in a wonton wrapper and fry for about 10 seconds on each side, or until golden brown and crispy. Remove and place on paper towels to drain. Repeat with the remaining wrappers. Set aside.

To make the crêpes, whisk together both types of flour, water, and salt in a mixing bowl until smooth and lump-free. Add water as needed to create a thin, crêpe-like batter. Heat a lightly greased large nonstick skillet (the bigger, the better) over low heat. Drop about 1/3 cup of the batter into the pan and quickly swirl the pan so that the batter spreads evenly. Use a spatula to spread the batter as thinly as possible.

After 1 minute, drop 1 tablespoon of the eggs onto the crêpe surface and spread around using a spatula. Sprinkle some cilantro and green onion over the top. Cook the crêpe for about 1 minute, or until the egg begins to set, then use a spatula to flip the crêpe over. Brush the crêpe with some of the Chinese sweet noodle sauce, leek flower sauce, red fermented bean curd, and chili sauce. Place a crunchy wafer in the center of the crêpe and fold each edge of the crêpe inward, like a package. Use the end of a spatula to break the wafer in half and then fold the whole crêpe in half. Transfer the Jian Bing Crêpe to a serving plate and sprinkle with sesame seeds. Repeat this process with the remaining crêpe batter and fillings. Serve immediately.

CRUNCHY WAFERS
Oil, for deep-frying
4 square wonton wrappers

CRÊPES
½ cup all-purpose flour
½ cup mung bean flour
1½ cups water
¼ teaspoon salt

FILLING
2 large eggs, lightly beaten
4 teaspoons minced fresh cilantro
1 green onion, green and white parts, chopped
2 tablespoons Chinese sweet noodle sauce mixed with 1 tablespoon water
2 teaspoons leek flower sauce
4 teaspoons red fermented bean curd
2 teaspoons Asian chili sauce, such as sriracha sauce
Sesame seeds, for sprinkling

CRICKETS AND OLD BEIJING

"Intent on disturbing the gloomy sleepless soul, the cricket moves toward the bed chirp by chirp."

—LISTEN TO THE CRICKET,
Bei Ju Yi, Tang Dynasty

Somewhere between taking my first bite and asking for my check at a Beijing restaurant, a man two tables over pulled a gourd out of his sleeve, placed it next to his teacup, and began poking it occasionally with premasticated cabbage. Then the gourd chirped.

"Ack! Is that a bug?" I asked my bemused Chinese friend. Crickets, some lauded for their song, others heralded for their fighting skills, have a 2,000-year history as pets in China. Soon I began noticing them everywhere—hanging from bikes, peeking out of pockets, tucked under hats—and I knew I had to get one.

The search for my new companion began with selecting a cage at an open-air market—dusty books and rugs stacked as high as walls and junk galore filled the market stalls. An old-timer with green vest and Coke-bottle glasses unfurled a wool blanket displaying various and sundry insect paraphernalia: ornate collectors' cages made of jade, ivory, bone, brass, or sandalwood; and "ticklers," beard-grass brushes used to provoke crickets before fights. He showed me his favorite cage, a clay pot carved with a dragon and fitted with a brass-hinged lid crafted for small fighting crickets (*qu qu*). However, I was already set on adopting the much larger singing cricket (*guo guo*) despite my fear of their six-inch antennae and mouse-size bodies. After deciding on a simple bamboo woven cage and a name,

Chang Ger, or "Sing Song," came to live with me in my lonely thirteenth-floor apartment.

Cricket lore attributes the origins of cricket captivation to the women of the Imperial Court. The Emperor's three thousand or so concubines spent their entire lives within the walls of the Imperial Palace. When the autumn rains came, they would catch crickets in golden cages and keep them near their pillows. At night, the haunting voice of the cricket would sing their parallel stories to the heavens, the tale of a vivacious life kept in constant emotional distress by the walls that caged them. The elite adopted this chic hobby, followed by the commoners. Soon crickets were bred for tenacity and aggression, and cricket fighting became a favorite sport. In the thirteenth century, the Emperor even appointed a national Cricket Minister, Jia Shi-Dao. Today, the arena sport still draws enormous gambling bets.

I didn't realize Chang Ger's nocturnal nature or the loudness of his chirp until my first night with him at home. His all-night chirping was as loud as a parrot screeching, and I found it impossible to sleep with him around. I tried remedying the situation one night by setting him on the outside of my windowsill. I woke up in the morning well rested, and I threw open my window (a little too fast) to look at the glorious day. Chang Ger had sung his last song.

LYCHEE MARTINI · 荔枝马天尼

Lychees are an unusual tropical fruit native to southern China. They grow in grape-like bunches and have a distinctive flavor—floral, sweet, and tart. To get at their translucent juicy centers, you must peel away their rough purple skin and remove the seed inside.

We first tasted lychee at a dinner party in Beijing. Our host and friend, Li Bijia, brought a bundle to the table as a sweet finale to the meal. I loved the fruit and quickly reached for another . . . and then another. As the peels piled high on my plate, the other dinner guests were amused, but Bijia was not. With a grave face, she warned me that eating too many lychees could cause my eyes to bleed! I suddenly felt quite full.

Bijia went on to explain the Chinese philosophy of yin and yang as it applies to food. Yin and yang is about the unity of opposites, and foods are divided into two opposing categories: "cold" (yin) and "hot" (yang) foods. Despite their names, hot and cold do not refer to temperature. Rather, hot foods are calorie-rich fats and sweets and are thought to stimulate the body's organs and blood flow. Lychees are one of these hot foods. Raw vegetables and most fruits are classified as cold foods and are believed to have the opposite effect, slowing the body's internal processes. A diet of too many hot foods can lead to heart attack and fever, while a diet consisting mainly of cold foods can lead to depression and lethargy. Good nutrition in this philosophy is based on achieving a balance between yin and yang.

These lychee martinis won't make your eyes bleed. They probably won't even throw off your qi, but too many will guarantee you a hangover.

SERVES 2

Bring the water to a boil in a small saucepan and stir in the sugar. Once the sugar is completely dissolved, remove from the heat and let cool to room temperature.

Fill a cocktail shaker with the ice cubes. Add the sugar syrup, vodka, lemon juice, and lychee syrup. Give the cocktail shaker a few good shakes and strain into 2 chilled martini glasses. Garnish each glass with 2 whole lychees and serve.

¼ cup water

¼ cup sugar

Ice cubes

½ cup premium vodka

2 tablespoons freshly squeezed lemon juice

¾ cup lychee syrup from canned lychees

4 lychees, peeled and pitted

CHOCOLATE-SESAME BALLS · 芝麻球

Chocolate is a Western invention and has only been produced in China since the 1980s. We found a restaurant in Beijing that serves chocolate-filled sesame balls. Sesame balls are an ancient Chinese dish traditionally stuffed with sweet red bean or sweet lotus paste. The chef responsible for this creative invention blends old, new, north, south, east, and west flavors and style.

People eat sesame balls for good luck during the Chinese New Year. Because the dough balls expand in the hot oil, tripling in size, they are seen as a metaphor for a successful investment.

MAKES ABOUT 10 BALLS

2 cups glutinous rice flour
⅓ cup rice flour
⅓ cup sugar
1 cup warm water
¾ cup coarsely chopped milk chocolate or sweet red bean paste
¾ cup sesame seeds
Oil, for deep-frying

Mix together both types of flour in a large mixing bowl. In a small bowl, dissolve the sugar in the water, and then slowly stir the mixture into the flour. Use your hands to knead the dough in the bowl until is has a consistency like cookie dough.

Use your hands to form the dough into golf ball–size balls. Then use your thumb to make a deep indentation in each ball, and fill the holes with a heaping teaspoon of chocolate. Pinch the hole closed with your fingers so that the filling is sealed inside. Roll the balls between your hands until they are smooth and round. Spread the sesame seeds on a plate or a flat surface and fill a medium bowl with water. Lightly dip each dough ball into the water and then roll the balls in the sesame seeds until completely covered. Use your hands to press the seeds into the dough balls if needed.

Heat 2 inches of oil in a wok over low heat. Fry 5 balls at a time in the oil for 20 minutes, constantly turning the balls with a spatula. Take care not to let the oil get too hot or the balls will burn! When the dough balls start to puff up, very lightly apply pressure on their tops with the spatula to help them grow larger. Remove the balls with a perforated strainer and place on paper towels to drain. Repeat the process with the remaining balls. Serve immediately.

THE CULTURAL REVOLUTION AND BEYOND

Professor Yang stood by the window, his eyes focused on some far-off time or place. When he finally spoke, he addressed the rain. "I was a member of the Red Guard during the Cultural Revolution," he said as my classmates and I shifted in our seats. "We threw books at our schoolteacher, we hit him with our fists. He was teaching the old ways. We were the new China, making way for our future. We thought we were right, of course."

Mr. Yang was my professor during my first semester at Tsinghua University in Beijing. It is the rare occasion that a person who lived through China's Cultural Revolution (1966–1976) opens up about his or her experiences, much less admits to being in the Red Guard. China's Cultural Revolution was a time marked by widespread fear and creative repression. Chairman Mao Zedong, "Champion of the People" and founder of the Communist People's Republic of China, told the youth and peasants of China to rebel against their oppressive government and to throw off

the chains of their past, the Confucian ideals of their fathers: harmony and stability.

"Revolution is not a dinner party," Chairman Mao warned the people. "A revolution is an insurrection, an act of violence by which one class overthrows another." The result was a national patriotic frenzy of destruction. Mao's most loyal and zealous followers, the Red Guards, waged war against the "four olds"—customs, habits, culture, and thinking. They smashed temples, entire buildings, and ancient works of art. Schools were shut down for years, and educated urbanites were forced to the countryside to "learn from the peasants." Self-expression and anything Western was demonized. Pianos were burned. Menus were censored. Authors and artists were killed, and then China, the roaring wizened Giant of the East, fell silent; Mao severed the nation's ties with the world.

Thirty-plus years have gone by since the Cultural Revolution, and the Chinese have started to regain a sense of individualism. People are experimenting with their own creativity and capitalism. An entrepreneur in Beijing actually turned the Cultural Revolution into a dinner party. Appropriately named for the Red Guard's de facto anthem, The East Is Red restaurant and dinner theater is more nostalgic than celebratory and worth a visit (or two).

We sat near the stage and ate heaping portions of Cultural Revolution–era food: basic stir-fried potatoes served in an earthenware bowl, steamed white fish on a rustic metal platter, and Mao's favorite red braised pork with steamed bread buns. Meals during the Cultural Revolution were prepared with simple ingredients and presentation was never ostentatious. Even the names of the dishes on The East Is Red restaurant menus read like propaganda from the time: "The Peasant Family Is Happy" and "Recalls Past Suffering the Food" and "The Self-restraint Does the Intestines."

Mid-meal, the red paper lanterns covering the ceiling dimmed and the show began. Actors dressed in drab peasant clothing paraded out on stage with crimson armbands and defiant fists. Young men wearing green Red Guard uniforms brought the Cultural Revolution propaganda posters to life before our eyes, and Mao's Communist slogans were set to song. Waving rifles above their heads, rosy-cheeked girls sang "Serve the people!" and "To rebel is justified!" Red Guards armed with Mao's *Little Red Book* of quotations policed the audience for resistors of the cause. All the while, Chairman Mao's radiant face looked down upon us benevolently from a gigantic mural above the stage.

Toward the show's end, an old tractor made its way onto the stage. Peasant farmers clambered aboard, waving guns and pitchforks in the air and singing "The East Is Red":

"The east is red, the sun is rising.
China has brought forth a Mao Zedong.
He amasses fortune for the people,
Hurrah, he is the people's great savior."

A few old-timers in the audience, nostalgic for their youth, sang along with the words and waved red flags above their heads, tears in their eyes.

Each generation leaves its mark, Professor Yang told us. "You are the future now," he said.

MAO'S FAVORITE PORK (Hong Shao Pork) ▪ 红烧猪肉

Look at a picture of Chairman Mao Zedong and you will know he was a dictator who enjoyed his food. Mao had government chefs in Beijing re-create dishes from his home province of Hunan, an area known for bold culinary flavors. One of Mao's favorite dishes was *hong shao zhu rou,* or red braised pork. The dish gets its deep red color from the dark soy sauce added to the tangy barbecue-like sauce. After an hour and a half of braising, the meat is tender and succulent and melts in your mouth. Traditionally this dish is made with pork belly, which is basically bacon. Pork belly is extremely flavorful but may be too fatty for some tastes. If you are not a dictator or are watching your waistline, you can substitute pork loin for the pork belly. Serve with white rice or sandwich the pork between Chinese steamed bread buns.

SERVES 4

If you are using pork belly, blanch it first in a pot of boiling water for 2 minutes, then drain well.

Combine the oil and sugar in a wok over medium heat, stirring until the sugar caramelizes. Raise the heat to high, add the pork, and brown for 3 minutes. Then add the dark soy sauce, light soy sauce, rice wine, ginger, star anise, chiles, and cinnamon. Add enough water to the wok to cover the pork. Bring to a boil, and then decrease the heat and gently simmer, covered, for 1½ hours.

Remove the pork with a slotted spoon. Discard the ginger, star anise, chiles, and cinnamon. Stir the cornstarch slurry into the remaining liquid, raise the heat, and boil until it reduces to about 2 cups of sauce. Serve the pork over bowls of white rice and drizzle generous spoonfuls of the sauce over the meat. Garnish with a heap of chopped green onions.

1½ pounds pork belly or pork loin, cubed

2 tablespoons vegetable oil

2 tablespoons sugar

2 tablespoons dark soy sauce

2 teaspoons light soy sauce

2 tablespoons Shaoxing rice wine or dry sherry

1 (1-inch) piece ginger, sliced

1 star anise

3 dried red chiles, seeded

1 (2-inch) cinnamon stick

2 teaspoons cornstarch, dissolved in 1 tablespoon cold water

2 cups cooked white rice, for serving (see page 257)

2 green onions, green and white parts, chopped, for garnish

STIR-FRY POTATOES AND PEPPERS · 酸辣土豆丝

Beijing is on the same latitude as Philadelphia, and it shares Philly's harsh winters and freezing temperatures. This cold weather coupled with an extremely dry climate makes farming in and around Beijing difficult. Farmers grow hearty crops such as wheat, cabbage, and potatoes. In this dish, potatoes are cut into slivers and quickly stir-fried with chiles, bell pepper, and a splash of vinegar. This Beijing basic is as addicting as Philly cheese steaks.

SERVES 4

Soak the potatoes in a bowl of cold water for 20 minutes to draw out the starch. Drain and pat very dry with paper towels. Combine the soy sauce, rice vinegar, sugar, salt, and sesame oil in a small bowl.

Heat the vegetable oil in a wok over medium heat until a piece of a chile sizzles when added to the oil but doesn't turn black. Add the garlic and chiles and stir-fry for 20 seconds. Add the potatoes and bell pepper and stir-fry for 2 minutes. Toss in the soy sauce mixture and stir-fry for an additional 5 minutes, or until the potatoes are cooked yet still crunchy. Serve hot.

2 medium potatoes, peeled and sliced into matchsticks
2 tablespoons light soy sauce
3 tablespoons clear rice vinegar
1 teaspoon sugar
½ teaspoon salt
1 teaspoon toasted sesame oil
2 tablespoons vegetable oil
3 cloves garlic, minced
2 dried red chiles, seeded and slivered
1 small green bell pepper, seeded and slivered

BEIJING SUMMER SALAD · 豆腐酱油生菜

In China, cold dishes are almost always ordered as appetizers before the main meal. If you are at a Beijing restaurant and only order entrées, expect your waitress to ask confusedly, "Don't you want to order any cold dishes?" She will likely insist that you do.

We like this custom and usually order a small plate of cold pickled vegetables, shredded sour cabbage, or seasoned tofu. This tofu salad is a combination of a few cold dishes we like and is guaranteed to hit the spot on a hot summer day.

SERVES 4

Chop the lettuce leaves into bite-size pieces and place in a large salad bowl. Toss in the tofu, bean sprouts, green onions, and cilantro leaves.

Whisk together the lemon juice, ginger, soy sauce, honey, and sesame oil in a small bowl. Toss the salad with the dressing until everything is evenly coated. Sprinkle with sesame seeds and serve.

1 small head romaine lettuce, cored
1 pound firm tofu, cut into 1 by ½-inch strips
½ cup fresh mung bean sprouts or soybean sprouts
3 green onions, green and white parts, chopped
Handful of fresh cilantro leaves, coarsely chopped
1 tablespoon freshly squeezed lemon juice
1 tablespoon minced fresh ginger
3 tablespoons light soy sauce
1 teaspoon honey
1 tablespoon toasted sesame oil
Sesame seeds, for sprinkling

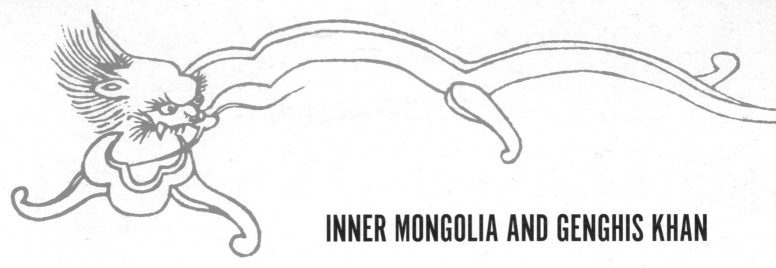

INNER MONGOLIA AND GENGHIS KHAN

Raging across the 500,000 square miles of the tumbling dunes of the Gobi Desert, fierce winds gather speed and sand, traveling 150 miles south before dumping on Beijing. These sandstorms transform vibrant Beijing into a hazy ghost town, reminding residents of the country to the north that shares their tumultuous, violent past: Mongolia.

Having been caught in these powerful Beijing spring sandstorms on more than one occasion without so much as a handkerchief for cover, the desire was born in me to journey north to see Inner Mongolia's Gobi Desert and experience its historical connections to China firsthand. Mongolia and China have been in conflict for as long as their histories have been recorded. Most notably, in the thirteenth century, Genghis Khan united the nomadic Mongols and, riding in on horseback, conquered northern China. Today, Mongolia is demarcated as Outer and Inner Mongolia. Outer Mongolia, or Mongolia, is an independent country, while Inner Mongolia is an official Autonomous Region of China. Nate and I packed our bags and readied ourselves for a week of nomadic living with the Mongols. What ensued was one of the strangest holidays I have ever taken, and not for the obvious reasons of breathtaking landscapes and intriguing cultural experiences, of which there were many.

A hired car took us to a remote area of the grasslands, but it turned out that this was not a novel idea. Inner Mongolia is a popular tourist destination among Chinese nationals, and there was already an entire Shanghai tour group complete with matching red baseball caps (all Chinese tour groups wear these same hats) awaiting our arrival at the Mongol village—ten yurts, or white canvas tents trimmed with royal blue Buddhist symbols, poking up from the surrounding green grasslands. As soon as we exited the comfort of our car, we were greeted by an unobstructed cool breeze and cheering people dressed in traditional Mongolian silk robes with gold and red embroidery who thrust shots of *bai jiu* (clear 80- to 150-proof liquor with a flavor akin to lighter fluid) into our hands. "To the sky!" they joyously voiced, prompting us to dip our fingers in the liquid, point to the sky and earth, dip again, and touch our foreheads. "Drink!" This choreographed routine continued until our foreheads were dripping wet and our bellies on fire.

Thoroughly sloshed, we were ushered into a nearby yurt with a formal yet modest dining room interior where more drinks were poured and we feasted on an entire slow-cooked lamb. In the center of the room, a young man played a two-stringed wooden instrument with a horse head carved on top. A *min kuurg*, he called it, a Mongolian violin of sorts, with each lingering note seemingly designed to ride the winds of the plains.

Over the next several days, we witnessed various traditional ethnic Mongolian activities, including

full-body wrestling and horse racing. Though staged for our viewing enjoyment, these spectacles were nonetheless entertaining and Mongolian. On the last night, we holed up in our yurt, exhausted and not wanting any more food or anything to do with the evening's festivities. Soon a knock came at our yurt door/flap. "Please join us," said a rosy-cheeked man with a full-length wool coat pulled up around his nose. "We think you are upset," he said. Not wanting to offend anyone, we ventured out for another night of laughter and lamb and didn't look back until the next morning. A boom box blaring old Michael Jackson and Celine Dion hits set the field of colorfully clothed Mongolians, Shanghai partiers, and the two

of us in motion as we sang along and watched people shoot off fireworks straight out of their hands. Close-range fire spilled down over our heads, and a bottle rocket streaked past my face so close I felt the heat. As relieved applause filled the air, the clearest roof of starry galaxies twinkled above in the night between bursts of man-made light.

Despite the odd superficiality of the trip, I did encounter a sense of nomadic life—a raw sense of self-sustainability, a life that stems from the land beneath my feet. Some of the Inner Mongolians we met had lived in this place their whole lives, the roaming sheep, growing vegetables, and grazing horses providing their sustenance and transportation. Also sprouting

up in the grasslands around us were hundreds of giant modern white windmills. Most of them had stopped whirring and fallen into disrepair as China shifted its energy investment focus in Inner Mongolia from wind power (which proved largely unsuccessful) to solar power. China is now building one of the largest solar farms in the world in Inner Mongolia in an effort to ease the country's heavy energy burden. It is expected to be completed by 2019 and will cover 16,000 acres in Ordos City.

Our Inner Mongolian adventure continued as we boarded an overnight sleeper bus for the edge of the Gobi Desert. Four people were to lie down across an unrolled bamboo mat in the back of the bus. Six

of us fit. Fortunately, the destination justified the eight-hour stuffy bus ride. Alone, we wandered the desert's rolling valleys on foot and later swayed wearily atop its golden hilltops from loose-fitting camel saddles. At the end of the day, we were stranded at the Gobi Desert without a ride home after our bus left without us. In 102°F heat, we sluggishly walked to the nearest highway and hitchhiked our way back to Hohhut, Inner Mongolia's heavily industrial capital city. To return to Beijing, we decided to splurge on first-class *ruan zuo* (soft sleeper) train tickets, but of course those were sold out, and we spent the twelve-hour return ride to Beijing on hard, immobile chairs.

MONGOLIAN HOT POT · 内蒙古火锅

Legend has it that Mongolian Hot Pot originated on the sand dunes of the Gobi Desert. Genghis Khan's Mongol warriors of the thirteenth century would throw meat, spices, and whatever else they had into their helmets and boil it all together over a fire. Their protein-rich diet kept them strong and allowed them to skip meals when food was scarce. Well fed and ruthless, they conquered northern China and most of central Asia, bringing with them this rich culinary tradition.

Hot pot is hands down our favorite meal to make for dinner parties. You'll need a large fondue pot or an electric wok (see Essential Cooking Equipment on page 252). Guests enjoy selecting ingredients to drop in the pot, waiting for them to cook, and then fishing them out with chopsticks. We enjoy the short prep time and lack of dirty dishes. To do it right, cover the dining table with newspaper (Chinese newspaper if you can get it) to catch any stray drips. Give each guest chopsticks, a small bowl to put the cooked food in, and access to the amazing dipping sauce. Use the ingredients list as a guide, but don't be afraid to be creative and add other cut-up vegetables and meats to the spread. Genghis Khan's warriors certainly were not afraid to mix it up.

SERVES 4 TO 6

To make the broth, combine the stock, water, cumin, salt, ginger, garlic, green onions, mushrooms, and jujubes in a large fondue pot or electric wok on high heat. Bring the contents to a boil, then decrease the heat to a gentle simmer.

To prepare the dipping ingredients, soak the bean thread noodles in warm water for 10 minutes, drain, and place on a serving plate. Place the sliced lamb, spinach leaves, cabbage leaves, potatoes, and any optional ingredients on separate serving dishes around the fondue pot.

Give each guest a small bowl of dipping sauce topped with cilantro and a bowl of rice. Raise the fondue pot's heat and instruct your guests to add ingredients to the bubbling broth with their chopsticks. When the ingredients are cooked (usually after a few short minutes), pluck the food from the broth using chopsticks (or a slotted spoon) and dunk in the dipping sauce before eating. Add boiling water from a kettle to the hot pot whenever the level of liquid dips too low.

BROTH

6 cups Chicken Stock (page 262) or low-sodium chicken broth
2 cups water
1 teaspoon ground cumin
½ teaspoon salt
1 (1-inch) piece ginger, sliced
4 cloves garlic, sliced
3 green onions, halved
2 dried Chinese black mushrooms
6 dried jujubes

DIPPING INGREDIENTS

4 ounces bean thread noodles
2 to 3 pounds boneless lamb, sliced paper-thin and against the grain (you can ask the butcher to slice it for you, or partially freeze it before slicing with a sharp knife)
8 ounces spinach leaves
8 ounces napa cabbage leaves, halved
3 large potatoes, peeled and thinly sliced

OPTIONAL DIPPING INGREDIENTS

Thinly sliced lotus root, cubed winter melon, cubed squash, frozen dumplings

■

Sesame Dipping Sauce (recipe follows)
Handful of fresh cilantro leaves, coarsely chopped
4 cups cooked white rice, for serving (page 257)

SESAME DIPPING SAUCE 芝麻酱小料

The perfect hot-pot dipping sauce—peanut buttery and creamy with a touch of heat. It also tastes fantastic with grilled meats like chicken or steak. If you are feeding hungry eaters, double the recipe.

MAKES 3¼ CUPS

Whisk together the sesame paste, peanut butter, black rice vinegar, water, garlic, and chili bean sauce in a large mixing bowl until well blended.

½ cup Asian sesame paste
½ cup smooth peanut butter
2 tablespoons Chinese black rice vinegar
2 cups hot water
2 cloves garlic, minced
1½ tablespoons chili bean sauce

SPICY STIR-FRY PEANUTS 炒花生米

Experts agree: If you can pick up one (and only one) peanut with your chopsticks, you are a chopstick expert yourself. Bowls of stir-fried peanuts are a fixture on Beijing home-style restaurant tables, and they make a delicious snack to keep on hand. They are a tasty way to practice using chopsticks, or to show off your mad skills. We like 'em hot and spicy. These peanuts will keep in a sealed container for up to 1 month and make a great gift.

SERVES 8 TO 10

Soak the Sichuan peppercorns and chiles in hot water for 20 minutes, and then drain and pat dry with paper towels. Use a pair of kitchen scissors to cut the chiles into small pieces. If the peanuts are whole, use your hands to break them apart into halves.

Heat the oil in a wok over medium heat until a piece of a chile sizzles when added to the oil but doesn't turn black. Add the peanuts, Sichuan peppercorns, and chiles to the oil and stir-fry for 4 minutes, or until the peanuts are a light golden brown. (Be careful not to burn the spices.) Toss in the salt, sugar, and liquor and stir until well combined. Remove the wok from the heat and let the peanuts cool before serving.

1 tablespoon Sichuan peppercorns
6 dried red chiles
1 pound raw peanuts, shelled and skinned
¼ cup peanut oil
1 teaspoon salt
1 tablespoon sugar
2 teaspoons *bai jiu* liquor or brandy

SHANGHAI
上海

"Hi, I'm Lavender Chase."

"And I'm Shanghai Lil..."

"We're here for the photo shoot," said the two beautiful burlesque dancers in unison, both in English with thick Australian accents. Already dressed for the show about to start, they wore matching sequined bikinis and towering feathered headdresses that ruffled and sparkled. It may have been just me, but it sounded as though they said everything in unison too.

"I'm from Australia... and I'm from Shanghai," they said.

They even seemed to move as one, together elegantly posing inside the red- and gold-satin-wallpapered private box on the club's mezzanine while Nate struggled to work our new camera in the low light. A wink here, a flip of the wrist there, a laugh, a finger bite, their hair always falling in place just right.

Nate blushed, his voice dropping an octave. "This is great, ladies. Can I ask you ladies to please take a seat? Or if you ladies don't want to, that's okay too," he said, gesturing to a sofa.

"Of course," they said, giggling and kneeling on the textured crimson velvet cushions as though they were mirror images of each other.

Oh, brother, how did I get here, I thought. It had been Nate's idea to come here on our first night in Shanghai. One of his friends from high school, a beautiful blonde girl from Virginia, had married the owner of a popular New York nightclub, the Slipper Room. Together she and her husband had moved to Shanghai to open a burlesque club designed to hark back to the Shanghai of old during its high-kicking heyday in the 1920s and 1930s—a glamorous, dangerous, scandalous time when the East and West met in history. Miss Amelia, as she is known now, was kind enough to offer Nate and me the opportunity when we were in town to see the show cover-free at her club, called Gosney & Kallman's Chinatown, and to meet some of the dancers for photographs.

As the trumpets and big band music picked up on the speakers, we said good-bye to Lavender Chase and Shanghai Lil and walked down the grand iron staircase to take our seats with the other audience members. For the first time I got a good look around me. Built in the remains of a 1930s Shinto temple, the room was transformed to look like one of the many dance halls from Shanghai's heyday. Art Deco gold sunburst motifs, etched highball cocktail glasses—it could have also been a cabaret theater on 42nd Street during the roaring '20s in New York City, when dancers took the stage to kick up their heels and skirts for a packed house of tuxedoed men and fancy women. On the day that World War II began in 1939, there were more than 200 nightclubs like this in Shanghai—the Casanova, the Venus, the Paramount—still with customers clinking glasses and dancing the fox-trot.

I ordered an absinthe cocktail with pineapple and lemon juice called a Miss Tickle at the bar and half expected Nicole Kidman to bust out from behind the tall red velvet curtains singing songs from *Moulin Rouge.* Instead I watched as the handsome British

emcee in tailcoat and top hat took the stage. "My friends, welcome to Chinatown!" he said, swinging a cane and smoking a cigarette at the same time. Lavender Chase and Shanghai Lil came out dancing to Frank Sinatra's crooning lyrics, "That's why the lady is a tramp!" The show was fun and at times hilarious—more vaudevillian than burlesque—and even the family of tourists with teenagers in the front row didn't seem too out of place. The Communist government may be getting hipper, but its Ministry of Culture makes sure dancers have sequins covering all the right places. This is certainly different from how things used to be in the early twentieth century, a time when a missionary was quoted as saying, "If God allows Shanghai to continue, he owes an apology to Sodom and Gomorrah."

If you were anybody in the 1920s or 1930s, you were in Shanghai. Movers and shakers came from around the world to seek their fortunes in the city and live the high life; it was a city of vice, glamour, pleasure, and commerce above all else. Foreign colonial powers occupied the city, which was divided into three separate areas: the French Concession, the International Settlement, and Greater Shanghai. In effect, there were three separate, self-governing cities within Shanghai. If you wanted to ride a trolley from the French Concession to another area, you had to change at the border. These foreign trade settlements had been established in Shanghai as a result of China's defeat in the Opium Wars. The British Empire had won the right to traffic illegal drugs in the country as well as occupy it, and China had been weakened to a point that it could do little to stop other foreign nations from sweeping into the port city to set up trade settlements of their own. Laws were flexible for the rich and fabulous, and gangsters ruled the streets.

At the time, there was also no need to show a passport to enter Shanghai. Boatloads of Jews escaping Nazi Germany and turned away elsewhere arrived in the city. Thousands of Russian refugees fleeing the Communist Russian Revolution also flooded Shanghai in need of a country to call home. Known as the White Russians, the men became bodyguards to the Chinese gangsters, and the beautiful Russian women were popular escort dancers at the city's many dance halls. However, in 1949 the Communist Party took over China, and the freewheeling fun finally stopped. Foreigners were kicked out or taxed to a breaking point and Shanghai slumbered for thirty years. Even so, the expats left a lasting impression on the town they once ruled. On Shanghai menus today, borscht, the purple Russian beet soup, masquerades as *luo song tang* (罗宋汤), and French pastries and croissants can be bought at the countless bakeries across the city.

Noticing the good food on the tables around me, I picked up a menu from the bar and saw that, just like the club menus from Shanghai's heyday, the food was almost entirely Western; for the most part, foreign residents didn't eat the local Chinese food.

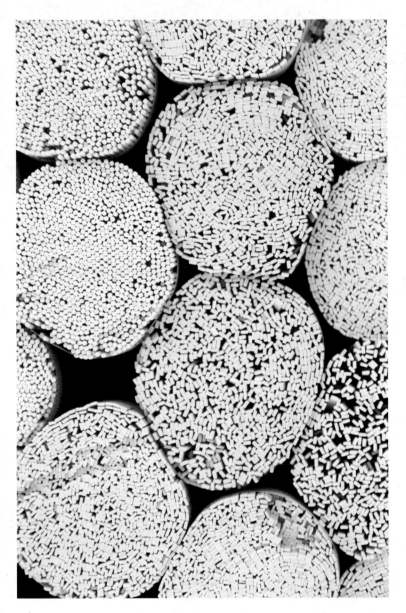

The food must have seemed quite strange to them—Chinese food was not well known around the world at that time, nor was it the burgeoning East-West fusion scene you find at Shanghai's trendy restaurants today. Foreigners ate the food of their home countries, and the cooks they employed learned to adapt foreign recipes using the local ingredients available in Shanghai. In a cookbook published in 1940 titled *Bon Appetit: Secrets from Shanghai Kitchens*, Lady Maze, the wife of a British inspector-general in Shanghai, provides recipes to her fellow expatriates for Spaghetti Bologna with Meat Sauce and an unfortunately named dish,

Minced Kidney on Toast. The Chinese were equally ignorant of Western food. Just before the turn of the twentieth century, the drug czar of China, Commissioner Lin, believed that the foreign "barbarians" literally could not survive without "tea and rhubarb."

When Nate and I asked the prolific author Tess Johnson, an American who first came to Shanghai in 1980 with the Foreign Service and stayed, what the difference is between the Shanghai of today and that of old, she said, "The great cycle of history has swung again. The foreigners are back. The businesses are back. The nightclubs are back. The vice is back. The schools are back."

Certainly the room around me was swinging again—the joie de vivre is back in Shanghai. Amid the laughing voices and clinking of glasses, I caught a few words of German from the bleached blonde in the booth across from me in a sparkling spaghetti-strap dress and gold cuffs as she leaned into the man with slick back hair next to her, whispering in his ear. Another woman, gliding by me in a white satin Empire-waist gown and speaking French to her friend, hurried to her seat before the show, balancing an olive-topped martini in hand. The twentysomethings seated at the table next to me were American expats who had just moved to the city to work on the soon-to-be-opened Shanghai Disneyland (one of the largest investments in China by a foreign country to date).

"I'll have what they're having," I said to the waitress. Hot dogs and champagne.

THE SHANGHAI LIL COCKTAIL · 上海鸡尾酒

One night Mary Kate and I found ourselves at the Glamour Bar, located along The Bund, Shanghai's historic riverbank. The fashionable cocktail bar offers a spectacular view of the Shanghai harbor and skyline through floor-to-ceiling windows. Women in chic short dresses and too-high stilettos and men in pressed tailored suits mingled about the room—it was clear that the days when Shanghaiers all sported the same soup-bowl haircuts and androgynous gray Mao suits were long gone. Shanghai now has a pervading culture of see-and-be-seen at the many places that awaken at night.

Here's a cocktail recipe we adapted from the bar at Gosney & Kallman's Chinatown, another club we hit up (see page 34). It's named for the club's star performer.

SERVES 2

Combine the gin, champagne, lemon juice, green tea, milk, rose water, and honey in a cocktail shaker and mix well with a spoon. Fill the cocktail shaker up with ice cubes and give it a few good shakes, then strain into 2 chilled champagne glasses. Garnish the rim of each glass with cucumber shavings and serve immediately.

¼ cup Hendrick's gin or other brand of premium gin
2 tablespoons champagne or sparkling white wine
2 tablespoons freshly squeezed lemon juice
3 tablespoons brewed green tea, cooled
2 tablespoons milk
1½ teaspoons rose water
2 tablespoons honey
Ice cubes
Cucumber shavings, for garnish

GUOTIE POT STICKERS · 锅贴

The word for "pot stickers" in Chinese is *guotie*, literally "pot-stick," a name they have earned from their cooking method. Chinese cooks first steam *guotie* in giant flat-bottomed iron pans. When all the water is absorbed by the dumplings, they are left in the pan to get crispy and "stick" to the pan. We recommend using a nonstick skillet when making these so that the dumplings don't actually stick to the pan forever. These Guotie Pot Stickers make amazing appetizers served with the dipping sauce. We like to make more dumplings than we can eat and freeze the extra for later.

MAKES ABOUT 36 DUMPLINGS

To make the dipping sauce, whisk together the black rice vinegar, ginger, sesame oil, cilantro, soy sauce, and sugar in a small bowl. Set aside.

To make the dumplings, combine the meat, soy sauce, cornstarch, ginger, green onions, sugar, sesame oil, and salt in a bowl and stir in one direction with a chopstick until just mixed. Fill a small bowl with some water. Hold a dumpling wrapper in the palm of your hand and place 1 heaping teaspoon of filling in the center. Dip your finger in the bowl of water and run it around the edge to help make a good seal. Lightly fold the wrapper over on itself, but don't touch the edges together. Starting at one end, use your fingers to make a small pleat on the side of the wrapper closest to you, then press the pleat into the other side and pinch together firmly. Keep making pleats down the dumpling opening in this way until completely sealed (see Dumpling Folding Tips on page 255). Repeat this process with the remaining filling and wrappers. Freeze any dumplings that you don't intend to cook immediately (see Dumpling Freezing Tips on page 256).

Heat 1 tablespoon of the vegetable oil in a nonstick skillet over medium-high heat. Place 12 dumplings pleat side up in the pan so that they are just touching each other. Cover and cook for 1 minute. Decrease the heat to medium-low, pour ¼ cup of the water into the pan, and cook, covered, for 8 to 10 minutes, until all the water is absorbed by the dumplings and their bottoms are crusty brown. Repeat this process 2 more times with the remaining dumplings, oil, and water. Serve the dumplings with a side of the dipping sauce.

DIPPING SAUCE

1 cup Chinese black rice vinegar

½ teaspoon minced fresh ginger

1 teaspoon toasted sesame oil

1 tablespoon minced fresh cilantro

¼ cup light soy sauce

1 tablespoon sugar

DUMPLINGS

12 ounces ground beef or ground pork

1 tablespoon light soy sauce

1 tablespoon cornstarch

1 teaspoon minced fresh ginger

¾ cup minced green onions, green and white parts

½ teaspoon sugar

2 teaspoons toasted sesame oil

Pinch of salt

About 36 round Dumpling Wrappers (purchased premade, or see page 258)

3 tablespoons vegetable oil

¾ cup water

BUDDHA'S DELIGHT · 罗汉斋

Sweet-smelling smoke curls from incense sticks, shaved-head monks in saffron robes busy themselves in the quiet courtyards, red paper lanterns dangle from distinctive Song Dynasty upturned roof eaves. The solace within the yellow-painted walls of Shanghai's Jade Buddha Temple is a world away from the bustling shopping malls and crowds over on nearby West Nanjing Road. The temple gets its name from the six-foot-tall, 2,000-pound, solid jade Buddha who sits inside the main hall, peering down at worshipers and tourists from atop his jewel-encrusted pedestal, and by the looks of his curvy figure, he enjoys his food.

Mary Kate and I entered the restaurant on the temple grounds (Buddhist traditionalists are vegetarians) and stole a glance at the menu: roast pork ribs, shark's fin soup, tripe, pig's feet, and dozens of other meats. We asked a waiter what was vegetarian, and he answered that everything was. The stir-fried kidneys were actually mushroom slices, and the roast ribs were fashioned from minced lotus root. The vegetarian life need not be any less interesting than that of a carnivore, the monks must have thought, fashioning vegetables like taro root and tofu into "mock meat."

Most restaurants in China make little effort to accommodate strict vegetarians. If you ask for a dish to be cooked without meat, chances are the broth or sauce used to cook the food contains meat products, and don't be surprised to find pieces of chicken in your veggie spring roll.

Here's our recipe for Buddha's Delight, a tasty vegetarian stir-fry that will make you forget about meat, at least for a little while.

SERVES 4

Wrap the tofu in 3 layers of paper towels, put on a plate, and cover with an upside-down plate. Place a 5-pound weight like a book or soup cans on top of the plate and let sit for 20 minutes to press out the water. This makes the tofu fry up golden and soak up the flavors of the dish. Remove the tofu pieces from the paper towels and slice into 1-inch cubes.

Heat 3 tablespoons of the vegetable oil in a nonstick skillet over medium heat. Fry the tofu pieces until golden brown on all sides, about 3 minutes. Transfer the tofu to paper towels to drain. Combine the soy sauce, vegetable broth, sugar, and oyster sauce in a small bowl and stir until the sugar is dissolved.

Wipe out the wok and heat the remaining 1 tablespoon of vegetable oil over high heat. Add the baby corn, snow peas, carrot slices, and asparagus and stir-fry for 1 minute. Stir in the soy sauce mixture, the mushrooms, tofu, bean sprouts, and cornstarch slurry, cover the wok, and steam for 1 minute. Season to taste with salt. Drizzle with sesame oil and serve.

8 ounces firm tofu

4 tablespoons vegetable oil

1 teaspoon light soy sauce

1/3 cup vegetable broth or low-sodium chicken broth

½ teaspoon sugar

1 tablespoon oyster sauce

½ cup canned baby corn

1 cup snow peas, trimmed

1 (3-inch) piece carrot, thinly sliced diagonally

8 thin asparagus spears, trimmed and cut into 3-inch segments

6 fresh shiitake mushrooms, stemmed and sliced

1 cup fresh mung bean sprouts or soybean sprouts

1 teaspoon cornstarch, dissolved in 1 tablespoon cold water

Salt

Toasted sesame oil, for drizzling

THE DRAGON'S HEAD

"Drop it like it's hot! Drop it like it's hot!" shouts Snoop Dogg from Nate's laptop speakers.

"Why do you insist on using that obnoxious song as an alarm clock?" I scream into my pillow. Nate's already out of his bed and in the shower singing. It's 4:30 A.M. and we have thirty minutes to get from our hotel room to the harbor if we want to catch the sunrise over the Shanghai skyline.

I chug a Diet Coke on the way out the door and we make it to the waterfront just in time to see the sun peek its orange head out from behind the soon-to-be-glittering skyscrapers. In the pale morning light, long before tourists flood the scene, a few old men zoom past us on motor scooters along the wide paved promenade next to the harbor, eager to park and unleash their homemade kites in the sky. I plunk down on a stone step to take in the view, and a man, still in his pajamas, strolls by me, walking backward (a common exercise in China), his confused toy poodle tagging along his heels on a leash. A woman, my

the old buildings of China's past along an area known as The Bund. The Bund is a row of Art Deco and neoclassical colonial buildings that look like they were transplanted from Europe and is the edge of an area that was once known as the International Settlement. After the Opium Wars, foreign countries came into Shanghai and exploited Chinese workers for their cheap labor, transforming the city from an inconsequential fishing village to a major world port and manufacturing center. Overnight, Shanghai became a booming metropolis and the first city in Asia to get electricity, running water, and telephones. Behind the high walls of the foreign trade concessions, the rich foreigners lived in the lap of luxury, driven around by chauffeurs in imported cars and cared for by maids in white aprons. On the other side of those walls, the dreadful living conditions of the underprivileged and have-nots became a breeding ground for Communist politics. It was here in Shanghai during this time that the Communist Party was first founded in China in 1921.

"Excuse me!" I holler as a middle-aged woman in blue gym shorts nearly knocks me to the ground. She shoots me a dirty look and rejoins her dance partner in a spin and twirl to the melody of a Stravinsky tune coming from their boom box nearby. I stop in front of the Bank of China building, the same area where, in 1949, part of The Bund was unexpectedly closed one night and guarded by armed soldiers. Under the cover of darkness, wooden crates containing gold by the ton were carried from Shanghai's bank vaults to awaiting ships in Shanghai Harbor. Clear that the Communists would win China's civil war, the leader of the Nationalist Party, Chiang Kai-shek, moved China's wealth in a mass exodus to the islands of Taiwan, where he would go on to found his government in exile. Shanghai was left for broke, and the Communists rolled in without a fight. The first thing they did was kick out

grandmother's age, slaps the trunk of a tree repeatedly with her palms, which according to Chinese medicine, purges bad qi from the body. As silly as it looks, I doubt I'll still be able to slap a tree with that much vigor when I'm eighty years old. To my left, a group of about thirty early risers practice Tai Chi and martial arts with handheld fans and even scarier weapons like swords and spears, their movements choreographed like a slow-motion dance. I wish I could capture these moments—old Chinese culture at its best. My camera just doesn't do them justice.

Nate runs to join the Tai Chi group, high kicking and punching the air. I am not nearly up for that at this hour, so I walk along the mile-and-a-half waterfront promenade. To my left, on this side of the harbor, stand the foreigners and send the intellectuals and capitalist-minded people to the countryside for "reeducation." For the next thirty years, anything Western was labeled "bourgeois" and strictly forbidden. Even dancing was outlawed in Shanghai until the 1980s.

On the other side of the harbor from where I stand, the Pudong side, Shanghai is a testament to China's impatience for the future. Deng Xiaoping, China's forward-thinking economic reformist, proclaimed Shanghai "the dragon's head" of China's economy in the '90s and urged the Chinese people to move to a more capitalist mind-set. "To get rich is glorious!" he declared. Foreign investments and government funds soon began pouring into the dragon's head, and construction broke ground. Neither has stopped since, and Pudong now boasts the world's third tallest television tower, the highest observation deck in the world located in the Shanghai World Financial Center, and one of the tallest buildings in the world—the 101-story Jinmao Tower. The list goes on. The skyscraper boom has happened so quickly that there aren't enough businesses to fill them. Much of the commercial office space on their many floors sit empty, as high as a 50 percent vacancy at times. The buildings are actually so heavy that the city is sinking one centimeter a year!

The sun is high and bright now and my stomach growls for breakfast. I see a few small fishing boats on their way out to sea and a tugboat pushing a barge with steel pipes and cables further down the river, no doubt bound for some construction site.

SHANGHAI FRIED NOODLES · 上海炒面

Shanghai life is notoriously fast paced—commuters fight traffic-congested streets and ride on crowded subways, business people work long hours at demanding jobs, and the city's young professionals are ambitious, stylish, and competitive. For meals, people often grab *xiao chi* (小吃), or "small eats," from the many small restaurants and street vendors that can be found in every nook and cranny of the city. *Xiao chi* is a catchall term that means anything that can be eaten on the go: fried stinky tofu cubes drizzled with hot sauce, *guotie* pot stickers, kebabs, soup dumplings, and spicy chicken wings. Our favorite Shanghai *xiao chi* are undoubtedly Shanghai Fried Noodles. The best we had were at Wujiang Road, a pedestrian paradise of dozens of stalls selling cheap, good eats. The chewy noodles came bathed in a dark and savory sauce mixed with flash-fried crispy snow peas and garlic slivers.

SERVES 4

Prepare the noodles according to their package instructions or boil until al dente. Rinse the noodles under cold water to get rid of any starch and then drain really well. Toss the noodles with the sesame oil until they are evenly coated and shiny.

Combine the dark soy sauce, light soy sauce, sugar, and cornstarch slurry in a small bowl.

Heat the vegetable oil over high heat. Add the ginger, garlic, green onions, and star anise and stir-fry for 10 seconds. Add the snow peas and cabbage and stir-fry for 1 minute, or until the snow peas are cooked but still a little crunchy. Add the soy sauce mixture and stir for 20 seconds. Toss in the noodles and stir until all the noodles are coated with the sauce and heated through. Serve immediately.

12 ounces fresh thick round noodles or Japanese udon noodles

2 teaspoons toasted sesame oil

2 tablespoons dark soy sauce

2 teaspoons light soy sauce

1 teaspoon sugar

1 teaspoon cornstarch, dissolved in 1 tablespoon cold water

1 tablespoon vegetable oil

½ teaspoon minced fresh ginger

4 cloves garlic, thinly sliced

3 green onions, white parts only, chopped

1 star anise

2 cups snow peas, trimmed

2 cups shredded napa cabbage

MA LA CRAWFISH (aka Spicy Little Dragon Shrimp) · 麻辣小龙虾

Crawfish, mudbugs, crawdads, langoustines, crawdaddies, ditchbugs, and yabbies . . . these crustaceans come with a lot of names, but I like their Chinese name the best: *xiao long xia,* or "little dragon shrimp." Not only do they look like little dragons, but once they are cooked in the spicy broth in this recipe, they are fire-breathing dragons as well. *Ma la* in this recipe's name means "mouth-numbing spicy," so be prepared for some heat. The 30 chiles might sound wildly inedible, but because of the hard shells on the small dragon shrimp, not too much spice actually permeates the meat.

This recipe feeds two people, but you can double, triple, or even gazunkle the recipe to feed a large group—just make sure your pot is big enough. Spread the crawfish out on a newspaper-covered table for serious chowing down and serve with some cold Chinese beer (Tsingtao is a good choice and available at most supermarkets).

SERVES 2

Combine the stock, rice wine, sugar, five-spice powder, soy sauce, and salt in a large bowl and set aside.

Heat the oil in a large pot over high heat. Add the ginger, garlic, bay leaves, and green onions and stir-fry for 20 seconds. Lower the heat to medium, add the chiles and Sichuan peppercorns, and stir-fry for 20 seconds, or until the peppers become aromatic. Turn the heat back to high and toss in the crawfish. Stir-fry for 3 minutes. Stir in the soy sauce mixture so that all the crawfish are coated, and then cover and let steam for 8 minutes, or until the crawfish are cooked through. Serve immediately.

2 cups Chicken Stock (page 262) or low-sodium chicken broth
1 tablespoon Shaoxing rice wine or dry sherry
1 tablespoon sugar
2 teaspoons Chinese five-spice powder
3 tablespoons light soy sauce
¼ teaspoon salt
¼ cup vegetable oil
1 (2-inch) piece ginger, sliced
10 cloves garlic
3 bay leaves
4 green onions, green and white parts, cut into 2-inch segments
30 dried red chiles
1/3 cup Sichuan peppercorns
4 pounds whole crawfish, rinsed well with fresh water

SHANGHAI SOUP DUMPLINGS · 小笼包

It's all about the soup when it comes to Shanghai Soup Dumplings (*xiao long bao*). Each dumpling is a little pocket of heavenly soup that literally bursts with flavor when you bite into it. The secret to getting the soup inside is adding cubes of congealed broth to the filling. The broth cools into what looks like soup ice cubes that melt inside the dumplings when steamed. Chinese cooks traditionally make the soup cubes by boiling pigskin, which contains natural gelatin. To cut down on time and hassle, we make our soup by simmering chicken stock with spices and gelatin, and it tastes just as great or better. You can buy premade dumpling wrappers for most types of dumplings, but we recommend making homemade dumpling wrappers for these. They will hold up better while steaming and won't leak any soup. To eat a soup dumpling, hold one with chopsticks over a soupspoon and gingerly take a bite out of the top of it. Let it cool for a second, and then slurp the soup out through the hole. Finally, dip the dumpling in pungent Chinese black rice vinegar and gobble the rest.

We ate at a restaurant in Shanghai that takes the soup obsession to a whole new level. Nan Xiang Steamed Bun Restaurant serves glorious softball-size soup dumplings filled with only soup, which you suck out through a straw.

MAKES ABOUT 30 DUMPLINGS

To make the soup, combine the stock, green onion, ham, rice wine, and ginger in a medium saucepan. Bring to a boil, and then decrease the heat and simmer for 30 minutes. Strain the soup and discard the solids. Return the soup to the saucepan, increase the heat, and boil until the liquid has reduced to 1 cup. Add the gelatin and whisk until it is completely dissolved. Transfer the soup to a shallow dish, cover, and refrigerate for 4 hours or overnight to allow the soup to congeal.

To make the filling, finely chop the congealed soup into tiny cubes. Combine the pork, green onion, soy sauce, rice wine, sesame oil, sugar, salt, white pepper, ginger, and soup cubes in a large bowl and stir in one direction with a chopstick until just mixed.

To form the dumplings, fill a small bowl with water. Place about 2½ teaspoons of filling in the center of a wrapper. Dip your finger in the bowl of water and run it around the edge to help make a good seal. Use your fingers to make a series of small pleats around the edge of the wrapper until all the pleats come together at the dumpling's top. Then twist the pleats shut to seal the dumpling (see Dumpling Folding Tips on page 255). Repeat this process with the remaining filling and wrappers.

Line a steamer tray with the cabbage leaves and place it in a wok or pot with enough water in the bottom to come just below the tray. Bring the water to a boil, cover, and let the leaves steam for 1 minute so that they become soft and flat. Remove the lid and arrange several of the dumplings on the cabbage so that they are well spaced. Cover and steam the dumplings for 12 minutes (see How to Steam on page 254). Combine the Chinese black rice vinegar and ginger slivers and serve the dumplings immediately with small bowls of the dipping sauce.

SOUP

2½ cups Chicken Stock (page 262) or low-sodium chicken broth
1 green onion, green and white parts, chopped
4 ounces cured Chinese ham or Virginia Smithfield ham, cubed
2 teaspoons Shaoxing rice wine or dry sherry
1 (1-inch) piece ginger, sliced
1½ teaspoons unflavored powdered gelatin

FILLING

1 pound ground pork
1 green onion, white parts only, minced
1 tablespoon light soy sauce
1 teaspoon Shaoxing rice wine or dry sherry
½ teaspoon toasted sesame oil
1 teaspoon sugar
½ teaspoon salt
¼ teaspoon freshly ground white pepper
1 teaspoon minced fresh ginger

About 30 round Dumpling Wrappers (page 258)
6 to 8 cabbage leaves, for steaming
Chinese black rice vinegar, for dipping
1 (1-inch) piece ginger, peeled and slivered into matchsticks

DOG ON AND OFF THE MENU

DOG ON AND OFF THE MENU

My good friend studying abroad with me in China, Krista, and I decided that it was very important to eat dog before the summer semester was over and we returned to the States. After class one day, we went on a mission to track some down. Going around to several restaurants and stores, we asked everyone in our beginner's Chinese, "We all want buy some dog?" The first few places turned us away, saying they didn't have any. Then we thought we were in luck.

A weary-looking clerk perked up behind the counter when we entered her otherwise empty store. "No, I don't have dog, but I do have cat," she said.

Krista and I looked at each other, giggling. "That's nearly as cool. Don't you think?" I said.

Krista turned to the clerk. "We'll take it," she said matter-of-factly.

The clerk gave us a long awkward look before walking from behind the counter and signaling for us to follow.

We trailed her through the grocery aisles and through a back door presumably for staff only or more probably where she lived. We found ourselves in a kitchen. *What would it taste like? Would it be dry, like jerky, or cooked rare and nearly raw?*

The woman knelt down and opened a cabinet below the countertop. Looking inside, we saw a mother cat with five or so kittens nestled up next to her fur, purring.

Krista and I shrieked in unison. "No! You don't understand," one of us said. "We want to eat it."

The woman caught herself on the counter. Her mouth dropped open. Clearly, we were the craziest foreigners she'd ever met.

My fuzzy brown-and-white spotted German Wirehaired Pointer dog, Nelson III, need not know about this, but Nate and I have since eaten dog meat,

and yes, I kind of liked it. Known as *gou rou*, dog meat comes from mixed Chinese breeds and European large breeds such as Saint Bernards and Pointers. It can be roasted, stir-fried, or served in a stew. No, it's not particularly great, but it's not bad either, rather like turkey or gamey beef. However, I don't think its average flavor is responsible for its long-standing popularity in China. Dog meat is not as common as most foreigners think but it is believed to have medicinal qualities and to improve blood circulation during the cold winter months. There's a Chinese proverb that goes, "Huajiang dog is better for you than ginseng." Huajiang dog meat is famous for its nutritional value (and ginseng root is an integral part of Chinese medicine).

Undoubtedly dog eating has a long history in China. A microbiologist in Sweden estimates that domestic dogs first evolved in East Asia possibly 14,000 years ago and then spread from there with migrating humans. In an ancient tomb dating back to 168 B.C. in the south of China, dog meat was found along with other funerary food offerings with the well-preserved remains of a noblewoman, and dog bones with knife marks have also been discovered at other archaeological sites. Millennia later, in 2009, China's first astronaut in space revealed his daily menu to include among other things rice, noodles, and dog meat specifically to help him keep fit.

Under Chairman Mao Zedong's rule and until he died in 1976, pet dogs were labeled bourgeois and forbidden. My Chinese friend Ai Li, who grew up in Beijing, told me of a time in the 1990s when her family had to send their two dogs outside of the city to live with distant relatives for a month. During this time the government deployed door-to-door task forces throughout the city after deciding that there should only be one dog allowed per household. "If they saw you had a second one, they would thump it on the head and kill it right in front of you," she said. Ironically enough, her father was a policeman.

In my on-and-off travels in China since 2001, I have felt fortunate enough to watch a nation change and transform at an unprecedented rate, and as always, Shanghai is at the forefront of the mainland's innovations and social trends. The increase of personal incomes over the years and the rise of the DINK (double income, no kids) couples, especially in the metropolitan areas like Shanghai, have led to expendable cash, hobbies, and pampered pets. Spending on pet food and pet care is up by more than 100 percent since 2004, experts say. It was in Shanghai where I first gawked at a straight-faced middle-aged businessman in a pressed suit and tie walking a Chihuahua dressed in pink booties and a sparkly pink raincoat. I don't even flinch now when I see a fluffy dog bleached and dyed to look like a giant panda or a striped tiger or when I see a Pekingese in a Burberry plaid shirt out for her morning constitutional, pushed along in a baby stroller. Outlandish dressing and fur dying of dogs in China is clearly all the rage and perhaps a way for owners to distance their beloved pets from more than just meat on a menu.

I snap a picture of one Mr. Zhang and his pooch exiting a restaurant on a corner near the People's Park in Shanghai. Mr. Zhang hugs the little guy tight in his arms and tells me, "He's so smart sometimes I think he will talk." In between takes, the pup tries to snag a dumpling out of his master's to-go doggie bag.

SOY SAUCE CHICKEN · 酱油鸡

I appreciate good barbecue sauce. Mary Kate and I grew up visiting our relatives in Little Rock, Arkansas, feasting on pulled pork smothered in the tangy sauce—the best barbecue sandwiches below the Mason-Dixon Line. If I learned anything, it's that perfect barbecue-sauce flavor strikes a balance between sweet, tangy, and spice. We've yet to find an exact Chinese equivalent to American barbecue sauce, but the sauce in this chicken smacks of brown sugar, ginger, and cinnamon and comes pretty darn close, with an added Asian panache. Soy Sauce Chicken is traditionally from Guangdong, but the sauce is identical to the duck version served all over Shanghai—except for the duck, of course.

SERVES 4 TO 6

Heat the oil in a large skillet over medium-high heat. Brown the chicken pieces in batches for 3 minutes on each side, transferring to paper towels to drain as each batch is browned.

In a large pot, combine the water, Sichuan peppercorns, star anise, and cinnamon and simmer for 15 minutes. Let cool, then strain the liquid, discard the spices, and return the liquid to the pot.

Add the soy sauce, rice wine, clear rice vinegar, and brown sugar to the pot over high heat. Stir until the sugar is dissolved. Add the chicken, green onions, and ginger. Bring to a boil, then decrease the heat and simmer, covered, for 20 to 25 minutes, or until the chicken is cooked through. Remove the chicken from the pot. Increase the heat and bring the remaining liquid to a boil, add the cornstarch slurry, and stir for 5 to 10 minutes, until it reduces to about 2½ cups of sauce. Drizzle some of the sauce on the chicken and serve the rest alongside for dipping.

2 tablespoons vegetable oil

3 to 4 pounds chicken pieces (with skin and bone), such as thighs, breasts, and drumsticks

6 cups water

1 tablespoon Sichuan peppercorns

2 star anise

1 cinnamon stick

1½ cups dark soy sauce

¼ cup Shaoxing rice wine or dry sherry

1 tablespoon clear rice vinegar

5 tablespoons brown sugar

4 green onions, tied in a knot

3 slices ginger, smashed with the side of a knife

1 tablespoon cornstarch, dissolved in 2 tablespoons cold water

TEA EGGS · 茶鸡蛋

These distinctive colored eggs simmer in roadside pots all over China and sell for a mere few cents to passersby. The eggs are first lightly boiled and then tapped with a spoon to create cracks in the shells and a marbled appearance when simmered in the pot with loose black tea, dark soy sauce, and aromatic spices. We like to make a few batches and brown-bag them to work for lunch or have them on hand to slice over a salad.

MAKES 8 EGGS

In a large saucepan, cover the eggs with cold water, bring to a boil, then decrease the heat and simmer for 6 minutes. Remove the eggs with a slotted spoon and set aside.

To the same pot of water, add the soy sauce, tea leaves, cinnamon, star anise, sugar, salt, bay leaves, and dried tangerine peel, if using, and simmer for 15 minutes.

When the eggs are cool enough to handle, tap the shells with the back of a spoon to create cracks in the shells. You want the eggshells covered with cracks, but still intact.

When the tea mixture is done simmering, return the eggs to the pot, bring to a boil, and then decrease the heat and simmer gently for 45 minutes. Turn off the heat and let the eggs cool in the liquid. Store the eggs in the tea liquid in the refrigerator for up to 6 days.

8 large eggs, or 16 quail eggs

½ cup dark soy sauce

2 tablespoons loose black tea leaves

1 cinnamon stick

4 star anise

2 tablespoons sugar

1 tablespoon salt

2 bay leaves

2 (about 2-inch-square) pieces dried tangerine peel (optional)

WONTON SOUP · 馄饨汤

Just east of the French Concession, we stopped off at a hole-in-the-wall restaurant where wonton soup was the only thing on the menu and the dining area doubled as the kitchen. With one eye on his soap opera flickering on a tiny TV set above the door, the cook plunged two handfuls of wonton dumplings into a large steaming pot of broth. After cooking them for just a few minutes, he spooned them into two bowls and ladled over the broth, topping the bowls with a heap of cilantro leaves and chopped green onions. The wonton soup at this local joint was better than any we tried at famous restaurants in Shanghai. Nate adds hot sauce and Chinese black rice vinegar to his, but I prefer the light taste of the shrimp- and pork-filled wontons floating in the gently flavored, clear broth.

SERVES 4

To make the broth, heat the oil in a large saucepan over high heat. Add the garlic and ginger and stir-fry for 10 seconds. Add the green onions and stock, bring to a boil, and then decrease the heat and simmer for 20 minutes. Season with salt to taste.

To make the wontons, combine the shrimp, pork, water chestnuts, ginger, soy sauce, clear rice vinegar, salt, and egg yolk in a large bowl and stir in one direction with a chopstick until just mixed.

Lay a wonton wrapper in front of you so that it is in the shape of a diamond. Fill a small bowl with water. Place a teaspoon of the shrimp filling in the center of the wrapper. Dip your finger in the bowl of water and moisten the edges of the wrapper. Fold the bottom corner of the wrapper up to form a triangle shape and press the edges to seal. Bring the lower two corners together and pinch between your thumb and index finger to form a wonton. Repeat with the remaining wrappers and filling. Freeze any dumplings that you don't intend to cook immediately (see Dumpling Freezing Tips on page 256).

Bring a large saucepan of water to a boil. Add the wontons and cook for 5 minutes. Remove the dumplings and divide among the serving bowls. Blanch the spinach in the dumpling water for 30 seconds and then divide among the serving bowls. Ladle the broth over the dumplings and serve with the Chinese black rice vinegar and Asian chili sauce as condiments.

BROTH

1 tablespoon vegetable oil

2 cloves garlic, minced

1 teaspoon minced fresh ginger

2 green onions, green and white parts, chopped

6 cups Chicken Stock (page 262) or low-sodium chicken broth

Salt

WONTONS

4 ounces shrimp, shelled, deveined and coarsely chopped

4 ounces ground pork

1/3 cup water chestnuts, minced

2 teaspoons minced fresh ginger

2 teaspoons light soy sauce

2 teaspoons clear rice vinegar

¼ teaspoon salt

1 egg yolk

About 30 square wonton wrappers

3 cups firmly packed spinach leaves, shredded

Chinese black rice vinegar, for serving

Asian chili sauce, like sriracha sauce, for serving

CHICKEN FEET AND PIZZA: A COLLEGE LIFE

In the chill of the sparsely heated dorm room, I wrapped my scarf a second time around my neck and scooted over on the edge of the bed to make room for three others to sit. "Dinner's almost ready!" Wen Chao declared as he rushed about his room stuffing clothes in a cabinet and toppling textbooks over on the card table set in front of me. His room was not nearly as nice as my private room in the foreign students' dormitory wing. Only one small mirror and a few coats hung from hooks next to the three bunks (six beds) on the otherwise bare cinder-block walls, and there was only one shared computer on a desk in the corner. A roommate sat intently typing away, deep in an instant-messaging conversation—*click, click, beep-click.*

Wen Chao was my Chinese-language partner, and on this night he had invited my classmate Scott and me over for dinner—he and his new wife, Hui Liang, had some exciting news to announce. I wondered if their news was that the two of them had finally been able to get an apartment together. For the time being, Hui Liang was still living in the girls' dorm across the Tsinghua University campus. "Not only is my wife a brilliant biochemist, she is a brilliant cook!" Wen Chao had bragged the previous week. Still I had no idea how she would cook for us, as none of the school dormitories were fitted with kitchens, but there perched on Wen Chao's windowsill was my answer: a lone rice cooker. Hui Liang stood nearby, spoon in hand, dishing out the dinner she had prepared entirely in the 2-quart electric appliance: rice, spinach, egg and tomato stir-fry, and duck soup spread out in bowls.

"Nate, you will be happy. We made your favorite!" Wen Chao said, lifting the plastic lid of the rice cooker to reveal a mess of rubbery yellow flesh and toenails. "*Feng zhua* [chicken feet]!" he beamed.

"What a surprise," I said, gripping my chopsticks and peering at the horror show. "Thanks," I added.

Scott raised his eyebrows. "Chicken feet are your favorite?" he asked in his Australian lilt. Scott had also just moved to China a few months before, and we were both timidly exploring the new and odd Chinese foods that we happened upon like American toddlers branching out into the scary world of vegetables.

"Of course!" I said, perhaps too enthusiastically. The truth was I'd never eaten a chicken foot in my life and the closest I had ever come to one were the ones still attached to the birds—walking around and scratching in the dirt. I racked my brain for how this miscommunication could have happened. "Chicken feet," I had told Wen Chao, were the only Chinese food that I did *not* care to eat. I must have left out the *bu* (no) in the phrase *zhen de bu xi huan* (definitely do not like). I vowed right then to stop skipping Chinese class so often.

Scott was the first to reach for one of the feet. "Nate, how do you eat them?" he asked. All eyes were on me as I began fumbling with a foot in my hand. "So, let's see . . . you tear off a toe like this. . . ." Wen Chao mercifully stepped in to show us the right way, chewing the tender skin off a toe and spitting out the delicate bones on his plate. I reached for another and was pleasantly surprised. The tendons of the foot had become very juicy and succulent after being stewed for a long time, and the meat fell right off the bone. In China, chicken feet are regarded as "phoenix talons" and are a *dim sum* delicacy popular across the country.

Halfway through the meal, Wen Chao could not contain his excitement any longer. "Both of our visas have been approved!" he said. He and Hui Liang had already been accepted to graduate programs in America, but the difficult visa interview process and

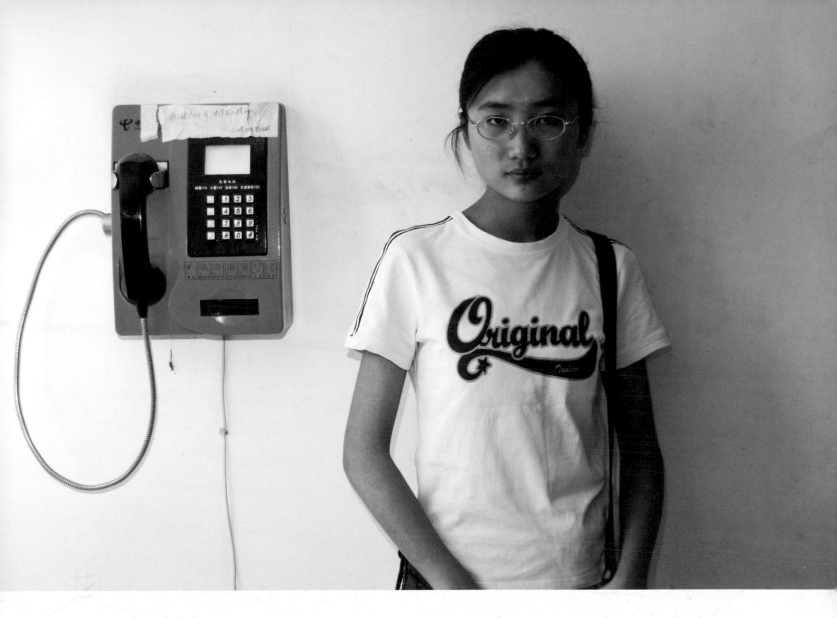

the limited number of visas given is often the deciding factor. Now they were one step closer to their dream of going to America. The news was bittersweet, however. Wen Chao would be moving to California, while Hui Liang would be attending a university in another state. Still, I was glad for them. My year studying abroad was turning out to be one of the best of my life.

Mary Kate also found her time as an exchange student inspiring, and while we were in Shanghai one summer, we rode the train to visit her alma mater in the nearby city of Nanjing. One of her good friends from school, Ling Long, or Betty as she goes by in English,

met us at a Pizza Hut where we had offered to take her out for pizza—a food she had never tried before. We piled into a booth and ordered a half pepperoni and half shrimp pizza, and Betty picked up a knife and fork for the first time. She wrapped the pizza's cheese around the tines of the fork and watched in bewilderment as the goo stretched all the way to her mouth. "How do I eat it?" she asked.

Even with our time spent as exchange students, the student experience in China is so different from that in the West that it still perplexes us. We once attended a lecture given by the Pulitzer Prize–winning photojournalist Liu Heung Shing, who was discussing his book titled *Shanghai*. It is a city he thinks perhaps most symbolizes China's progress over the past few decades. Liu clicked through a slide show of photographs and we watched as the last half century of China's history passed before our eyes: angry faces of students rebelling during the Cultural Revolution (a time when schools were shut down altogether in the country), university graduates working in the fields of the countryside, young students shouldering bayonets, crowds of people destroying books in the streets. Then as policies changed toward education, so did the photos. One picture stands out in my mind. On a night in 1980 after university entrance exams were reinstated, Liu snapped a picture in Tiananmen Square, where a sea of youths crowded the square reading books under its electric lights (they likely had none at home). Liu said he kept his camera's shutter open for several seconds, but the scene appears crisp instead of blurry, because the students sat so still, engrossed in their books.

The Chinese have never looked back, Liu said. Now parents encourage their kids to study relentlessly, and in Mary Kate's and my observations, critical thinking often takes a backseat to memorization. (When Mary Kate was an English teacher, her first-graders stayed later at school than she did, often pulling twelve-hour days with no weekends off.) Few people who have never been to China can understand the frenzy, Liu said. The Chinese people have seen the world, and they want to catch up.

YANGZHOU FRIED RICE · 扬州炒饭

Chinese home cooks have long riffed on the humble fried rice to create new and exciting variations. In this recipe, bits of shrimp, egg, peas, and vegetables get stir-fried in a hot wok with long-grain rice to create a colorful party on your plate. It is great as a side dish or as the main event. Stir-frying can transform day-old rice and last night's leftovers into a delightfully tasty meal. The only rule is that you first stir-fry any raw meat and hearty vegetables to cook through and then toss in the rice at the end. Make sure all the ingredients are prepped before you start cooking, because once you start, it's go, go, go!

SERVES 4

Bring a small pot of water to a boil. Blanch the peas in the boiling water for 4 to 5 minutes, or until they turn bright green and are cooked through. Drain and set aside.

In a small bowl, combine the oyster sauce, sugar, rice wine, soy sauce, and sesame oil. Use a chopstick or fork to break up the clumps in the cooked rice.

Heat the vegetable oil in a wok over high heat. Add the shrimp and green onions and stir-fry for 10 seconds. Add the eggs and scramble until they are just set, and then immediately toss in the rice and stir until well mixed. Add the oyster sauce mixture, the peas, and mushrooms, and stir-fry for about 2 minutes, or until the mushrooms are soft. Stir in the black pepper. Remove the wok from the heat and let rest for 4 minutes before serving.

1 cup peas (fresh or frozen)

1 tablespoon oyster sauce

½ teaspoon sugar

1 tablespoon Shaoxing rice wine or dry sherry

2 teaspoons light soy sauce

½ teaspoon toasted sesame oil

2 cups cooked long-grain white rice, chilled (see page 257)

1 tablespoon vegetable oil

6 ounces shrimp, peeled, deveined, and coarsely chopped

4 green onions, green and white parts, chopped

2 large eggs, lightly beaten

3 fresh shiitake mushrooms, caps only, cut into pea-size cubes

¼ teaspoon freshly ground black pepper

YOUTIAO FRIED DOUGH STICKS · 油条

If China has a national breakfast food, it has got to be *youtiao*. These deep-fried dough sticks are like puffy, airy doughnuts. The dough hits the oil and expands to several times its original size with the help of an ingredient called alum. You can find powdered alum in the spice section at specialty grocery stores. *Youtiao* are traditionally a street-vendor fixture, but the ever-popular KFC fast-food chain has now gotten in on the *youtiao* action by adding them to its breakfast menu. Sprinkle with sugar, dip into a piping-hot bowl of soy milk, smash inside an egg omelet, or eat with congee rice porridge. I like cinnamon and sugar.

MAKES 15 STICKS

3½ cups all-purpose flour
1 tablespoon salt
½ tablespoon baking soda
1½ tablespoons alum
11/3 cups warm water
Oil, for deep-frying
1 cup sugar

Sift together the flour, salt, baking soda, and alum in a large bowl. Slowly stir in the water until well combined, and then let stand for 15 minutes.

Turn the dough out onto a lightly oiled work surface and knead for 10 minutes, until it is smooth and elastic. Add a small amount of water or flour if necessary.

Divide the dough in half, and then use a rolling pin to roll each half into a (15 by 4-inch) strip. Use a sharp knife to cut each strip into 15 (1 by 4-inch) strips. Stack the strips on top of each other in sets of two. Then use a chopstick to press down lengthwise on the strips to fuse them together.

Heat 4 inches of oil in a wok over medium heat until a small piece of bread added to the oil turns golden brown after 30 seconds. Pick up a strip of the dough by holding both ends. Gently stretch the dough to a length of 8 inches while at the same time twisting the strip twice, and then slide the dough into the oil. Repeat with 2 more dough strips, constantly turning the dough in the oil with chopsticks for 1 minute, or until the strips are puffed up and golden. Using a perforated strainer, transfer to paper towels to drain. Sprinkle generously with the sugar. Repeat with the remaining dough strips and serve immediately.

FUJIAN

福建

FUJIAN: COUNTRY COOKING 福建

We began noticing the bees about a mile back. At first it was just a mild buzzing and the occasional wooden box near the roadside with "蜂" (the Chinese character for "bee") stenciled in red ink on its lid—nothing to worry about. Then the hives became closer together and more frequent, as many as one every three feet (I lost count at sixty), and untold stinging insects darted in and out of their openings and around our heads as we made our way up the narrow mountain lane that snaked along the edge of the cliff, a rushing river roaring far below in the subtropical valley. This was a much bigger honeybee farm operation than what Mary Kate and I had going in our backyard as kids. We harvested honey (which is much harder than it looks) from our four hives and sold jars of it door to door in the neighborhood with handmade labels reading "Tate & Tate Honey, Ain't Nothin' Sweeter."

I reached a small tent pitched on the side of the road where a man and woman sat playing cards, a beekeeper's hat and a smoker nearby. The man looked up. "What are you doing here?" he asked. I couldn't say much; he spoke an obscure Fujianese dialect and very little Mandarin. Cut-off and remote areas like this in Fujian Province have dialects that vary from valley to valley, but I managed to explain that I was on vacation. We had just left Shanghai and were in the middle of our weeklong biking adventure down the southeastern coast of China.

"Vacation?" he asked. This seemed very hard for him to accept. The only bikers who rode through these mountains were smart enough to ride on ones with motors—the steep roads were designed for powerful

military vehicles and heavy trucks laden with granite from nearby quarries—and for all he could tell I was alone. Mary Kate was still way back down the mountain puttering along at an unbelievably slow pace even for her. It was getting late in the day and we were far—"too impossibly far," as my beekeeping friend pointed out—from the city of Putian, our night's destination. "*Jia you! Jia you!*" I called out to Mary Kate as she rounded the corner. *Jia you* literally means "add oil" and is the Chinese way of saying "hurry up!" She shot me a dirty look and continued muttering to herself as she trudged up the hill pushing her bike. "I'm starving . . . I hate bees . . . I can't breathe. . . ." We had come to understand the meaning of the well-known Fujianese saying *ba shan yi shui yi fen tian* (Fujian is eight parts mountain, one part water, and one part farmland).

I think the man pitied us and our sorry idea of a vacation, because he filled an old Sprite bottle that he had on hand with fresh honey and offered it to me. "*Man zou* [walk slowly]," he said as a polite way of saying goodbye. We rode on and finally reached the peak of a most grueling slope and pointed our handlebars down the other side of the equally steep and winding mountain lane. Wind and adrenaline flushed our faces. This was real-life Mario Kart—speeding down an open road cut through red mud cliffs, then over wooden bridges, past banana trees and lychee orchards, dodging bees and the occasional car around hairpin turns, ears popping along the way. The sun went down and the moon went up. Then everything stopped—for me anyway.

Bam! My bike hit a pothole head-on and I was jolted forward on my face. I lifted my chin to inspect the damage to my bike, but just at that moment I saw the two glowing yellow eyes—the bared teeth, the barking—hurtling toward me. Most guidebooks recommend that backpackers carry pepper spray to ward off feral dogs in the rural areas of China. I had a bottle of honey. Swinging my leg back over the bike seat, I punched my foot down on the pedals. *Glub glub glub*—the tire wobbled under the strain of an obvious flat. By now the dog had a friend, and the two of them lunged at my tires and snapped their jaws inches from my legs. I grabbed the honey from the side of my pack and desperately threw it in their direction, only to hear it land with a thud and putter across the gravel road. I called to Mary Kate for help but she was long gone. All I could see of her was the flashlight bungeed to the back of her bike disappearing in the darkness ahead.

I hadn't seen Mary Kate move that fast all week. When I caught up to her 300 yards down the road, she was screaming "Nooo!" into the now-quiet night and brandishing a tree branch. "I was going to come back for you! I promise!" she cried. I couldn't blame her too much, though. Three dogs from the stray pack had decided to chase her, and she was obviously rattled by the one who had put holes in the heel of her right shoe.

We fixed my tire on the side of the road by flashlight, and after midnight (our day had started at six that morning) we hit a much-needed stroke of luck. Wading through a muddy field, we found ourselves one stand of trees away from civilization and a humongous factory complex. Fujian's interior is mainly made up of rural countryside—fruit plantations, cabbage patches, duck farms, crystal blue lakes and streams, stray dogs—but near its coast, where we found ourselves that night, Highway 324 runs down the length of the province connecting its main port cities of Fuzhou, Quanzhou, and Xiamen. The busy road is not a fun place for a bike. Exhaust-spitting trucks blast by while transporting products made at the multitude of industrial factories that dot its roadside.

There out in front of the tall, fortress-like metal gates, a sign read "Putian shoe factory," and a group of young workers just off their late-night work shift stood around a noodle vendor—texting and talking on their cell phones—waiting for their *sha cha* noodles. As we approached, slowing our bikes to a stop and walking up to the food cart, all eyes followed us.

I suddenly felt self-conscious, and a quick glance at Mary Kate told me that we might even appear frightening to them. Her hair, mud splattered and wildly wavering in the wind, combined with her red sunburned face beaming in the dim moonlight and the tree branch that she'd never put down to give her the appearance of a modern-day Medusa walking forth from the wilderness.

"Where are you from?" a teenage boy wearing a zip-up hoodie and high-tops piped up from the crowd.

"America," I answered. A slew of questions relating to why we were in Putian followed, and after Mary Kate explained that we had just pedaled our way down from Fuzhou, the northern capital city of Fujian, one of the guys pointed at her, declaring her "*li hai!*"—a slang word with many different connotations, but here we took it to mean "badass."

"Do you know *Le Bu Lang Zhan Mu Si*?" he asked.

We shook our heads. His friend, a girl with a pink handbag slung over her shoulder, spoke up. "No, no! Tell them his nickname . . . *Xiao Huang Di!*" she said expectantly.

That name translated as "Little Emperor," but we were still in the dark. "Le Bulang James . . ." another guy prompted.

"Lebron James! Yes, of course we know of him," Mary Kate answered, but that was about all we could say because they all knew loads more about the NBA than we did.

The sweet-smelling noodles we ordered were up, and I resisted the urge to kiss the noodle vendor. I was so happy to finally eat. We soon said good-bye to our new friends, as we still had a ways to go and they were headed back within the factory walls to their work-unit dorms. Their day had surely been longer than ours. In the actual city of Putian, ten miles away, a city of maddening traffic with 3 million people and all of maybe five street signs, shoes were for sale everywhere, many of them labeled "Nike" and "Adidas." (I even saw Nike Air Max Lebron kicks for sale.) Putian, we discovered, is renowned for its international export trade of high-end sneaker knockoffs.

We came to Fujian expecting to eat the elaborate Fujianese dishes touted in Chinese cookbooks with names like Buddha Jumps Over The Wall (a complex mix of dozens of ingredients including shark's fin, sea cucumbers, quail eggs, and abalone) and Green Island Covered with a Hundred Flowers (seasoned shrimp with crab ovaries and digestive glands, water chestnuts, and pork). However, in our travels around the province we found that simple stir-fries and basic dishes, literally known as *nong jia cai* or "peasant food," is what most people eat everyday. Cooks draw on the abundant seafood and produce available to make easy, down-home, hearty meals. A restaurant owner in the Hakka village of Yongding told us as he prepared a whole fish to be steamed with ginger and soy sauce, "No matter how simple the dish, if you start with fresh ingredients the taste will show."

SHA CHA NOODLES · 沙茶面

Not to be confused with Thai satay peanut sauce, Chinese *sha cha* sauce is made with ground soybeans, garlic, and brill fish. The sauce is used by Fujianese and Taiwanese cooks to infuse soup broth with a sweet and savory flavor. Make sure you stir the sauce in the jar well before spooning it out, as the ingredients have a tendency to separate between uses.

SERVES 4

Chop the chicken into bite-size pieces. Combine the stock, rice wine, ginger, sha cha sauce, and green onions in a large pot and bring to a boil. Drop in the chicken, decrease the heat, and gently simmer for 20 minutes. Season with salt to taste.

Meanwhile, cook the noodles according to their package instructions or boil them until they are al dente. Drain and place in 4 bowls. Top each bowl with the bean sprouts and bok choy and use a slotted spoon to place the chicken on top. Then pour the hot broth over everything. Drizzle a little sesame oil over the bowls and sprinkle with cracked black pepper before serving.

1 pound boneless, skinless chicken thighs

6 cups Chicken Stock (page 262) or low-sodium chicken broth

1 tablespoon Shaoxing rice wine or dry sherry

3 slices ginger, smashed with the side of a knife

3 tablespoons sha cha sauce

3 green onions, white parts only, chopped

Salt

14 ounces fresh round noodles or 11 ounces dried egg noodles

Handful of fresh mung bean sprouts or soybean sprouts

3 cups lightly packed bok choy leaves, shredded

Toasted sesame oil, for drizzling

Freshly cracked black pepper

RADISH AND BABY CORN QUICK PICKLES 泡白萝卜玉米笋

China has been plagued by wars, natural disasters, and famine throughout its long history. In times when food was scarce, Chinese cooks expertly preserved food through smoking and pickling. At any given Chinese grocery store, even Wal-Mart, the produce section is loaded with jars and bowls of pickled vegetables that come in all shapes and colors. We like to use Chinese pickled vegetables as a briny condiment on sandwiches or salads or just to snack on with chopsticks. These quick pickles will keep for up to 10 days in the fridge.

SERVES 4

Thinly slice the daikon radish into rounds, and if it's a very large radish, slice the rounds in half. Toss the radish slices with the salt in a bowl and let sit for 30 minutes to draw out the excess moisture. Rinse the radish slices under water, drain, and pat dry.

Heat the vinegar and sugar in a small saucepan over medium heat. Bring to a boil and stir until the sugar is completely dissolved. Remove the saucepan from the heat and allow the vinegar mixture to cool. Stir in the oil, ginger, and chile. Toss the radish slices, baby corn, and cilantro in a large bowl until well combined and then transfer to a large jar. Pour the vinegar mixture into the jar, cover, and refrigerate overnight before serving.

1 pound daikon radish, peeled
1 teaspoon salt
1 cup clear rice vinegar
2/3 cup sugar
2 tablespoons vegetable oil
1 (1-inch) piece ginger, peeled and
    sliced into matchsticks
1 dried red chile, seeded and chopped
1 cup baby corn, cut into 1-inch
    segments
3 tablespoons minced fresh cilantro

POPIAH ROLLS · 薄饼

Zhong Shan Street in the city of Xiamen is a shopping area during the day, but at night it turns into an eating paradise. Fujian snacks of every kind are sold from vendor stalls: oyster omelets, fried taro cakes, sweet fried cheese dumplings, fresh watermelon juice, and fried conch. We were particularly taken with these healthy rolls. They are basically spring rolls with wrappers that are not fried. Fujian cooks use a variety of fillings in popiah. Our recipe uses flaked white fish tossed with carrots, bean sprouts, and daikon radish slices. Feel free to substitute chicken for the fish.

SERVES 4

Season both sides of the fish fillets with salt and pepper. Heat 1 teaspoon of the oil in a nonstick pan over medium heat. Cook the fillets in the pan for about 3 minutes on each side, until the fish is cooked through and no longer translucent. Remove the fish from the pan and let rest for 5 minutes. Then use a fork to flake the fish into chunks. Set aside.

Pulse the peanuts a few times in a food processor, until they are crushed into a coarse powder. You can also achieve the same result by spreading the peanuts on a counter, covering them with a clean kitchen towel, and then pounding them with a heavy object like a wine bottle. Set aside.

Heat the remaining 1 tablespoon of oil in a wok over medium heat. Add the ginger and stir-fry for 10 seconds. Then add the carrot and radish and stir-fry for about 1 minute, or until tender. Add the bean sprouts and oyster sauce and stir-fry for another 30 seconds. Remove the vegetables with a slotted spoon and drain well.

Place a spring roll wrapper in front of you so that one of the corners is pointing toward you and the wrapper is in a diamond shape. (Cover the rest of the wrappers with plastic wrap so they don't dry out.) Lay a lettuce leaf horizontally in the center of the wrapper. Place one-quarter of the vegetable filling and one-quarter of the fish on top of the lettuce leaf and sprinkle with the crushed peanuts. Spoon a little chili sauce on top of the filling and then place another lettuce leaf on top. Fold the bottom corner of the wrapper upward. Then fold the short sides inward. Last, roll the pouch away from you to seal. Place the roll with the loose ends facing downward on a plate so that it doesn't unroll. Repeat with the remaining 3 wrappers, then serve.

12 ounces flaky white fish fillets, like sole or cod

Salt and freshly ground black pepper

1 teaspoon plus 1 tablespoon vegetable oil

1/3 cup roasted peanuts

1 tablespoon minced fresh ginger

1 small carrot, peeled and slivered

1 cup peeled and slivered daikon radish or thinly sliced red radishes

2 cups fresh mung bean sprouts or soybean sprouts

2 tablespoons oyster sauce

4 (8½-inch) spring roll wrappers

8 romaine lettuce leaves, stems trimmed so that each leaf is 6 inches long

Asian chili sauce, such as sriracha sauce

HAKKA AND TINY TEACUPS

My first thought at breakfast in Yongding was that the teacups were too small. Each time we took a sip, they had to be refilled. Our host, Mr. Li, didn't seem to mind, but we felt like a bother and wondered why a people would ever design cups to hold only one sip at a time.

Getting to Yongding in itself was an adventure—a bumpy bus shared with two chickens to a town in the mountains and then motorcycles the rest of the way. On a break, I tasted *yang mei*, a small red fruit, set out to dry roadside on bamboo trays. The flavor was a mix of sour and salt, making me curious to see what other unusual fruits and dishes awaited us. Coming around a bend as we entered Yongding, I noticed my first of many *tu lou*, or "earth buildings." The *tu lou* were mysterious, giant octagonal, square, circular, and triangular buildings resembling fortresses and built of packed earth. Inside, bedroom corridors lined the walls, centering around the main ancestral hall. This central hall was designed to support all types of family gatherings—weddings, banquets, funerals, and even entertaining guests.

The Hakka minority (*ke jia*), or literally "visitor people," live here in clans and have done so for generations. The architecture of these *tu lou* have withstood the test of time. Nate and I stayed in a comfortably cool room on the second floor of a nineteenth-century *tu lou* (some date back as far as the thirteenth century). Our window reminded me of a castle window—the packed earth walls were three feet thick. The Hakka people, as their name suggests, are used to being visitors. The Hakka have a tradition of migrating and have moved beyond the walls of their *tu lou* by the millions, settling in all four corners of the globe.

Distinct communities of Hakka can be found in the rest of China, Taiwan, the United States, Britain, and France, among other places.

Meals here were like eating with family. Mr. Li wanted to hear all about what was going on in our lives. I told him about university life in America and showed him Texas on a map. He smiled and said, "Yao Ming plays there!" Mr. Li's older brother showed us how to kill a fish by whacking its head with the handle of a knife, and his sister-in-law gave us a tour of their vegetable garden. Yongding's main industry is agriculture, and its mountain-ous landscape is a collage of tiered tobacco, carrot, bamboo, and rice fields, with personal gardens creep-ing into almost every backyard. In addition to tea at dinner, we drank a sweet long-grain rice wine that Mr. Li makes at home.

Just like their homes suggest, family is central to the Hakka cul-ture. Serving others and making guests feel welcome is a priority, a meal just another opportunity to show they care. After spending a few days with the Hakka people, I understood their teacups. Sure, mine was tiny, but it was always full. Refilling it again and again was just another way Mr. Li let me know that he was attending to every detail and not to worry about a thing.

FARMHOUSE OMELET ▪ 西红柿炒鸡蛋

Traveling is stressful, especially when you are constantly moving from town to town and waking up in different beds. Our accommodations in the Hakka village of Yongding found us in a 120-year-old farmhouse complete with wooden boards for beds and a rooster outside the window for an alarm clock. His 4:30 A.M. wake-up call and no sleep-button option had Nate and me out the door and hiking in the surrounding green hills in time to catch the sunrise. By lunchtime we were starving and we found our way back to the farmhouse. The mother of the household whipped up these stir-fried eggs and tomatoes in her wok, a simple but deceptively tasty dish. Minced pungent fresh ginger gives the eggs a little kick, and the sugar stews with the tomatoes to bring out their natural, savory umami flavor.

Some of my Chinese friends say this was the first dish they learned how to cook because it is so easy to prepare. Our recipe makes one large omelet and is perfect for those lazy times when you want an easy hot meal that cooks in a minute.

SERVES 1 TO 2

Bring a pot of water to a boil. Plunge the tomatoes into the boiling water for 30 seconds to loosen their skins. Remove, drain, and when they are cool enough to handle, peel them. Cut the tomatoes in half through the middle so that the seed chambers are exposed, squeeze out their seeds, then coarsely chop the tomatoes.

Whisk the eggs and ¼ teaspoon of the salt together until well blended. Heat 2 teaspoons of the oil in a wok or frying pan over medium heat and swish the oil around so that it coats the bottom of the wok. Pour in the eggs and scramble with a spoon until the eggs are just set, then remove from the wok. Heat the remaining 2 teaspoons of the oil in the wok over high heat, add the green onion and ginger, and stir-fry for 10 seconds. Toss in the tomatoes, the remaining ¼ teaspoon of salt, and the sugar and stir for 30 more seconds. Stir in the scrambled eggs until heated through and serve immediately.

3 medium tomatoes

3 large eggs

½ teaspoon salt

4 teaspoons vegetable oil

1 green onion, green and white parts, chopped

½ teaspoon minced fresh ginger

1 teaspoon sugar

CORN AND PINE NUT STIR-FRY · 松仁玉米

Chinese cooks have used pine nuts for hundreds of years. They are extracted from the pinecones of evergreen trees and have a light, piney flavor and smooth texture. The little ivory-colored nuts are full of vitamin E and protein; however, their high fat content makes them extremely perishable, so keep them in the refrigerator until you're ready to use them. This very simple country stir-fry is healthy and delicious.

SERVES 4

In a small bowl, combine the sugar, salt, and water and stir until dissolved. Set aside.

Heat 2 teaspoons of the vegetable oil in the wok over medium-low heat. Add the onion and rice vinegar and sauté them for 10 to 15 minutes, or until they caramelize. Remove the onion from the wok.

Heat the remaining 2 teaspoons of vegetable oil and the sesame oil in the wok over medium heat. Toss in the corn, carrots, peas, and stir-fry for about 6 minutes, or until the corn and carrots are tender. Mix in the sugar mixture, pine nuts, and onion and stir-fry for 1 minute longer. Serve hot.

½ teaspoon sugar
½ teaspoon salt
2 tablespoons water
4 teaspoons vegetable oil
1 medium onion, chopped
1 tablespoon clear rice vinegar
1 teaspoon toasted sesame oil
2 cups corn kernels (fresh or frozen)
2/3 cup peeled and chopped carrots
2/3 cup peas (fresh or frozen)
½ cup pine nuts

CHOP SUEY AND FUJIAN ABROAD

"Chop Suey Resorts: Chinese Dish Now Served in Many Parts of the City. Many New Yorkers Like It—Provides a Cheap and Substantial Meal—Chinese Waiters Indifferent to Tips."

—THE NEW YORK TIMES, *November 1903*

The restaurant looked more like an aquarium with bubbling fish tanks stacked high in the front windows. Red plastic buckets spread out on the patio swirled with swimming sea creatures: shrimp, turtles, crabs, eels. This was, in effect, the menu. The owners, a husband and wife wearing navy blue aprons, stood by the restaurant door waiting for us to choose our lunch. "We'll have those," I said, pointing to a bin of mussels. Then, like always, I asked if we could follow them into the kitchen and observe how they cook. "Why?" Mr. Zhang asked. "Just sit out here," he said. Mary Kate pretended not to hear him so that I would have to be the one to launch into our lengthy, heavily rehearsed speech of why we were here in Fujian's southern city of Xiamen looking for recipes, but Mr. and Mrs. Zhang didn't need much convincing. "Well," I began, "I'm visiting from New York City . . ."

"New York? We have friends there! Yes, yes, come cook with us," Mr. Zhang said.

"We haven't heard from them since they left for New York two years ago," said Mrs. Zhang, scooping out an armful of the black mollusks with a net and carrying it to the kitchen.

"Do people there know of Fujian?" Mr. Zhang asked.

I had some difficulty explaining the concept of a Chinatown. "There's an area of the city where a lot of Chinese immigrants live, er . . ." I fumbled with my words. It seemed too simplistic to equate China's influence, specifically that of Fujian, on America to just Chinatowns. "Yes," I added, finally deciding on my answer. "People know Fujian's influence in America even if they don't know the province by name."

Mr. Zhang seemed pleased with this answer and began vigorously scrubbing the mollusks with a cloth and tearing off their wiry beards. "What is Chinese food like in America?" he asked.

"It has more oil, more meat, and less vegetables. You wouldn't recognize it," I answered.

Mrs. Zhang quickly stir-fried some garlic, ginger, and chiles, filling the pint-size kitchen with a wonderful aroma. Then she readied the hot wok with a splash of rice wine and a touch of soy sauce. Steam whooshed up as she tipped in the mussels, dropping a lid on top.

Chinese immigrants, many of whom were laborers who had come to work on the transcontinental railroad, first arrived in America on the West Coast during the mid-1800s. As they began opening restaurants, Chinese cooks learned to use the unusual

American vegetables (broccoli is a good example) in place of Chinese ones, as well as how to adapt the flavors of their dishes to local tastes. It is said that chop suey was invented during this time when Chinese food was Americanized. *Chop suey* literally translates as "odds and ends" or basically "leftovers" and was more or less stir-fried chopped meat and vegetables served over rice. No two cooks made it the same way. The popularity of chop suey spread from San Francisco and the West Coast to the East Coast, where the twenty-five-cent offbeat stir-fry continued to make a splash—dispelling American prejudices of exotic Asian food and starting a culinary revolution. Soon New York City had "gone 'chop-suey' mad," according to *The New York Times*, and then the rest of the country succumbed to madness for what had become American Chinese food. Later, immigration reform and Nixon's visit to China in 1972 sparked a reinvention of Chinese food and new appreciation for it. Everybody wanted to try what the President was eating, and for the first time people started venturing into Chinatowns to seek out undiscovered dishes like Peking duck, Sichuan spicy fish, and soup dumplings.

Mr. and Mrs. Zhang joined us as we sat down to our lunch under the red glow of the patio awning. "If you two ever open a restaurant in New York, you will have to serve these black bean mussels and Fujian *sha cha* noodles. The overseas Fujianese will eat them up. A taste of home," he said.

I think America is in the midst of another Chinese culinary revolution. A shift in immigration that started in the 1990s has changed the landscape of China's presence in America. In the past, most immigrants arrived from Hong Kong and Taiwan. Today, they come mostly from the mainland, the majority specifically from Fujian Province. I've watched the change unfold on the streets of Chinatown in

New York. Where I used to hear only Cantonese spoken on the streets, the language of Guangdong and Hong Kong, I now hear more and more Mandarin.

The food is also changing. Chinatown restaurants used to serve almost exclusively Cantonese food. Now I am starting to see more food from the rest of China that has previously never been seen before as cooks from other regions of the country open up shop: Fujianese handmade noodles, steamed clams, Fuzhou-style fish balls, Sichuan hot pot, Xian roast pork sandwiches. For amazing tasting Xinjiang-style lamb kebabs, visit the food cart below the Manhattan Bridge on the corner of Forsyth Street and Division Street.

GINGER-STEAMED FISH 姜蒸鱼

Riding the ferry across the water to Gulangyu Island was a reminder of just how many people there are in China. In a small waiting room, we were slammed together with 200 or so other passengers waiting to board the next boat. When the doors slid open, everyone raced through them, pushing and shoving to guarantee a seat on the boat.

Stepping off onto the island was a different story. No cars or bikes are allowed on the island, and we wandered the quiet, meandering pedestrian streets between crumbling European colonial mansions, banyan trees with sprawling branches, and small restaurants serving fresh seafood dishes to tourists. The street scenes were so beautiful that I counted no less than eight couples posing for wedding pictures—in front of manicured flower hedges, atop steps leading up to a mansion, and behind a fountain.

This recipe makes fillets that taste light and moist. The honeyed marinade enhances the fish's flavor, and flash-fried ginger and garlic slices add a zesty crunch. Even though a white fish is traditionally used, we love to sometimes swap it for Atlantic salmon fillets.

SERVES 4

4 (6-ounce) firm white fish fillets, such as halibut or sea bass
Freshly ground black pepper
2 tablespoons light soy sauce
2 tablespoons Shaoxing rice wine or dry sherry
2 teaspoons honey
2 teaspoons toasted sesame oil
3 green onions, green and white parts, chopped
1 (2-inch) piece ginger, peeled and slivered into matchsticks
2 tablespoons vegetable oil
6 cloves garlic, thinly sliced
1 dried red chile, seeded and slivered

Place the fish fillets skin side up on a heatproof plate that will fit into a steamer tray. Lightly score the tops of the fillets with a knife. Season each fillet with black pepper and rub into the fish.

In a small bowl, whisk together the soy sauce, rice wine, honey, and 1 teaspoon of the sesame oil and pour over the fish fillets. Sprinkle the green onions and one-third of the ginger over the fish.

Pour 2 inches of water into the base pot of a steamer and bring to a boil. Place the plate with the fish fillets on a steamer tray and place in the steamer. Cover and steam for 6 to 10 minutes, until the fish is cooked through and no longer translucent (see How to Steam on page 254). Remove the fillets and place on 4 serving plates. Pour the remaining juice from the steamer tray over the fish.

In a wok or small saucepan, heat the remaining 1 teaspoon of sesame oil and the vegetable oil over high heat until very hot. Drop in the remaining two-thirds of the ginger and the garlic and stir-fry for about 45 seconds, or until they turn light brown and crunchy. Toss in the chile and stir-fry for another 10 seconds. Pour the hot oil mixture over the fish fillets and serve.

THE GOOD CHINA

One afternoon in Beijing, over tripe and a sour soup with wood tree ear fungus, a friend and former coworker of mine, Xiao Gao, balked at the idea that I was truly interested in Chinese food. "You need to see for yourself how and where china dishes are made to fully understand our food," she solemnly insisted. Even though I had grown up eating on a different set of our family's "good china" on every special occasion and with a mother whose attitude is that "one can never have too many dish sets," I had never once considered how china was made. "Where do we go?" I asked. The answer was Jingdezhen, a southern city in Fujian's neighboring province of Jiangxi and the porcelain capital city of the world with 1,700 years of pottery-production history.

Xiao Gao completely arranged Nate's and my trip. She had *guanxi* with someone in Shanghai who had a business connection with somebody who knew a porcelain factory owner in Jingdezhen. (*Guanxi* is a name given to the complex personal relationships and favors that play a factor in business and in getting things done in general in China.) The whole thing was confusing, as *guanxi* often is, but Xiao Gao said that everything would be fine if we called Maggie—the factory owner—when we arrived in Jingdezhen and said that "Mr. Wu" sent us. Not only was everything fine but Maggie and her assistant Suzie also treated us to two amazing days of seeing the ins and outs of porcelain making, starting with a hands-on experience at Maggie's factory.

Passing through a quiet workshop of painters and into a hall humming with the sound of spinning pottery wheels, I sat down on a tiny bamboo stool to my own wheel. Taking cues from the potter next to me, I dunked my hands in a bucket of murky water and slicked the spinning lump of clay into a cone between my hands. Then I formed an opening at the top and used my thumbs and fingers to pinch and pull it wider into a bowl. Then my bowl began to lean and wobble and fold in on itself. *It had looked so easy.*

Suzie rushed in to catch my gray blob before it completely tumbled off the wheel. "Don't worry," she said, centering the bowl and beginning to throw it into an hourglass vase. "It takes practice. I've been learning in school for four years already," she said.

"If you're just painting pottery, no problem, but if you want to make pottery, you need to know something about physics and chemistry," Suzie said. Taking a finished teacup out of its box, Suzie held it over a lightbulb to show me the thin delicateness of each piece. Then she banged it forcefully against another to show me the strength of the material and the rich resonating sound it produced. "Animal bone powder is mixed in with these to make them extremely durable," she explained. To make Chinese porcelain, clay and ground stone are mixed with water to form a gray-colored clay. The clay is hand-thrown into pots, bowls, or what have you, dried for five days in the sun, and then fired for a short time in a kiln to remove impurities from the clay. After being painted with colored glazes, the vessels are finally fired in a blazing-hot kiln.

On our second day, we toured an ancient wood-lit kiln in Jingdezhen that dated back to the early Qing Dynasty (1644–1911). The kiln was a large egg-shaped room the size of a racquetball court, with a dome brick ceiling and a gravel floor. During the Qing reign, when Jingdezhen's kilns were burning hot, artisans fired hundreds of thousands of porcelain pieces to feed a growing mania in Europe for Chinese porcelain, especially the blue-and-white painted wares. Europe did not yet have the technology or the skill to make china, and the mysterious heatproof material became as desired

as gold. Topping the list of the porcelain-obsessed was Queen Mary II of England, who decked out her palaces with hundred of pieces of china and commissioned one-of-a-kind porcelain objects. By the mid-1600s, all the fashionable people of Europe were eating off hand-painted china. Centuries even before this time, Chinese junks laden with porcelain set sail for the rest of the world from Fujian's maritime Silk Route port city of Quanzhou, the largest port city of Asia at that time. Chinese porcelain was met with such success throughout the world that it became synonymous with China, its country of origin.

On our last evening in town, Maggie presented us with a banquet of food on dishes hand-painted with dragons that could have literally pleased an emperor. Up until the last dynasty, Jingdezhen was responsible for creating the royal wares. The town's history is so centered around ceramics that its foundation is built upon millions of pottery shards and its streets are lined with lampposts that are covered with hand-painted porcelain—blue-and-white mountain landscapes, orange persimmons, and pink peonies. "Our artists could have painted even more spectacular ones," Maggie told me. "But the artist who got the job has *guanxi* with the mayor."

PEEL 'EM AND EAT 'EM SHRIMP WITH
CHILE-SOY DIPPING SAUCE 蒸虾蘸辣酱油汁

On Gulangyu Island, just off the coast of Xiamen, we met a man named Hong who lived in an old colonial brick home. He was a tour guide by day and an online stock-market trader by night. We went out to eat with Hong and a few of his friends on the island and ordered a plate of steamed shrimp. I was surprised to see them shell the shrimp and tear off the heads before eating. This was a different story than in most other places in China, where people prefer to eat the head and the shell whole. I mentioned this to Hong. "Eww," he said, "that would not have a fresh flavor. It would be the wrong consistency and ruin the taste." Fujian cooks pride themselves on cooking light and fresh foods that are never greasy.

These shrimp are the perfect finger food, and the chile-soy dipping sauce tastes like summer. Peel first.

SERVES 4 TO 6

To make the shrimp, toss the shrimp in a bowl with the lemon, salt, bay leaves, and onion. Set aside to marinate, covered, for 15 minutes.

Meanwhile, make the dipping sauce. In a small bowl, mix the soy sauce, rice vinegar, sesame oil, vegetable oil, honey, chiles, cilantro, ginger, and garlic. Let sit for 30 minutes to bring out the flavors.

Pour 2 inches of water and the rice wine into the base pot of a steamer and bring to a boil. Place the shrimp in the steamer tray and put in place in the steamer. Cover and steam for 5 minutes, until the shrimp is bright pink and cooked through (see How to Steam on page 254). Serve the shrimp with the dipping sauce.

SHRIMP

2 pounds shrimp, shells on but heads removed

1 lemon, thinly sliced

½ teaspoon salt

2 bay leaves

1 small onion

DIPPING SAUCE

¼ cup light soy sauce

¼ cup clear rice vinegar

1 teaspoon toasted sesame oil

2 tablespoons vegetable oil

2 tablespoons honey

4 dried red chiles, seeded and coarsely chopped

2 tablespoons minced fresh cilantro

1 tablespoon minced fresh ginger

2 cloves garlic, minced

¾ cup Shaoxing rice wine or dry sherry

STIR-FRY SUGAR SNAP PEAS · 炒甜豌豆荚

Snow peas have a tendency to get a little limp when stir-frying, but sugar snap peapods maintain their crunchy texture. The heat from the wok brings out their natural sweetness. This is a beautiful, brightly colored stir-fry. Three minutes and you're eating.

SERVES 4

Heat the oil in a wok over high heat. Add the garlic and stir-fry for 10 seconds. Add the snap peas and stir-fry for 1 minute. Add the carrot, rice wine, and salt and stir-fry for about 2 minutes, until the beans are soft yet still crunchy and bright green. Serve immediately.

2 teaspoons vegetable oil
4 cloves garlic, thinly sliced
1 pound sugar snap peas, trimmed
1 medium carrot, peeled and slivered
    into 3-inch lengths
2 tablespoons Shaoxing rice wine or
    dry sherry
½ teaspoon salt

新昌

海 茸 蔴 昌

楊北海

RESTAURANT

HONG KONG
香港

HONG KONG 香港

Fresh off the bus from mainland China and through Hong Kong's immigration checkpoint, Nate and I wearily pile into a red and silver cab on a glitzy skyscraper-lined street on Hong Kong Island. "Chungking Mansions," I say to the driver, naming the complex of ultracheap guesthouses where we always stay when we come here—a place that is about as far away from the idea of a mansion as one could imagine.

"Okay," the driver says. "But I should tell you, I just heard on the news that a foreigner has been shot and killed there tonight!" he exclaims, motioning to the dashboard radio. I strain my ears to hear the animated broadcast, but it is in Cantonese—Hong Kong's official language—and I can't understand a word. Nate and I rack our brains for another option, but before we know it, we are through the Cross-Harbor Tunnel to Hong Kong's peninsula territory Kowloon and rolling up to the wide, steel-gated entrance of the Chungking Mansions. Nefarious characters and rough-looking men with tattoos shuffle in and out of the door, and a handful of cops mill about the front steps.

"Nothing looks different. I'm sure it's fine," Nate says, unloading our bags from the trunk.

The infamous Chungking Mansions tenement building is a seventeen-story tangle of businesses, restaurants, home residences, and a hundred or so guesthouses. Every night thousands of international people sleep within its walls, and according to the anthropologist Gordon Mathews, as many as 130 countries have been counted at one time on its guest registries: Japanese hippies, laborers arriving from the Philippines and India, backpackers like us, African and Pakistani traders in town for business or just passing through for a weekend to get their visas for mainland China. Phones, watches, electrical goods, gold, and other products (legal and otherwise) are sold on the ground floor between international food stalls that dish up Indian curries and chapatis, Southeast Asian food, pastries, and fried rice. Cops are never far—a fact we learned during our last trip here, when three policemen busted into our nine-dollar windowless guest room (the door lock had been smashed long ago) and demanded our passports during a building-wide raid for illegal immigrants. The only thing that appears different tonight at the Chungking Mansions is the TV van parked out front and the news crew covering the scene.

I shove a wad of Hong Kong dollars through the cab's lowered window. "Look!" the driver says, pointing to a news cameraman setting up his tripod behind me. "If you stay the night, maybe you'll be on TV," he says, laughing and speeding off as I begin to worry. Hong Kong Chinese people don't typically venture into the Chungking Mansions. Tales of illicit goings-on inside have given the place a notorious reputation among locals as a den of iniquity. My favorite Chinese movie director, Wong Kar Wai, grew up in the Tsim Sha Tsui area around the Chungking Mansions. His parents wouldn't allow him to visit the place as a kid, but that didn't stop his enduring fascination with the mysterious international hub. The complex was later

an inspiration for his movie *Chungking Express*. The plot centers on drug smugglers, murderers, cops, and a noodle-shop cook. Many of its scenes are filmed within the building's claustrophobic labyrinth of smoky rooms and slippery back hallways. In interviews, Wong has summed up his inspiration for using the Chungking Mansions in his film by saying, "That mass-populated and hyperactive place is a great metaphor for the town herself."

"There's no way I am staying in that building tonight," I tell Nate, putting my foot down on the

matter. Nate slams his pack on the sidewalk. "No way," I add. "Maybe later in the week, but not tonight."

"Then where do we go?" he demands.

"I know exactly the place. And it's not where anyone got shot tonight!" I slam back as I march north on Nathan Road without the slightest idea of where I'm going or where to find a place in our budget.

"Oh, I can't wait to see it!" Nate says, falling in line behind me. A guesthouse owner from within the Chungking Mansions follows us past the Rolex store on the corner, no doubt desperate to fill his recently vacated rooms. "Okay, okay. No lower, but fifty percent off for you. I'll even give you fresh towels," he pleads. "Clean sheets!" he says. We don't stop. Gritty hustlers in leather and gold slink from the shadows: "DVD, DVD . . . Copy watch? Copy watch?" A man with a low-billed baseball cap and cigarette corners Nate: "A tailored suit for you, sir?" he whispers. These guys never sleep. I walk right past the ritzy Hyatt Regency hotel and skip the four-star Holiday Inn. I glance over my right shoulder as I cross the street by the Kowloon Mosque, making sure I don't get run over tonight by the city's high-speed traffic that drives on the left side of the road, a leftover from Hong Kong's British rule. Now we're passing a row of glamorous stores—Gucci, Fendi, Dolce & Gabbana, Prada. I catch my reflection in the Chanel boutique window and wish I hadn't. I look like I've just been on a restless fifteen-hour bus ride with no air-conditioning and Chinese pop songs playing at full volume the entire way. Next time I'm flying from Fujian to Hong Kong.

Ducking into a small twenty-four-hour eatery with Nate in tow, I slump into a booth, resigning myself to the fact that we will just go back to the Chungking Mansions. "At least let me eat a last meal," I say, grabbing a menu and immediately turning to the drinks section.

We order, and bowls of fresh noodles and crispy roast duck arrive at our table. I spoon tangy green onion–ginger sauce over everything and drain my glass of Hong Kong iced milk tea in nearly one gulp. This is why I keep coming back to this city. Lulled into a food coma, I stare out the restaurant's steamy window and let my mind wander. A hipster couple passes by on their way to or from dinner, her hot pink pumps impossibly fashionable and his slim-cut black suit and skinny tie so cool. Across the street, a four-story high Kate Moss looks down at me smugly from an illuminated billboard, modeling a

slinky white dress without a care in the world. I doubt *she's* staying at the Chunking Mansions tonight.

Arriving in Hong Kong from mainland China is always a shock for me and one I'm not always prepared for. Even though the city maintains its Chinese character, it feels more like New York than Shanghai. Prices are higher, and the sprawling metropolis is international, fashionable, current, and much less interested in me. Many Western ideals like capitalism, free speech, and individualism remain from the city's 156 years under British rule, and the energy in the streets is infectious. Its alleys literally glow red, green, and blue from the layered neon shop and restaurant signs that stretch farther, higher, brighter above the streets, competing and screaming for people's attention and begging us to *buy buy buy*. I am easily swayed and end up buying too much and eating too much whenever I'm here, and I'm not the only one.

Locals of all ages pride themselves on having a keen sense of style and knowing great food. Hong Kong has the freest market economy in the world, zero sales tax, trendy fashion boutiques, and restaurants that serve a seemingly endless variety of food, including the famed *dim sum* cuisine. At night in the shadows of the skyscrapers, market stalls illuminate the alleys of Hong Kong, selling raw meat, live seafood swimming in buckets set on the sidewalks, and fresh tropical fruit loaded on wooden carts. People bustle home from work carrying shopping bags and grocery sacks. Also lit up at night is what I consider to be one of the most impressive, sprawling skylines in the world. Best viewed from the top of Victoria Peak, a mountain on Hong Kong Island, the panoramic city is breathtaking. Modern glass skyscrapers jut up into the sky like mountains themselves on the Island, and across Victoria Harbor, Kowloon continues for as far as I can see, and ever in the distance are the 234 outlying islands that make up Hong Kong's New Territories region—the city's best-kept secret of beautiful natural beaches, subtropical forests, and roaming water buffalo.

HONG KONG MILK TEA ▪ 香港奶茶

The British may have left Hong Kong in 1997, but in their wake they left a love of black tea taken with milk and sugar. Milk tea is the most popular drink in Hong Kong and can be drunk hot or cold. Every restaurant has its own secret combination of types of tea leaves. I've seen some use five different tea blends in one pot. We prefer English Breakfast or Orange Pekoe, but you can use whatever black tea you have on hand. The leaves are simmered with an eggshell to prevent any bitterness. Hong Kong Milk Tea's alternate name—"silk stocking tea"—gets its name from the stretchy, hosiery-like filter used to strain the tea, but you can use cheesecloth as an alternative.

SERVES 4

Combine the water, tea, and eggshell in a small pot or saucepan. Bring to a boil, then lower the heat and simmer gently, covered, for 30 minutes. There should be about 3 cups of tea remaining in the pot. Strain the tea through cheesecloth or a coffee filter. Mix in the sugar, stirring until it is dissolved, then chill in the refrigerator.

Divide the chilled tea evenly into 4 highball glasses and add ¼ cup evaporated milk and ¼ cup whole milk to each glass. Drop about 5 ice cubes into each glass and stir the tea. If you want to make bubble tea, add 3 tablespoons rehydrated tapioca balls to each glass and serve with a wide straw or long-handled spoon.

4 cups water

4 tablespoons loose English Breakfast or Orange Pekoe tea

1 eggshell, rinsed

5 tablespoons sugar

1 cup evaporated milk

1 cup whole milk

Ice cubes

¾ cup large black tapioca balls, rehydrated according to their package instructions (optional)

CHAR SIU ROAST PORK ∙ 叉烧肉

Hong Kong restaurants proudly display the day's roast pork (and whole roast geese) strung up behind street-level windows to tempt passersby. When an order for *char siu* pork is made, the butcher pulls the succulent roasted meat down—chop, chop, chop—and carves it up on a platter or stuffs it in a Styrofoam take-out container for those on their way home from work. The pork can be eaten inside steamed buns (see recipe on page 105) or over noodles, or it's great served on top of white rice and drizzled with its sweet barbecue-like sauce.

This recipe's marinade infuses the meat with a deep savory flavor, and the dish gets its tangy undertones partly from the addition of *bai jiu* (白酒), a type of Chinese clear liquor. If you can procure some Chinese *bai jiu*, we recommend doing it up Chinese-style and kicking back a few shots. It is customary for the host to drink as much as his guests.

SERVES 4 TO 6

2 pounds boneless pork loin
¼ cup hoisin sauce
¼ cup light soy sauce
1 tablespoon dark soy sauce
1/3 cup honey
1 tablespoon sugar
1½ teaspoons Chinese five-spice powder
1 tablespoon *bai jiu* liquor or brandy
1 tablespoon vegetable oil
1 teaspoon cornstarch, dissolved in 1 tablespoon cold water

Slice the pork loin lengthwise and then cut the 2 strips in half crosswise to make 4 strips. Score the meat all over with a knife to help the marinade soak in.

In a large bowl, mix together the hoisin sauce, light soy sauce, dark soy sauce, honey, sugar, five-spice powder, liquor, and oil until well blended. Toss in the meat and use your hands to massage the marinade into the meat, making sure all the pieces are coated. Cover the bowl and marinate in the refrigerator for at least 4 hours (overnight is even better).

Preheat the oven to 425°F. Add a wire rack to a roasting pan and fill the pan with ½ inch of water. Place the pork strips on the rack, reserving the remaining marinade. If you don't have a roasting pan and rack insert, place a pan filled with ½ inch of water on your oven's lowest rack to catch the roast's drippings. Then place the pork strips directly on your oven's center rack.

Roast the pork for 10 minutes. Turn the strips over and baste both sides with the reserved marinade. Lower the heat to 325°F and roast for an additional 20 minutes, or until the meat is cooked through and no longer pink inside.

To make the sauce, boil the liquid in the roasting pan or dripping tray, along with any extra marinade, in a small saucepan until it reduces to about 1 cup. Add the cornstarch slurry and simmer for 1 minute while stirring.

Let the roast rest for 5 minutes, and then slice thinly and serve.

CHICKEN AND MUSHROOM CONGEE · 香菇鸡粥

Hong Kong stays up well after its bedtime, especially in the Kowloon area, and besides bars and dance clubs, movie theaters are packed. Back in mainland China, the government permits only twenty foreign films to be played in cinemas each year, and there are no foreign movies or TV shows allowed on television. When Mary Kate and I are visiting Hong Kong from the mainland, we usually end up going to see as many movies as there are out. I think there is no better way to end a movie night in Hong Kong than by stopping by an open all-night restaurant and grabbing a hot bowl of rice congee.

If you like Italian risotto, chances are you'll like Chicken and Mushroom Congee. Both are made with short-grain rice that simmers down to a creamy texture. The ingredients added to the plain congee are up to the individual cook and are often served as condiments, making it a fun dish to experiment with. Every congee eater and their sister seem to have an opinion on the congee style they prefer. You can make sweet congee, savory congee, thick congee, runny oatmeal-like congee, and any combination of these. This savory congee recipe made with sautéed shiitake mushrooms, salty chicken, sweet peas, and chicken stock makes for a hearty soup.

SERVES 4

2 tablespoons salt
1 (4-ounce) boneless, skinless chicken breast
1 teaspoon vegetable oil
1 cup chopped fresh shiitake mushrooms, stemmed
1½ tablespoons light soy sauce
1 cup short-grain white rice
3 cups Chicken Stock (page 262) or low-sodium chicken broth
5 cups water
1 slice ginger, smashed with the side of a knife
½ cup peas (fresh or frozen)
2 green onions, green and white parts, chopped

Bring a pot of water to a boil. Add the salt and boil the chicken in the water for 10 minutes, or until the chicken is cooked through. Drain the chicken and let rest until it is cool enough to handle. Shred the chicken by pounding it a few times with a rolling pin and then pulling it apart into shreds with your fingers. Set aside.

Heat the oil in a medium skillet over high heat. Add the mushrooms and soy sauce and sauté for 1 minute, then remove and set aside.

Combine the rice, stock, water, and ginger in a large saucepan. Bring to a boil, then decrease the heat and simmer gently, covered, for 45 minutes. Stir the rice every 5 to 10 minutes to keep the rice from sticking to the bottom of the pan.

Add the peas to the saucepan and cook for 5 more minutes. The congee should have a runny, oatmeal-like consistency. If the congee becomes too thick, add a little water, or if it's too soupy, simmer it for a little longer, uncovered, until it thickens up.

Serve each bowl of congee topped with the shredded chicken, mushrooms, and chopped green onions.

CHAR SIU PORK BUNS · 叉烧包

A local cook rented us an empty room in her Hong Kong Island apartment and gave us a lesson on how to make these Char Siu Pork Buns. Her apartment was tiny, like most Hong Kong homes, and space was used efficiently. The kitchen sink doubled as counter space when she laid a bamboo cutting board over its top. The fluffy buns puff up like white clouds after they are steamed, and their sweet roast pork filling is heavenly.

MAKES 16 BUNS

To make the dough, combine the water and milk in a small bowl. In a large bowl, combine the flour, sugar, and baking powder and stir until well combined. Slowly stir in the water mixture, and when it is absorbed, stir in the shortening and vinegar. Turn the dough out onto a lightly floured work surface and knead for about 10 minutes, or until the dough is very smooth and elastic. Cover the dough with plastic wrap and let rest for 1 hour.

Meanwhile, cut sixteen 2-inch squares from a roll of parchment paper.

To make the filling, whisk together the soy sauce, sugar, ketchup, honey, and oyster sauce in a bowl until the sugar is dissolved. Heat the oil in a wok over medium heat. Drop in the green onions and sauté for 30 seconds. Add the pork and soy sauce mixture and stir for 2 minutes. Add the cornstarch slurry and cook for 1 more minute, or until most of the liquid has evaporated. Remove the wok from the heat and let cool.

Roll the dough into a 12-inch-long cylinder and cut it into 16 equal pieces. Use a mini rolling pin to roll the dough pieces into 3-inch diameter disks. Cover the disks with plastic wrap so they don't dry out. Place 1 tablespoon of pork filling in the center of a dough disk. Pleat the edges of the dough and pinch the pleats together at the top to seal the filling inside. Repeat with the remaining dough disks and filling.

Pour 2 inches of water into the base pot of a steamer and bring to a boil. Place several of the buns on parchment squares and arrange on the steamer tray at least 2 inches apart to give them room to expand. Place the tray in the steamer, cover, and steam for 12 to 14 minutes, until the buns are all puffed up (see How to Steam on page 254). Repeat with the remaining buns. Serve warm.

DOUGH

¼ cup water
5 tablespoons milk
2¼ cups cake flour
½ cup sugar
3¼ teaspoons baking powder
2 tablespoons vegetable shortening, melted
1 teaspoon white vinegar

FILLING

2 tablespoons light soy sauce
2 teaspoons sugar
1 teaspoon ketchup
2 teaspoons honey
1 tablespoon oyster sauce
1 tablespoon vegetable oil
4 green onions, white parts only, minced
1½ cups chopped Char Siu Roast Pork (page 102)
1 teaspoon cornstarch, dissolved in 1 tablespoon water

DRINK MORE TEA, EAT MORE DIM SUM

A cute old lady with a speckled gray ponytail and jade earrings strolled past me three times on the narrow footbridge as I stood watching the fishing boats pace by below, returning from the sea—each time she passed, her pushcart was piled a little higher. On either side of the riverbank where she walked, fishermen docked their flat-bottomed sampan boats and lugged bucket after bucket of splashing fish, squid, and other sea creatures onto the land. Sorting through their haul and selecting a handful of crabs and a few fish, she loaded her small cart with seafood. Other villagers sorted through the bins as well—some just out of curiosity of what the morning's haul had brought and some bartering for their selection.

My stomach growled for breakfast, and I wandered through the quaint fishing village of Tai O and entered the nearest teahouse. It was not even seven in the morning, but the round tables inside were packed and the room was abuzz with gossip (everyone knew everyone's name). Porcelain clinked as old-timers

dunked their teacups in bowls of hot water to warm them before filling them with green tea. I joined the only table with an empty seat and sat between a man who never once looked up from his newspaper and the lady I recognized from the bridge. "Where's your pushcart?" I asked. "I took it home," she answered. I knew she couldn't live far, as most of the homes in Tai O are built upon stilts along the scenic river waterfront.

Taking notice of the handwritten *dim sum* menu on the wall, I ordered myself enough of the tiny appetizers to feed a family of five. Sipping my tea, chatting with the people around me, and eating to my heart's content, it occurred to me that this must be how *dim sum* was invented. When teahouses sprung up along the Silk Road in China to cater to tired travelers wanting rest and *yum cha*, the ancient Chinese tradition of "drinking tea," someone must have thought of adding a snack to go along with the tea, and thus these tiny morsels came about. *Dim sum* translates as "touch the heart" and are meant to just be small bites, not a full meal. Diners order as few or as many of the small, toothsome, sweet and savory dishes as they want: mango pudding, steamed rice wrapped in a lotus leaf, chicken feet. One fisherman told me that every morning he wakes up early to drink tea and eat *dim sum* before he goes out fishing. "And when I come back," he said, "I drink more tea and eat more *dim sum*!"

I felt a world away from the skyscraper-laden Hong Kong Island while sitting there on Lantau Island—an island of palm trees and sandy beaches. However, it had only taken me three hours by ferry and bus to make the trip. Lantau Island is one of the 234 outlying islands that make up Hong Kong's New Territories region and is a reminder of what all of Hong Kong used to be like not so long ago. During the Ming Dynasty,

Hong Kong and its surrounding areas were famous for growing incense trees and exporting incense products, which led to the name Hong Kong (*xiang gang,* 香港), or "Fragrant Harbor." When the British took it over in 1841 as a spoil of the first Opium War, Hong Kong Island had fewer than 10,000 residents and was described by Queen Victoria's Foreign Secretary as "a barren rock with nary a house upon it."

During the next century and a half under British rule, while the mainland concurrently struggled with bloody civil wars, invasion, and Communist-driven creative oppression, Hong Kong established itself as a world financial center and pioneered a new filmmaking genre with kung fu films made popular around the world by Bruce Lee and Jackie Chan. Hong Kong's population also increased dramatically, and this influx was due in large part to mainland refugees. For years, many families lived on the sampan boats they first arrived on, anchored in the harbor. Now the city's use of space can be taken as a sign of efficiency (certainly

not poverty), with its real estate extending high in the sky and outward in every direction. Families live in old apartment high-rises and hang their clothes outside their windows to dry, damp linens and underwear dangling in the wind above a new Louis Vuitton store on the first floor. Instead of seeming like a hypocrisy, it fits with the times.

As the city's population has ballooned to 7 million, so has the locals' appetite for *dim sum*. The *dim sum* "halls," as they are called in metropolitan Hong Kong, are not the laid-back gatherings of Tai O, but rather rowdy, dizzying places with mind-boggling selections of food. Around the round tables in the restaurant, women push trolleys stacked precariously high with bamboo steamer trays full of tempting *dim sum* dishes like velvety white steamed buns that, when broken open, reveal tangy barbecue pork (*char siu bau*). Diners yell out for more hand-pleated pork dumplings topped with pink beads of crab roe (*siu mai*) or simply grab a tray off the cart for themselves. Mary Kate and I have even been in restaurants that are so slammed at lunchtime that diners resort to going straight into the kitchen to serve themselves, and at some of the larger halls there can be a hundred items to choose from.

Unfortunately, it's not very feasible to make *dim sum* at home, as most of the dishes are extremely time-intensive. Sometimes we just make one or two dishes and serve them as fantastic appetizers or cocktail starters. We've included only a few *dim sum* recipes in this book, but if you can find a *dim sum* hall near you, here are a few can't-miss dishes to order: *har gao* (translucent shrimp dumplings, considered to be the benchmark for any *dim sum* restaurant), *loh bak goh* (steamed turnip cakes flavored with Chinese bacon), *luo mai gai* (steamed lotus leaf parcels containing rice and chicken), *cheung fan* (steamed rice noodle rolls of shrimp or barbecue pork). In the meantime, be a hero and make our *dim sum* recipes for your friends: Char Siu Pork Buns (page 105), Black Bean Spareribs (page 110), Mango Pudding (page 110), and Chicken Spring Rolls (page 113).

MANGO PUDDING · 芒果布丁

My favorite part about *dim sum* is that it's okay to eat dessert first without the guilt. There's no rule (not even among parents) that you have to wait until all your vegetables are eaten before you can get to the good stuff. It's perfectly acceptable to choose desserts from the individual dishes that come around on the *dim sum* cart whenever you want. Mango Pudding is creamy, velvety goodness loaded with chunks of fresh mango and topped with fresh strawberry slices—something worth eating at the beginning and the end of a meal.

SERVES 4

To make the pudding, bring the water to a boil in a medium saucepan. Add the sugar and powdered gelatin and whisk until completely dissolved. Remove from the heat. Combine the coconut milk, cream, sugar mixture, and salt in a large bowl. Gently whisk in the mango puree and lime juice until smooth. Toss in the diced mango and mix well.

Slowly pour the pudding into 4 martini glasses or water goblets, filling them to the rim. Chill the puddings in the fridge for at least 4 hours, or until set.

To make the whipped cream, whisk the cream and sugar in a large bowl until soft peaks form. Cover and refrigerate until ready to use. (This can be prepared up to 4 hours ahead of time.) Top each pudding with the whipped cream, strawberries, and a sprig of fresh mint. Serve chilled.

PUDDING
1 cup water
½ cup sugar
1 tablespoon unflavored powdered gelatin
½ cup coconut milk
½ cup heavy whipping cream
¼ teaspoon salt
1½ cups fresh ripe mango puree (about 3 cups diced fresh mangoes blended in a blender)
1 teaspoon freshly squeezed lime juice
½ cup diced fresh mango

WHIPPED CREAM
1 cup heavy whipping cream
1 tablespoon sugar

1 cup sliced strawberries
4 sprigs mint, for garnish

BLACK BEAN SPARERIBS　豉汁蒸排骨

These are not made with South American black beans like the black beans and rice I used to cook all the time in my apartment in college. Instead, these Chinese black beans are soybeans that have been left to ferment until they turn black. Their hearty, savory flavor complements meats well.

This *dim sum* dish that traditionally uses whole black beans, though we prefer adding the easier-to-find Chinese black bean sauce. (Substitute chili bean sauce if you want them spicy.) Steaming the ribs makes the meat extra juicy and moist. Ask your butcher to cut the ribs into chopstick-friendly 2-inch segments.

SERVES 4

In a large bowl, mix together the black bean sauce, rice wine, cornstarch, baking soda, ginger, garlic, sesame oil, and honey. Toss in the bell pepper and spareribs and marinate for 30 minutes in the refrigerator.

Pour 2 inches of water into the base pot of a steamer and bring to a boil. Place the bell pepper and spareribs in a heatproof shallow dish on the steamer tray and put in place. Cover and steam for 20 minutes, or until the ribs are cooked through (see How to Steam on page 254).

3 tablespoons Chinese black bean sauce
1 tablespoon Shaoxing rice wine or dry sherry
3 tablespoons cornstarch
½ teaspoon baking soda
½ teaspoon minced fresh ginger
2 cloves garlic, minced
2 teaspoons toasted sesame oil
1½ teaspoons honey
1 small red bell pepper, seeded and chopped into 1-inch squares
1½ pounds pork spareribs, cut into 2-inch segments

SWEET AND SOUR SHRIMP ▪ 甜酸虾

"Haaaaa—yah!" That's the immortal sound of Hong Kong kung fu film star Bruce Lee screaming in the classic film *Enter the Dragon* as he opens a can of you-know-what on the movie's dastardly crime-lord villain. Hong Kong is a creative powerhouse famous for producing some of the best pop music and movies in Asia, and Hong Kong kung fu films have had a tremendous impact on today's Hollywood movies.

Hong Kong is also famous for its sweet and sour sauce, which is served on pork, chicken, and shrimp. The best versions harmoniously balance the sweet and sour flavors. Our recipe for Sweet and Sour Shrimp achieves that balance but also has that great tang. Haaaaa—*yah*!

SERVES 4

1 tablespoon Shaoxing rice wine or dry sherry
2 tablespoons cornstarch
2 teaspoons toasted sesame oil
1½ pounds medium shrimp, peeled and deveined
2 tablespoons clear rice vinegar
1½ tablespoons sugar
3 tablespoons ketchup
3 tablespoons pineapple juice
1 teaspoon light soy sauce
3 tablespoons vegetable oil
2 cloves garlic, minced
1 tablespoon minced fresh ginger
3 green onions, white parts only, chopped
1 small green bell pepper, seeded and chopped into 1-inch squares
1 small red bell pepper, seeded and chopped into 1-inch squares

In a large bowl, combine the rice wine, 1 tablespoon of cornstarch, and the sesame oil. Stir until dissolved. Toss in the shrimp and let marinate for 30 minutes. Drain the shrimp and set aside.

In a medium bowl, mix together the rice vinegar, sugar, ketchup, pineapple juice, soy sauce, and the remaining 1 tablespoon of cornstarch. Set aside.

Heat 1 tablespoon of the vegetable oil in a wok over medium heat. Toss in the shrimp and stir-fry for about 1 minute, or until they turn pink and are cooked through. Remove the shrimp and wipe out the wok. Heat the remaining 2 tablespoons of vegetable oil in the wok over medium-high heat. Add the garlic and ginger and stir-fry for 10 seconds, then add the green onions and green and red bell peppers and stir-fry for 2 minutes, or until the peppers are tender. Pour in the vinegar mixture and simmer for 1 minute. Toss in the shrimp until they are coated with the sauce. Serve hot.

STIR-FRY BABY BOK CHOY ▪ 炒小油菜

I'm used to cooking with bok choy, slicing it up and putting it in soups and stir-fries, but I rarely think to use its smaller cousin, baby bok choy. The flavor is slightly sweeter than mature bok choy, and as vegetables go, it's pretty darn cute.

SERVES 4

¼ cup Chicken Stock (page 262) or low-sodium chicken broth
1 teaspoon cornstarch
½ teaspoon sugar
2 tablespoons vegetable oil
2 cloves garlic, minced
1½ pounds baby bok choy, sliced in half lengthwise
Salt

In a small bowl, mix together the stock, cornstarch, and sugar until dissolved.

Heat the oil in a wok over high heat. Add the garlic and stir-fry for 10 seconds. Toss in the bok choy and stir-fry for 30 seconds so that the leaves are coated with the oil. Add the stock mixture and lower the heat to a simmer. Cover the wok and cook for 2 minutes, or until the bok choy is tender and bright jade green. Season to taste with salt and serve.

CHICKEN SPRING ROLLS · 春卷

Spring rolls are traditionally eaten during the Chinese New Year Spring Festival (which is how they get their name), but fortunately you can find them year-round at *dim sum* joints or make them at home. To make vegetarian spring rolls, replace the chicken with an equal amount of chopped mushrooms.

Worcestershire sauce is a common dipping sauce for spring rolls in Hong Kong. The British first brought the tangy, pungent sauce with them from the British colonies in India.

MAKES ABOUT 20 SPRING ROLLS

Heat 2 tablespoons of the vegetable oil in a wok over high heat. Swish the oil around and toss in the chicken. Stir-fry for 1 minute, or until the chicken is no longer pink, using a spatula to break the chicken into tiny pieces. Remove the chicken and wipe out the wok. Heat the remaining 1 tablespoon of vegetable oil in the wok over medium-high heat and stir-fry the garlic, ginger, and green onions for 20 seconds. Add the mushrooms and stir-fry for 2 minutes. Stir in the oyster sauce, hoisin sauce, sugar, and cornstarch and cook for 1 minute, then remove the wok from the heat. Toss in the chicken and mix well.

Place a wrapper in front of you so that one of the corners is pointing toward you and the wrapper is in a diamond shape. Place about 2 tablespoons of the chicken filling just below the center of the wrapper in a horizontal line. Fold the bottom corner of the wrapper upward. Roll the pouch upward to just below the center of the diamond and then fold the two sides inward. Last, use your finger to moisten the top edge of the wrapper with the egg and then roll the pouch upward to make a seal. Repeat with the remaining wrappers and filling.

Wipe out the wok, pour in 2 inches of oil, and heat over medium-high heat until a small piece of bread dropped in the oil fries golden brown in 30 seconds. Slide 5 spring rolls into the wok and fry for 2 to 3 minutes, until they are crispy and golden brown. Using a perforated strainer, transfer the spring rolls to paper towels to drain. Repeat this process with the remaining spring rolls.

Serve hot with a side of Worcestershire sauce for dipping.

3 tablespoons vegetable oil
1 pound ground chicken
2 cloves garlic, minced
2 teaspoons minced fresh ginger
2 green onions, green and white parts, chopped
4 fresh shiitake mushrooms, sliced
2 tablespoons oyster sauce
½ tablespoon hoisin sauce
¼ teaspoon sugar
1 tablespoon cornstarch
20 (5-inch-square) spring roll wrappers
1 large egg, beaten
Oil, for deep-frying
Worcestershire sauce, for dipping

DEMOCRACY NOW

If I'd known I was going to be interviewed on camera by a live international news network in Hong Kong, I would have rethought eating that messy barbecue pork at lunch. Too late now. The camera is rolling. The reporter is asking important questions about the state of the world and I am wearing a dirty napkin for a shirt—wrinkled from weeks of being wadded up at the bottom of my pack and carried from one miserable hostel to another. "Are you here as Americans today to support democracy around the world?" the reporter asks. I can't answer. I can't breathe. I can't take my eyes off the suffocating camera lens inches from my face to answer the reporter. All I can think about is someone somewhere in London can see me trembling on the television set.

"No," Nate responds, "we're just here to eat as much as we can and to write a book with recipes and food and stuff." A nice plug for our cookbook, but the subject of the interview definitely isn't us. It's the 100,000-plus banner-bearing, outraged protestors pressing in around us in Victoria Park on Hong Kong Island.

The truth is that Nate and I aren't here for political reasons. We just came from brunch at a *dim sum* restaurant and were on our way to get some freshly squeezed sugarcane juice at Time Square in Causeway Bay when we found ourselves in the midst of a massive protest with a microphone in our faces. At least we are able to glean from the reporter what is going on. Today is July 1, the anniversary of Britain's handover of Hong Kong back to China. Hong Kong was owned by Britain and under British rule for 156 years until the land lease expired in 1997. Hong Kong people gather every year on this date for the "7-1 March" to voice their political concerns and to demand "Democracy Now" from their Communist owners in Beijing.

Our interview of a nearby protest marcher goes much better. Maggie Lo, a young businesswoman, shares her individual thoughts on the day. "We are here because we want to fight for democracy," she says. She goes on to explain that pro-democratic residents like her have been fighting for universal suffrage for many years. Britain had begun to create more and more general-election positions, but since the handover, Hong Kong has lost much of its democratic self-control, with even its Chief Executive appointed by Beijing. She said that this disregard for the people goes against the Chinese government's promise to allow the self-governing capitalist Hong Kong an unchanged lifestyle. Deng Xiaoping, the former Chinese leader who orchestrated the Sino-British agreement that led to the handover, called for "one country, two systems," promising to allow Hong Kong a high level of political autonomy for "at least fifty years."

Maggie hopes that by the time fifty years goes by, China's politics look more like Hong Kong's than the other way around. "Democracy now is the first step," she says, a wry determined smile forming on her lips as she turns to join the sea of yellow armbands parading by.

Over a loudspeaker and aided by charismatic singers on a central stage, the fight song from the musical *Les Miserables* rings out: "Do you hear the people sing? Singing the song of angry men. It is the music of a people who will not be slaves again!" Another chant in the crowd picks up: "Our home! Our place! Our dream! Democracy now!" Anyone who knows mainland China or has heard of the 1989 Tiananmen Square incident in Beijing, when a student-led protest turned into a massacre, knows that a rally like this would be impossible anywhere in the mainland, but this is not the mainland; this is Hong Kong. Never has this distinction seemed more apparent to me than today.

CHICKEN LETTUCE CUPS · 生菜包

Chinese cooks don't use a lot of raw vegetables, but instead prefer to stir-fry or braise them. There are a few exceptions, however, and in Hong Kong cooks fill crisp iceberg lettuce leaves with savory minced pigeon meat. Since we have no intention of domesticating the pigeons outside my New York City apartment window (pigeon meat is hard to find in the United States), we've substituted chicken in this recipe, which tastes equally as delicious. Chuck all the filling ingredients in a food processor if you're in a hurry, but larger chunks of mushrooms and water chestnuts add texture. Don't forget the fresh cilantro leaves heaped on top.

SERVES 4 TO 6

Combine the soy sauce, hoisin sauce, rice vinegar, salt, and sugar in a small bowl and mix together until the sugar dissolves.

Heat 1 tablespoon of the oil in a wok over high heat. Stir-fry the garlic and ginger for 10 seconds. Add the onion, mushrooms, and water chestnuts and stir-fry for 2 minutes. Remove the contents of the wok.

Heat the remaining 2 tablespoons of oil in the wok. Swish the oil around, add the chicken, and brown for 1 minute, or until no longer pink. Add the cooked vegetable mixture back to the wok, decrease the heat, and stir in the sauce mixture. Stir for 1 minute, or until the sauce is heated and the chicken is cooked through.

Spoon the filling in equal amounts into the lettuce cups. Top each lettuce cup with cilantro and sprinkle with chopped cashews. Serve warm.

2 tablespoons light soy sauce

1 tablespoon hoisin sauce

2 tablespoons clear rice vinegar

½ teaspoon salt

½ teaspoon sugar

3 tablespoons vegetable oil

2 cloves garlic, minced

2 teaspoons minced fresh ginger

1/3 cup minced red onion

1 cup chopped canned button mushrooms

½ cup water chestnuts, minced

1 pound boneless, skinless chicken breasts, minced

8 to 10 inner leaves iceberg lettuce, edges trimmed and chilled

Handful of fresh cilantro leaves, coarsely chopped

¼ cup unsalted roasted cashews, coarsely chopped

COCA-COLA CHICKEN WINGS · 可乐鸡翅

I'm kind of an obsessive Coca-Cola investor and junkie. Whenever I see something Coke, I have to get it. I've bought some of the most ridiculous Coke collectibles at antiques shops and on eBay, and when I came to China for the first time, I brought home a carry-on full of heavy Coke bottles and cans just because I liked the Chinese characters printed on them. *Ke kou ke le* (可口可乐) is a phonetic translation of "Coca-Cola" and translates literally as "makes mouths happy." When I found Coca-Cola chicken wings in Shenzhen, Guangzhou Province, I flipped out. Coke in food? Yes! The Coca-Cola Company was the first American company to distribute its products in China after the statesman Deng Xiaoping opened the country to foreign investors in 1979. By now the cola is a fixture in every convenience store across China.

Typically, a can of Coke is the only ingredient for the wings. The secret combination of ingredients in Coke boils down to a reduced sauce not unlike barbecue sauce and gives the meat a rich flavor. In Hong Kong, however, we found a few variations on the dish. Our favorite was a version with soy sauce, ginger, and garlic. Even with a few extra ingredients, these wings are still ridiculously easy to make, and you don't have to own a first-edition Coca-Cola miniature die-cast scooter bike to think these wings are fabulous.

MAKES ABOUT 20 WINGS

Rinse the chicken wings under cool water and pat dry. Toss the wings with the rice wine in a bowl and let marinate for 20 minutes.

Heat the oil in a wok over medium-high heat. Stir-fry the garlic and ginger for 10 seconds, and then add the chicken wings and stir-fry for 2 minutes. Add the soy sauce, Coca-Cola, and star anise to the wok and bring to a boil. Decrease the heat and simmer, uncovered, for 40 minutes, or until the liquid has reduced to about 3 tablespoons. Sprinkle the wings with sesame seeds, if using, and serve.

2 pounds chicken wings (about 20), tips removed
¼ cup Shaoxing rice wine or dry sherry
1 tablespoon vegetable oil
3 cloves garlic, minced
½ tablespoon minced fresh ginger
¼ cup light soy sauce
1 (12-ounce) can Coca-Cola
1 star anise
1 tablespoon sesame seeds (optional)

HOT GINGER-LEMON COKE · 热姜汁柠檬可乐

The vending machine at the Hong Kong Island ferry dock sells "typhoon resistant umbrellas—guaranteed!" Having been in Hong Kong during a typhoon, somehow I can't imagine these little plastic umbrellas holding up in the wild winds and sheets of rain that I watched rock ships and shake buildings. With the notoriously wet and wild weather in Hong Kong, seafarers have long known the soothing power of gingerroot. Just chewing on a piece of ginger can prevent seasickness on the bumpiest of boat rides. The Chinese have known the health benefits of gingerroot for centuries. In this simple, modern-day remedy for the common cold, Coca-Cola is boiled with ginger and lemon for a soothing, restorative drink. But it is also great to drink anytime. Unfortunately, Diet Coke does not work as a substitute.

MAKES 1 SERVING

1 (12-ounce) can Coca-Cola
½ lemon, thinly sliced
1 (1-inch) piece ginger, peeled and thinly sliced

In a small saucepan, bring the Coca-Cola, lemon slices, and ginger to a boil, then decrease the heat and simmer gently for 8 minutes. Serve hot or chilled in a highball glass with the ginger and lemon slices.

CHEATER'S ROAST DUCK SOUP · 懒汉烤鸭汤

Visit your local Chinese restaurant and pick up a large take-out portion of crispy roast duck to make this Cheater's Roast Duck Soup. Spread the crispy-skinned duck slices over noodles and broth and sprinkle with chopped green onions. It'll be the easiest meal you've ever made, and cleanup is a breeze.

SERVES 4

1 pound fresh round noodles or 10 ounces dried egg noodles
5 cups Chicken Stock (page 262) or low-sodium chicken broth
1 tablespoon Shaoxing rice wine or dry sherry
3 slices ginger, smashed with the side of a knife
3 green onions, white parts only, chopped
3 cups firmly packed shredded bok choy leaves
1 pound Chinese roast duck with crispy skin, chopped into bite-size pieces
Handful of fresh mung bean sprouts or soybean sprouts
Toasted sesame oil, for drizzling

Prepare the noodles according to their package instructions or boil until al dente. Drain well and divide among 4 bowls.

Combine the stock, rice wine, ginger, and green onions in a large pot and bring to a boil, then decrease the heat and simmer for 10 minutes. Add the bok choy to the pot and simmer for 1 minute, or until the leaves are wilted and turn bright green. Use a slotted spoon to remove the bok choy from the pot.

Top each bowl of noodles with the roast duck. Heap the bean sprouts and bok choy on top and then pour the broth over everything. Drizzle a little sesame oil over the bowls before serving.

THE HEART OF SOY SAUCE

Ken Wong plunged his hand into the over-sized pot of mushy brown ick. "Smell this," he said, shoving a handful of crumbling, moldy beans in my face. I breathed in and perceived an invigorating, earthy aroma redolent of maple and molasses. "It smells like soy sauce!" I exclaimed.

Mr. Wong chuckled. Of course it smelled like soy sauce. We were visiting Kowloon Soy, his soy sauce factory in the New Territories, an underdeveloped region of Hong Kong, and we were standing in the middle of a field lined with row upon row of ancient ceramic pots large enough for me to sit in, all of them full of fermenting soybeans. "How many pots are there?" I wondered aloud.

Taking off his Oakley sunglasses, Mr. Wong looked around. "You know, I've never counted. Too many to count," he said. "It's a shame you came today. Because it rained earlier, we still have the lids on. If not, all the pots would be open to the sun." I turned around to see that Mary Kate had taken the lid off another pot and submerged her arm up to her elbow in the coffee-colored goo. I decided to try it myself. As I reached down, I felt the soybean mixture become more and more liquid. For three months—sometimes up to six months depending on what is needed—the beans ferment in these pots with saltwater. Except for days like this when it might rain, the beans are exposed to the air to roast directly in the sun before being pressed, strained, bottled, and shipped to a grocery store near you.

Of all Chinese cooking ingredients, soy sauce has to be the ingredient with which Americans are most familiar. We use it as a condiment on rice, a flavoring in stir-fries, and an ingredient in meat marinades. Soy sauce has even found its way to Texas. The "secret" recipe of my favorite brand of Texas barbecue sauce includes vinegar, molasses, and soy sauce. But those ubiquitous little plastic packets of soy sauce that come with your Chinese takeout? They aren't the real thing. The liquid inside is actually just a mixture of water, salt, sugar, and coloring.

In China, soy sauce has been a cooking ingredient for more than 2,500 years, and the way it is made has remained relatively unchanged. The process is simple, Mr. Wong explained. "Anyone can get a recipe and make soy sauce." First, soybeans (Mr. Wong only uses organic) are boiled until they are soft and then combined with a little wheat flour. The mixture is fermented in a cool, dry place until it looks like a giant moldy chocolate cake. The cake is then broken apart, the pieces mixed with saltwater in earthen jars and set outside in the sun.

"If anyone can make soy sauce, why should I buy yours?" I asked, wondering if I've overstepped my bounds.

"Because we put our heart into making it. That is the difference. You can taste it." He answered matter-of-factly. Putting his heart into every bottle of Kowloon Soy soy sauce may not be the most economical method, but you can't argue with the superior, rich taste. Kowloon Soy is one of only four soy sauce companies in Hong Kong to still use the traditional method of fermenting soybeans in pots in the sun and having an experienced master walk the rows every day. "You see, here—this one is darker. I taste it. Smell it. Touch it. A practiced eye," Mr. Wong said, showing us the differing degrees of mushy. The pots are more than a hundred years old, with a patina inside from the thousands of batches of soy sauce that have passed through them, adding a depth of flavor that can't be fabricated in plastic barrels. Most soy sauce factories these days ferment the soybeans under controlled conditions inside a warehouse, adding chemicals to speed up the fermentation, sometimes to as short a time as three days.

Good soy sauce is like a fine red wine, full-bodied and complex with flavors. "We're like the Rolls-Royce of soy sauce!" Mr. Wong laughed. Of the two main kinds of soy sauce, light and dark, he uses only light. "I put it on everything. Rice, beans . . ." he says as he begins to count the foods he adds it to on his hands. "Oh, steak. I put it on that too." Light soy sauce is considered fresh soy sauce and is the product produced right after the beans are done fermenting. Dark soy sauce is made by aging light soy sauce for a longer time and adding sugar. It has a deep red color and is used to add color to a dish. Both light and dark are healthy, and Mr. Wong's ninety-year-old father, who still accompanies him to the factory on occasion, attributes his excellent health to his lifelong love of soy sauce. "My dad always carries around a little bottle," he said. "He takes it out at restaurants because he thinks theirs is no good."

DRAGON
PORTUGUESE
CUISINE

MACAU
澳门

MACAU: PORTUGUESE FUSION FOOD ON THE BEACH 澳门

I pushed open the hotel's front door expecting a lobby or reception area, but instead I found myself inside the remnants of an ancient Portuguese fort. The Pousada de São Tiago hotel and restaurant in Macau is a converted seventeenth-century fort once used to defend against pirates, and it's a curious mixture of Portuguese and Chinese food and history. However, so is all of Macau, a peninsula and two-island territory controlled by Portugal for 400 years, until 1999, when it was returned to China. In front of us, thirty or so stairs led up to a narrow stone cavern where it was easy to imagine the conversations of European explorers and the tales of pirates still echoing off the crumbling walls.

Mary Kate and I ventured up the foreboding stairs but actually neither stayed nor ate there. We couldn't afford it. A day at Macau's greyhound and horse races and a particularly comfortable row of stools on a slot-machine aisle on the first floor of the Casino Lisboa (we only gambled for research, of course) took what little funds Hong Kong hadn't, and we were left on an extremely tight budget, necessitating sleeping on bamboo mats on the floor of a roach-infested hostel and showering in an outdoor wooden shack. This dump was a far cry from the many famous and luxurious accommodations we grudgingly passed up in Macau. Spread across the peninsula and Taipa Island is one glamorous hotel and entertainment center after another, giving rise to the town's nickname, "Vegas of the East." You can watch the Cirque de Soleil aerial acrobats fly above the stage at the Venetian Macau, the largest casino in the world. The place is so big that they claim ninety Boeing 747 jumbo jets could fit within its doors, but instead it's packed with 3,000 gaming machines, 750 gambling tables, and water-filled canals complete with gondoliers serenading tourists with cornball Italian love songs.

Macau's reputation as a booming pleasure town preceded itself for me. I first wanted to travel here as a kid after seeing the James Bond movie *The Man with the Golden Gun*, in which Bond jets over the waves on a hydrofoil from Hong Kong to Macau (we took the one-hour ferry) to seek out an expert Portuguese gun maker in a shady back alley and to gamble at the Casino de Macau. Then I read the nonfiction book *Thrilling Cities*, written by the James Bond series author Ian Fleming, about his extensive world travels. Fleming says of Macau, "I have seldom left a town with more regret." Fleming (and James Bond) enjoyed the gambling and nightlife of the town, but when I finally arrived there, I found that Macau's real charm lies in its fascinating mix of Chinese and Portuguese culture. Portugal, Macau's former colonial ruler, has left much of its laid-back Mediterranean culture and architecture behind. I have a soft spot for Portugal and its food. Having lived in nearby Spain for a few years, I traveled to Portugal several times and always left with regret. On my visits, I wandered the charming meandering streets and tiled plazas of Porto and dined in the quaint cafés of Lisbon—I have a craving to this day for thick slices of vine-ripened tomatoes with black olives, olive oil drizzled on top, and torn pieces of crusty country-style bread to mop up the juices.

In Macau, the rustic baked breads and sublimely simple flavors of the Mediterranean are shaken and stirred with Chinese spices and cooking techniques. Whether you come to Macau as a high roller or as flat-broke backpackers like us, the soulful food, colorful Mediterranean architecture, and laid-back attitude is enough to warrant the trip. The best meal I had in Macau (even making my top ten list of all time) was also incredibly simple: sausage, bread, and fried rice. Ever conscious of our dwindling budget, we ordered the cheapest things on the menu from Fernando's, a restaurant near Hac Sa Beach, and spread out the plastic take-out containers directly on the soft black sand: chorizo sausage with crunchy bread, fried rice with bits of salt cod and olives, and a simple tomato salad with olive oil and vinegar. We splurged on some warm imported Portuguese beers from a bicycle vendor and tracked down some silverware (Macau restaurants mostly use cutlery). We ate and ate under the last of the sun as the incoming tide crashed against the rocky inlet just past our beach area, spraying salt and water high in the air.

Macau owes its complex culture to these inlets that first gave Japanese pirates a hideout and refuge from the formidable South Asian seas and monsoons. These infamous pirates terrorized the surrounding Chinese villages and islands, including Hong Kong and Taiwan, until the adept and better-armed Portuguese seafarers arrived from around the tip of South Africa's Cape of Good Hope. The Portuguese kept the pirates at bay and set up trade with Guangdong, a southern region of China, swapping European technology like eyeglasses for Asian silks and spices to send back to Portugal and the rest of Europe.

The Chinese were thankful for the presence of the Portuguese, as they brought peace to their lands, and eventually allowed the foreigners to use Macau as their trading base in the 1650s. Under the arrangement, the new Christian settlers took no time in intermarrying among the local Buddhists, and the two unlike languages mingled on the islands. Soon a new "Macanese" people and culture were born. Settlers brought herbs and spices from other colonies and outposts in Asia, Africa, Goa, Malacca, Timor, and even Japan. The Macanese people fused Portuguese cooking techniques with local produce to create what is arguably one of the oldest fusion cuisines in the world. Times are rapidly changing in Macau since China's takeover of the territory, but organizations like the Macau Culinary Institute are dedicated to preserving the local culture through Portuguese and Macanese cooking classes.

The sausage and bread reduced to crumbs and the Macanese fried rice now a fond memory, we sat through a warm subtropical summer downpour that crept up on us on the beach, knowing it wouldn't last long. "I don't want to leave," Mary Kate said. Was she thinking, like me, about ditching responsibilities and moving to Macau to make a fortune at the blackjack table and to get fat on Macanese Danta Vanilla Custard Tarts (page 132)? No, she said, she just dreaded returning to our sticky bamboo floor mats and our six-legged amigos that scurried across in the dark when our flashlights went out.

AFRICAN CHICKEN · 非洲辣鸡

I'm not going to lie, this dish isn't pretty. A thick, chunky brown sauce spooned over chicken will have you wondering what you've just cooked up, but the taste will have you and your guests swooning. I like to imagine this dish, with its Portuguese name *Galinha à Africana*, as a stowaway from the Portuguese explorer Vasco da Gama's voyage to India, via Mozambique. The chicken's savory sauce is a concoction of flavors from around the world: red chile, coconut, paprika, and peanut butter.

There are variations of this addictive sauce all over Macau, and we have come up with our own ultimate recipe. First of all, fresh coconut is a must (a bag of the pre-grated sweetened stuff won't cut it). Fortunately, fresh peeled coconut is available at most specialty grocery stores these days. If you can't find it, buy a whole fresh coconut, whack it with a hammer so that it splits into pieces, and drain out the water. Spread the pieces on a cookie sheet white side up and bake at 350°F for 15 to 20 minutes so that the white flesh separates from the brown shell. Pull the flesh away from the shell and use a vegetable peeler to peel any remaining thin brown skin. Grate with a cheese grater and there you go, fresh grated coconut! Thinly slice any leftover coconut and toast it with a little salt, sugar, and chili powder to make a fantastic snack.

SERVES 4 TO 6

To make the chicken marinade, mix together the chiles, paprika, and five-spice powder in a small bowl. Rub the spice mixture all over the chicken and marinate in the refrigerator for 2 hours.

To make the sauce, pulse the bell pepper, onion, coconut, and garlic in a food processor or blender so they are minced but not pureed.

Preheat the oven to 350°F. Melt the butter in a wok or saucepan over high heat, add the bell pepper mixture and the chiles, and sauté for 5 minutes. Add the stock, peanut butter, paprika, bay leaves, tarragon, salt, and sugar and bring to a boil, then decrease the heat to low and simmer for 10 minutes. Remove the bay leaves.

Heat the olive oil in a large skillet over medium-high heat. Brown the chicken in batches for 3 minutes on each side, transferring to paper towels to drain as each batch is browned.

Drizzle a little olive oil on a baking pan and place the potatoes, olives, and chicken, skin side up, on the pan. Spoon two-thirds of the sauce over everything and then bake for 30 minutes, or until the chicken is cooked through and is no longer pink. Warm the remaining sauce in a small saucepan over medium heat. Serve the chicken, potatoes, and olives with the sauce drizzled on top.

CHICKEN MARINADE

3 dried red chiles, seeded and minced

2 teaspoons sweet paprika

1 teaspoon Chinese five-spice powder

3 to 4 pounds chicken pieces (with skin and bone), such as thighs, breasts, and drumsticks

SAUCE

1 medium red bell pepper, seeded and chopped

1 medium onion, chopped

1 cup grated fresh coconut

6 cloves garlic

3 tablespoons unsalted butter

3 to 5 dried red chiles, seeded and minced

2 cups Chicken Stock (page 262) or low-sodium chicken broth

¼ cup creamy peanut butter

¼ cup sweet paprika

2 bay leaves

1 teaspoon dried tarragon

¼ teaspoon salt

2 teaspoons sugar

2 tablespoons olive oil

6 small white or red potatoes, halved

½ cup pitted black olives

MACANESE CRAB CURRY · 澳门咖喱蟹

My foot slipped on the rotten wood pier, sending me tumbling into the reedy marsh. I had just wanted a better view of the fishermen drawing in their sweeping nets with the day's catch, and now I was stuck in mud up to my shins. At least I didn't fall further out on the pier into the bay. Virtually untouched by the frenzy of tourists and new casinos rocketing up on the Macau peninsula and Taipa Island, much of Coloane Island remains a working fishing village, with flat-bottomed sampan boats gliding briskly on the water at sunrise. Macau (pronounced *ao men* in Mandarin) actually got its name from A-mah, the goddess of the sea. A sixty-foot-high jade statue of A-mah stands atop the Alto de Coloane on the island, blessing the Macanese fishermen who sail by.

Curry was brought over from India by Portuguese traders, so I was told by a local, and it has become an integral part of Macanese cooking. Traditionally, the crab is served in the shell and you have to really work to get tiny bits of meat out, so we've substituted lump crabmeat in this recipe to skip an unnecessary hassle. You can cook the curry broth ahead of time and just before you're ready to eat, drop in the crab. It cooks in minutes.

SERVES 4 TO 6

Combine the crabmeat, shrimp, and 1 teaspoon turmeric in a large bowl and toss with a wooden spoon until coated and yellow. (Don't use your hands—the turmeric will stain your fingers yellow!)

Heat the oil in a large pot over medium heat. Add the onion, bell pepper, ginger, and salt and cook for 5 minutes, until the onion becomes translucent. Add the remaining 1 teaspoon of turmeric, the cumin, and paprika, and stir and cook for another 2 minutes. Add the coconut milk, tamarind concentrate, and stock and bring to a boil, then decrease the heat to a simmer. Add the crabmeat and shrimp and simmer for 3 minutes, or until the shrimp is cooked through. Serve with a side of white rice.

1 pound jumbo lump crabmeat, picked free of any shell pieces

1 pound medium shrimp, shelled and deveined

2 teaspoons ground turmeric

1 tablespoon olive oil

1 medium onion, thinly sliced into half-moons

1 small red bell pepper, seeded and slivered

1 (1-inch) piece ginger, peeled and slivered into matchsticks

½ teaspoon salt

½ teaspoon ground cumin

3 teaspoons paprika

1 (12-ounce) can coconut milk

1½ tablespoons tamarind concentrate

2 cups fish stock or clam juice

2 cups cooked white rice, for serving (see page 257)

DANTA VANILLA CUSTARD TARTS · 蛋挞

Waiting in line behind a dozen other salivating folks inside Lord Stow's Bakery, I watch a baker pull yet another tray of custard tarts from the ovens. Each flaky pastry cup is filled with a rich egg and cream custard polka-dotted with blackened spots from the oven's heat. Clearly, I'm at the right place to eat my favorite Chinese dessert.

Lord Stow moved to Macau from England in the late 1980s and soon began churning out his version of the Portuguese *pastéis de nata* tarts at his eponymous bakery on Coloane Island. Today, the smooth and creamy custard tarts are considered a Macanese classic and have made their way to the mainland. They are so popular that when the fast-food chain KFC opened up shop in China years ago, they bought the secret recipe from a popular bakery in Macau and now sell the tarts in all their restaurants in China.

MAKES 12 TARTS

Preheat the oven to 350°F. Lightly beat the egg and egg yolks together in a large bowl and set aside.

Whisk together the egg yolk mixture, the milk, cream, sugar, salt, and vanilla in a saucepan until well mixed and yellow. Bring to a gentle simmer over medium-low heat and cook the custard, stirring constantly, for 6 to 8 minutes, until the custard thickens (but is not lumpy). Transfer the custard to a bowl and cover with a piece of plastic wrap, taking care to touch the plastic wrap to the custard's surface to prevent a skin from forming.

Place a sheet of the cold puff pastry dough on a clean work surface and cut the dough in half crosswise. Place one piece on top of the other. Starting from a short side, tightly roll up the dough to form a cylinder. Use your hands to roll the dough back and forth a few times so that the dough sheets seal together, and then flatten the ends with your hands. Chill in the freezer for 10 minutes to firm up the dough and make it easier to work with.

Use a sharp knife to cut the cylinder into 12 equal sections. Place the dough sections flat side down on a work surface and use a rolling pin to roll them into 4-inch disks. Place a disk in the well of a standard-size muffin pan and use your index finger to press the dough down directly against the bottom. Taking care not to trap any air bubbles, use your fingers to press the dough from the bottom up the sides until the dough reaches the top edge of the muffin well. Repeat with the remaining dough. If the dough becomes too elastic and difficult to work with, place it in the freezer for 5 minutes to firm up.

Fill each dough cup half full of custard. Bake the tarts for 20 to 25 minutes, until their centers are firm and their crusts are golden brown. Move the muffin pan to your oven's top rack, turn on the broiler, and broil them for 3 minutes, or until little burnt spots appear on their tops. Keep an eye on them so they don't burn too much. Serve the tarts warm or at room temperature. If there is any extra custard left over, we recommend eating it out of the bowl with a spoon!

1 large egg

3 large egg yolks

1 cup whole milk

1 cup heavy whipping cream

1/3 cup sugar

¼ teaspoon salt

2 teaspoons vanilla extract

1 (9-ounce) sheet frozen puff pastry, thawed but still cold

DRAGON FRUIT SANGRIA ▪ 火龙果桑格利亚酒

An aqua and white striped awning on the Ali Curry House patio mercifully shades me from the noonday sun as I sit, stuffed on sublime curried crab and shrimp toast. A wide saltwater lake sits behind a row of parked motor scooters, reflecting a bright blue sky and the shiny new Wynn casino building. I will regret drinking this pitcher of sangria at lunchtime, but with a view like this, it has to be ordered. And after a quick glance around me at the other restaurant tables, it looks like the thing to do.

Sangria, crisp and refreshing, is on every restaurant menu in Macau. The best sangria uses a no-frills red wine, a carbonated drink like Fresca, and cut-up fresh fruit by the handful. We like to use bright and colorful dragon fruit, which can be bought at specialty grocery stores or in Asian grocery stores, but you can also drop apple slices, pears, or even cut-up strawberries into the pitcher.

SERVES 4 TO 6

In a large pitcher, combine the wine, triple sec, brandy, Fresca, and frozen pink lemonade and mix well. Squeeze the juice of 1 orange, 1 lemon, and 1 lime into the pitcher and mix well. Leaving their peels on, thinly slice the remaining orange, lemon, and lime and drop them into the pitcher. Add the dragon fruit to the pitcher and chill in the fridge. When you serve the sangria, make sure every glass contains a few pieces of fruit.

1 (750-milliliter) bottle red wine, such as Chianti
½ cup triple sec
½ cup brandy
1 (1-liter) bottle Fresca
1 (12-ounce) can frozen pink lemonade concentrate
2 oranges
2 lemons
2 limes
2 dragon fruit, peeled and cubed

MACANESE ALMOND COOKIES ▪ 杏仁饼

After weeks with nary a decent cookie or slice of cake while traveling around China, Nate and I were ecstatic to find that cafés in Macau serve great fresh-baked pastries and desserts. I grabbed a box of these Macanese Almond Cookies at a bakery on Rua de Felicidade, the aptly named "Street of Happiness," and we promptly gobbled them down with milky coffee. (Green tea would also be a lovely accompaniment.) The cookies have a wonderful sweet almond flavor and the crunchy consistency of pecan sandies.

Macanese Almond Cookies are made in Macau with wooden molds that shape them into small jewel-like disks. Back in my apartment in New York, I don't have the traditional wooden molds (and I doubt you will either), so I used a small paper cup with the top cut off so that it's about ½ inch deep. They're not as ornate as the cookies sold in Macau, but it's the taste that counts.

MAKES ABOUT 24 COOKIES

Preheat the oven to 275°F and line 2 baking sheets with parchment paper. Use a sharp knife or a pair of scissors to cut away the top portion of a small paper cup, leaving only a ½-inch-deep cookie mold. Discard the paper scraps.

Place the flour, sugar, almond meal, and shortening in a food processor and process until well combined. Combine the water and almond extract in a small bowl and then add to the food processor. Pulse until thoroughly combined and the dough looks like sand. Transfer the dough to a large mixing bowl.

Place about 5 pieces of chopped almonds into the paper cup mold. Working over the mixing bowl, press a small handful of the dough into the mold and use your fingers to pack the dough into the mold and then level it off. Place the mold upside down on the prepared baking sheets and slowly remove the mold. Repeat this process with the remaining almonds and dough. Bake the cookies for 25 minutes. Let them cool on a wire rack for 1 hour before serving.

2 cups mung bean flour

1 cup confectioners' sugar

½ cup almond meal (about ½ cup peeled raw almonds ground in a food processor)

2/3 cup vegetable shortening

2 tablespoons water

1½ teaspoons almond extract

¼ cup roasted almonds, coarsely chopped

MACANESE CALDO VERDE SOUP · 薯茸青菜汤

Like a lot of good fusion food, Macanese cuisine came about from cooks adapting recipes to local ingredients. I imagine a Portuguese cook making this soup, not finding the kale or greens he wanted at the market in Macau and substituting bok choy leaves instead. This satisfying soup begins with a velvety potato base, and Portuguese sausage and shredded bok choy leaves are dropped in when it's hot. Then the soup is topped with a swirl of olive oil.

SERVES 4 TO 6

Heat the oil in a large pot over medium-high heat. Add the onion and garlic and sauté for 5 minutes. Add the water, salt, and potatoes and gently boil, covered, for 20 minutes, or until the potato slices are very mushy. Mash the potatoes in the pot with a potato masher until the soup is smooth. Add the bok choy and lemon juice and bring to a boil, then simmer for 2 minutes, or until the bok choy leaves turn bright green. Before serving, top each bowl with a few slices of chorizo sausage, a swirl of olive oil, and a sprinkling of cracked black pepper.

3 tablespoons extra-virgin olive oil, plus more for serving
1 medium onion, chopped
1 clove garlic, minced
8 cups water
2 teaspoons salt
6 medium potatoes, peeled and sliced
3 cups finely shredded bok choy, green leaves only
Juice of ½ lemon
½ cup thinly sliced chorizo sausage
Freshly cracked black pepper

THE DAIRY QUEEN LION DANCE

I don't remember what I noticed first: the smell of burning incense or the sound of clanging cymbals. Camera swinging around my neck, I had spent the day alone following the enchanting blue-and-white tile street signs, written in both Chinese and Portuguese, around Macau. Turning left at one, I found myself walking down a narrow street sandwiched between pastel-hued residential high-rises. Then I noticed a few street performers on the corner banging drums and behind them the Dairy Queen—a shiny new DQ restaurant decked out with flower bouquets and urns of smoking incense sticks. Paper signs written in Chinese read "Good Luck to the New 'Ice Empress'!" And in front of the ice cream shop's door was a skewered roast suckling pig on a folding card table. Shiny red apples topped its head.

A man in red silk pants banged a gong and a drumbeat followed, faster and louder, rising to a roar. Suddenly three lion figures, previously lying motionless on the ground, began to tremble and sway, then prance around before the gathering crowd. The "lions" didn't look like actual lions but more like the highly stylized lion statues that guard the Forbidden City in Beijing. Two men hid beneath each ornately crafted costume: a broad head of colors, fur made of silk and feathers, wild painted eyes, and a mane sparkling with silver. One man manned the rear of the lion and provided the creature's back legs (he must have lost a bet) while another man peered out from the lion's mouth, kneeling and standing, depending on the stance of the lion. At times when the lion reared its head in the air, I would catch a glimpse of the man below, his fingers rapidly tugging levers inside the head to control the creature's batting eyelids and chomping jaw. With each step the lions took, a cymbal sounded and then immediately a drum thudded, like a soundtrack to their movements.

Clang! Bong! Clack! Bang! A tiny pile of iceberg lettuce and a red envelope dropped on the cobblestone ground. The gold lion shook. Its tail spun, eyes blinked, ears lifted, the dancers' feet ready to pounce. Then, in a burst, its head roared and devoured the lettuce and envelope. Thrashing about, it sprayed the "chewed" food in the air followed by a red satin scroll that unfurled from its jaws reading "Prosperity and Success to the Cause!"

This wasn't the end. A man—resembling a longhaired Chinese Elvis Presley impersonator with huge sunglasses and a dance of his own—lit a string of firecrackers dangling from the sky on a red pole. As the sparks and debris flew, people jumped out of the way with much less alarm than me. And the lions went crazy—running, shaking, roaring. The purple dragon's front dancer stood on the shoulders of the other so that the lion's front legs rose completely off the ground, roaring at the Dairy Queen storefront from twelve feet in the air.

The dancers tore off their lion bodies, smiling widely for the cheering crowd. One of them, a boy with beads of sweat across his forehead, told me that it's incredibly hot under the costume's head (a fact I knew all too well from my six-month stint working at Disney World). Dairy Queen had commissioned the dance troupe to help with their opening ceremony because lion dances, with their roots in martial arts and acrobatics, are thought to bring good luck and to symbolize a fresh start. The pronunciation of the word "lettuce" in Cantonese, *sang choy*, is similar in pronunciation to the

Chinese words for "rising wealth," so when the lion eats and sprays the lettuce out, he is sending good luck to the business. And just to have all their bases covered, firecrackers are set off to scare away any lingering evil spirits. The troupe is paid with the money inside the red envelope, or *hong bao*.

Lion dancing began in China and is now also a popular Asian sport. Like international figure-skating competitions with judges, scores, and medals, dance troupes from Asian countries compete with dragon and lion dances in the international Asia Games that Macau periodically hosts.

I guess it was better that it was me who got to see the performance and not Nate. One of my short-lived jobs as a teenager was at a Dairy Queen in Ohio. If the DQ in Fairborn would have put on this show, let me tell you, it would have made the front page of the newspaper. In Macau, it was business as usual.

MACANESE FRIED RICE ▪ 澳门炒饭

Walking along the waterfront down the Rua das Lorchas, past pastel stucco apartment buildings splashed with freshly washed clothes dancing and drying in the sun and the occasional window box bursting with red and pink geraniums, the pungent smell of drying fish assaults my nostrils. All along the sidewalk, salted fish are laid out on woven wooden trays baking in the direct sunlight. Dried fish, especially *bacalao* (salt cod), is one of the many ingredients introduced by Macau's Portuguese colonists and is an important component in Macanese cooking. In the fifteenth century, Portuguese fishermen came up with a way to preserve surplus fish by salting and sun-drying them on the decks of their ships.

To me, this dish is the essence of Chinese-Portuguese fusion. Fried rice, a distinctly Chinese dish, is fused with Mediterranean black olives, chorizo, and salt cod. *Bacalao* is used primarily as a flavoring agent in Macanese fried rice; however, it is difficult to find and prepare. We substitute a dash of Asian fish sauce in its place in this recipe, which gives the rice a similar flavor, but if you can find *bacalao* (or its Italian equivalent, *baccalà*) at a fishmonger or specialty food store, substitute 3 ounces (rehydrated and chopped) for the Asian fish sauce.

SERVES 4 TO 6

In a small bowl, combine the sugar, Asian fish sauce, and lime juice and stir until the sugar is dissolved.

Heat the oil in a wok over high heat. Add the garlic and onion and sauté for 3 minutes, or until the onion starts to turn translucent. Pour in the eggs and scramble until they are just set, and then immediately toss in the rice and stir until well mixed. Decrease the heat to medium and add the bell pepper, corn, chorizo sausage, olives, and the sugar mixture, and stir-fry for 3 minutes. Remove the wok from the heat and let rest for 4 minutes before serving.

¼ teaspoon sugar

1 tablespoon Asian fish sauce

Juice of ½ lime

3 tablespoons olive oil

3 cloves garlic, minced

1 small onion, thinly sliced into half-moons

2 large eggs, beaten

3 cups cooked long-grain white rice, chilled (see page 257)

1 small green bell pepper, seeded and thinly sliced

½ cup corn kernels (fresh or frozen and thawed)

4 ounces chorizo sausage, thinly sliced

1/3 cup pitted green olives

PORK CHOP BUNS WITH CHILI-SOY MAYONNAISE 猪扒汉堡

A Portuguese baker named Mela let me in on a little secret in Macau. "Breads are totally different here because we import our flour from Europe," he said in English with a charming Portuguese accent. "The flour they use in China is nothing like this," he said, pointing to two 50-pound bags of flour with European labels on the kitchen floor. Mela's bakery delivers fresh-baked breads to restaurants and homes around town daily.

Pork chops sandwiched between two fluffy and crunchy buns are a Macanese specialty, and at the Café Tai Lei Loi Kei in Taipa village, waitresses carry large trays of them, sometimes two layers deep. The indoor restaurant has room for only two tables, but their outdoor seating area swells daily with locals and tourists who come mainly for the buns. The best time to eat them is at three o'clock, when the bread buns are hot out of the oven. But be sure to get there earlier, because they sell out fast. Purists eat the sandwiches plain with just the crispy fried pork cutlet and the toasted bun, but we like to punch things up a notch with a bolt of chili-soy mayonnaise and a thick slice of tomato.

MAKES 4 SANDWICHES

To make the chili-soy mayonnaise, mix together the mayonnaise, soy sauce, lemon juice, and chili powder in a small bowl and chill until ready to serve.

To make the pork chop buns, place the pork cutlets between two pieces of plastic wrap. With a meat mallet or the bottom of a heavy skillet, pound the cutlets until they are about ¼ inch thick. Rub the garlic salt on both sides of the cutlets. Heat ½ tablespoon of the oil in a medium skillet over medium-high heat. Fry 2 of the cutlets for about 2 minutes on each side, or until they are browned and cooked through. Repeat with the remaining ½ tablespoon of oil and the remaining 2 cutlets.

Meanwhile, preheat the broiler. Slice the sandwich buns lengthwise and then broil them for about 30 seconds on each side, or until they are just toasted. Spread the buns with the mayonnaise, place a pork chop and a slice of tomato on the bottom half of each, and add the bun tops. Serve immediately.

CHILI-SOY MAYONNAISE
½ cup mayonnaise
2 teaspoons light soy sauce
1 teaspoon freshly squeezed lemon juice
½ teaspoon Asian chili powder

PORK CHOP BUNS
4 boneless pork cutlets
1 teaspoon garlic salt
1 tablespoon vegetable oil
4 sandwich buns
1 large tomato, sliced

MACAU TABLE SALAD · 澳门沙拉

Supermarket cooking-oil sections in mainland China often stretch the length of an entire aisle, and the shelves are weighed down by gargantuan 5-gallon jugs of peanut oil, sunflower oil, and soybean oil for stir-frying and deep-frying, but there is one glaring omission: olive oil. Even with its health benefits and great taste that is appreciated in the West, olive oil has not caught on with Chinese cooks, but Macau is an exception. Macanese food has deep Portuguese roots, and olive oil is liberally added to dishes. At a *supermercado* on Taipa Island, I counted no less than twenty-seven different brands of olive oil on the shelves. I even bought a tin of the Portuguese olive oil brand Gallo so that I could make this salad back in Beijing. All Macanese restaurants serve some variation of this salad. It may be very simple, but the fresh ingredients with the tang of the olive oil and vinegar tastes like the Mediterranean on a plate. Buy the best-quality extra-virgin olive oil that you can get your hands on, and look for bright red vine-ripened tomatoes. Sometimes simple is best.

½ head Boston or romaine lettuce
3 large tomatoes, sliced
1 medium onion, thinly sliced into half-moons
¼ cup unpitted black olives
2 tablespoons clear rice vinegar
¼ cup extra-virgin olive oil
Salt and freshly ground black pepper

SERVES 4

Separate the lettuce leaves and spread them on a serving platter. Place the tomatoes on the leaves and then top with the onion and olives. Drizzle everything with the rice vinegar and olive oil and then season to taste with salt and pepper.

TAMARIND PORK STEW ▪ 罗望子炖猪肉

This wonderful stew gets its balance of sweet, salty, and sour flavors from brown sugar, tangy tamarind concentrate, and pungent shrimp paste. Shrimp paste, or *balichão,* is a pink sauce made from ground fermented shrimp and has a powerful stinky smell on its own. (The first time I opened a jar I wanted to chuck the whole thing out the window!) But simmer shrimp paste in a stew and it becomes a wholly different experience—mellow and savory, pleasantly aromatic. You can find shrimp paste sold in jars at Asian grocery stores.

SERVES 4

Combine the onion and shrimp paste in a food processor and blend until smooth.

Heat 2 tablespoons of the oil in a wok over high heat. Add the pork and stir-fry for about 4 minutes, or until browned on all sides. Remove the pork from the wok.

Heat the remaining 4 tablespoons of the oil in the wok over medium heat and sauté the onion mixture for 5 minutes. Mix in the sugar, garlic, and chiles and sauté for another 45 seconds. Add the stock, tamarind concentrate, soy sauce, and pork, and pour enough water into the wok to just cover the pork. Bring to a boil and then lower the heat and simmer gently for 1 hour. Serve the pork in its sauce, topped with cilantro leaves.

1 large white onion, chopped
1 teaspoon shrimp paste
6 tablespoons extra-virgin olive oil
1½ pounds pork shoulder, cut into
    1-inch cubes
2 tablespoons brown sugar
4 cloves garlic, minced
3 to 5 dried red chiles, seeded and
    thinly sliced
1 cup Chicken Stock (page 262) or
    low-sodium chicken broth
2 tablespoons tamarind concentrate
2 teaspoons dark soy sauce
Handful of fresh cilantro leaves

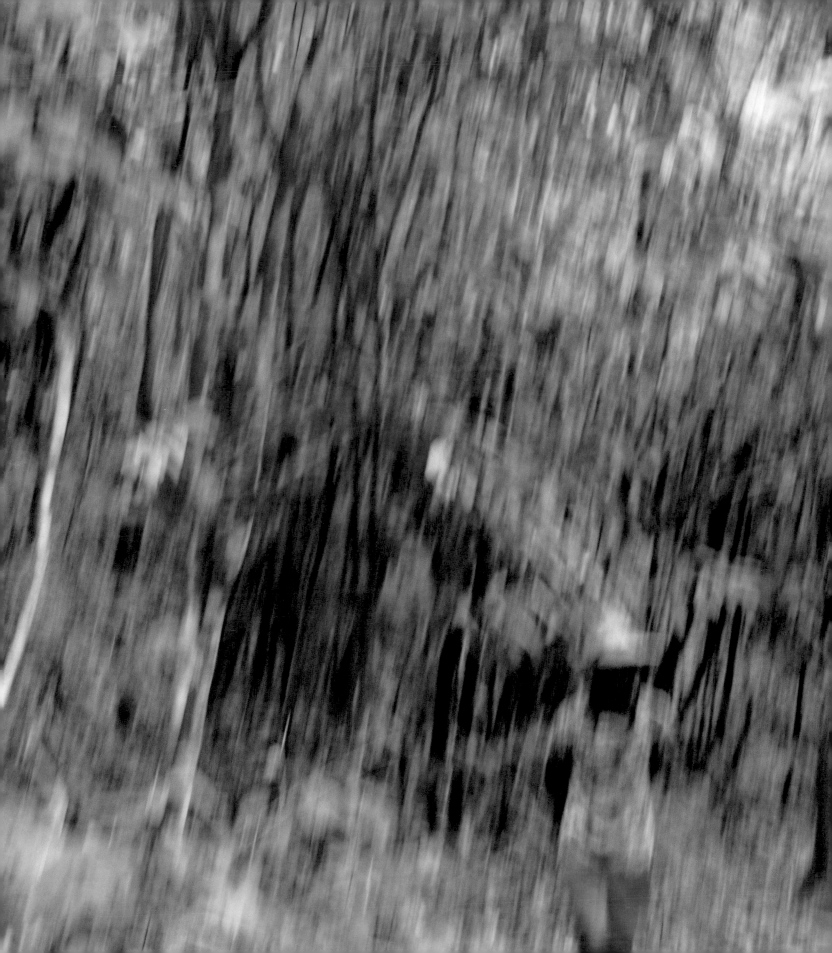

YUNNAN
云南

YUNNAN: JUNGLE FOOD 云南

You've got two bars on there! Quick!" I said, "call her before the signal fades again." The orange and red sun over the backdrop of endless rice paddies and mountains was setting along with my hope of survival. Nate fumbled with the keys on the phone and the Illinois area code and number while I sat down under the shade of a 3-foot-wide bamboo shack with open sides and held my breath. It was raining again, and that meant more mudslides along our footpath. "Mom! Mom, is that you?" Nate screamed. "It's me. We're lost in the jungles of Burma with no water or food!"

Whenever I tell this story, I never have to explain to the listener the stupidity of starting out an international phone conversation like this. I should have known to tell Nate. His prepaid cell phone cut out before he or I could say more, and our poor mother was left with no news from her only children for days. As she describes it, she could hardly drive home from Wal-Mart, where she'd gotten the call, and she was so worried that she started a prayer chain by contacting everyone she knew except for our dad. Even if we were lucky enough to escape the wild jungle cats, he would surely kill us.

Perhaps it's best she didn't know what transpired before we made it back to civilization. Our quest for danger that summer started in Kunming, the capital city of China's Yunnan Province. There we boarded a bus that took us on a twenty-two-hour drive through the topsy-turvy Himalayas to reach the jungles of Xishuangbanna. "Danger falling rocks" signs were posted all along the way and I timed the hours as if they were my last. The Xishuangbanna Autonomous Region in southern China borders Burma (now called Myanmar), Vietnam, and Laos and is home to the Dai Minority people and most of China's last remaining wild elephants and tigers. From there, motorcycles took us as far south as we could go and still be in China and, when they skidded to a halt, we watched our drivers disappear back along the muddy path. I was sixteen, a junior in high school in Ohio, and this was my first time away from my parents—this far, anyway. Nate had been living in Beijing for six months, and he promised that his Eagle Scout training, not high-tech gear or planning, of which we had neither, would get us through anything.

Alone in a vast valley, we headed out into the dense, rainy jungle. By nightfall, our hand-drawn map resembled a wet napkin, and we had given up on finding a village in which to stay the night. We'd passed

two, but the villagers had angrily told us to get off their land. Their dialect was unfamiliar to us, but their scowls communicated just fine. Just to be sure we got the hint, they followed us to the edge of their village. We decided that Nate's plastic tarp would have to double as a tent in a small clearing in the mountains. Nate promised that a fire would keep away the mosquitoes that might or might not carry malaria, and that the tarp, propped up by sticks, would protect us from snakes and other animals. I was not comforted. The fire never started, even after Nate burned one of my shirts (the Talbots blouse Mom had lent me) to get it going, and the tarp fell down from the sticks after ten minutes. Huddled together on the ground and arguing over the last stale cracker, all it took was one nearby animal screech in the pitch-black night

and we went running down the mountain, arms linked, with no flashlight, the tarp and most of our supplies left behind forever. We walked all night.

Lucky for us, stinky fruit trees grow in Xishuangbanna. Durian fruit, or stinky fruit as it is nicknamed for its spiky skin and putrid odor, helped sustain us over the next day as we searched for anyplace that resembled the faded doodles on our map. Finally, we stumbled upon a house on stilts where a young family—mom, dad, and two daughters—welcomed us for the night. Before falling fast asleep on the wooden floor, I heard a pig squeal from below the house, where the family kept their farm animals. We awoke in the morning to the smell of fresh pork sausage, a breakfast of simple sausage topped with a heap of cilantro leaves, steamed lotus root, and sweet mango slices prepared just for us. The youngest daughter, a girl of about five with a missing front tooth, covered a wicker table with jade green banana leaves and served the food in tin bowls. She marveled, wide eyes and open mouth, at how much we could eat.

Serving a sweeping spread of food with meat like this had been a tremendous expense for the family. They wouldn't accept our money, so instead we decided to offer a gift. I dug in my pack for anything that seemed American or interesting, but there was only one decent thing in there. I stepped forward, holding the gift high above my head, and bowed low to the ground. (I've since learned that bowing is more of a Japanese custom.) Nate translated for me: "We are wayward travelers and you took us in. Thank you from the bottom of my heart. I want you to have this special gift. It is a CD for an electronic music device called a CD player. The band is an American classic: Destiny's Child."

A couple of days and awful nights later, when we finally made it to Jinghong, the capital city of

President Jiang Zemin appeared on the screen to congratulate the country. The eagerness and the hope for China to step up on a world stage was apparent on the faces of the people around us listening to him speak. It was hard to imagine a country for which this honor would mean more. Though with the Games still seven years off, I could never have predicted what a success it would be for the emerging country.

Jubilation surrounded us there in Jinghong that night as we dined on fish grilled in banana leaves and toasted our survival with warm twelve-cent beers. Nate cleared his throat. "What do you think now about that cookbook idea that I've been telling you is so great?" he asked. I considered it seriously for the first time. "Yeah. Well, we'd have to come here. Nobody knows about the incredible food in Yunnan," I said.

Years later and we finally made it back to Yunnan—where it all began for us—in the midst of our intense gastronomic tour for this book. We returned to Xishuangbanna, this time with iodine tablets and a better hand-drawn map that kept us from thinking that we had accidentally crossed the border into Burma. We love the natural beauty of this part of the country and the region's largest ethnic group, the Dai Minority people, who live here. Cultural ideas are openly shared across the jungle-tangled borders of Southeast Asia, and when it comes to Dai culture, it is best to look at their not-too-distant neighbors in Thailand. The Dai language—written and spoken word—is very similar to that of the Thai language. Even Xishuangbanna is a Chinese phonetic translation of the original Thai name Sipsongpanna, or "12,000 rice fields."

Xishuangbanna, we saw mayhem and fireworks erupting in the streets. "They must be celebrating our return!" Nate said. I was too sore to roll my eyes. A mudslide-driven tumble halfway down a hill of rubber trees had left a dent in my humor and the right side of my face. We walked straight into the nearest restaurant before even considering a shower, and there on an old television set wedged above the register we saw footage of another celebration in Beijing's Tiananmen Square. An animated reporter nearly shouted to be heard over the noise: "Beijing will be the sight for the 2008 Olympic Games, beating out Toronto and Paris! The people of the People's Republic of China rejoice!"

Dai dishes are also similar to Thai food, often punctuated with lemongrass or mint leaves, and fresh fruit is frequently added to meat or rice dishes to create a unique sweet and savory combination. Still, when you get out in the rural areas of China like this one, for

云南 153

the most part the food is simple: peanuts, stir-fried greens, rice, vegetables, and fruits that happen to be in season. But in the towns and cities of Yunnan, like Jinghong, Lijiang, or its capital city Kunming, where access to ingredients is easier, you can find (in my humble opinion) the best and most creative foods available in all of Southeast Asia. We spent a lot of time exploring the rest of Yunnan and getting to know the foods and people of the other twenty-five ethnic minority groups (including the Naxi, who have a matriarchal society) that call the jungles and rain forest and mountains of Yunnan home. We think the recipes in this chapter capture the best Yunnan has to offer.

HEI SANDUO PORK AND GREENS STIR-FRY · 黑三剁

The light flickers and the shadow of my hand moves across the page. Coal and kindling meet; fire clashes against iron, and smoke rises between the wooden slats drying the assorted meats that hang above. All around us the animals are waking, each to his own tune: the rooster to the sun, the pig to his trough, the water ox to his work, the dog to his master. I lie in bed, wrapped in blankets on the floor, not knowing the proper etiquette of the village, and watch the father of the house cracking the eggs and boiling the rice for breakfast. His hands work fast and I can see fresh pork meat in his wok.

Hei sanduo traditionally calls for Chinese black pickled rutabaga (*meigui datou cai*, 玫瑰大头菜), a common ingredient in Yunnanese cooking. It is a difficult ingredient to find in the West, but if you have luck finding it at an Asian grocery store, replace the Chinese pickled mustard greens with the pickled rutabaga and forgo the soy sauce.

SERVES 4

1 tablespoon vegetable oil

2 to 3 dried red chiles, seeded and minced

2 cloves garlic, minced

1 teaspoon minced fresh ginger

8 ounces ground pork

3 medium green bell peppers, seeded and minced

1/3 cup Chinese pickled mustard greens, rinsed very well and minced

1 tablespoon light soy sauce

2 teaspoons clear rice vinegar

2 cups cooked white rice, for serving (see page 257)

Heat the oil in a wok over medium-high heat until a piece of a chile sizzles when added to the oil but doesn't turn black. Add the chiles, garlic, and ginger and stir-fry for 10 seconds. Add the ground pork and stir-fry for 1 minute. Add the bell peppers and pickled mustard greens and stir-fry for another minute. Use a wooden spoon to break apart the pork and mix it with the vegetables. Add the soy sauce and rice vinegar and stir-fry for 30 more seconds. Serve with white rice.

DAI TOMATO-MINT SALAD · 傣味凉拌薄荷

We stumbled upon this refreshing salad at a Dai restaurant in downtown Jinghong on a sweltering June afternoon. The spearmint sprigs are left whole and tumbled with a little chili oil, juicy cherry tomatoes, and punchy garlic. This dish is guaranteed to satisfy on a hot summer day.

SERVES 4

3 tablespoons vegetable oil

1 to 2 dried red chiles, seeded and coarsely chopped

3 cloves garlic, minced

3 cups loosely packed fresh mint, leaves and tender parts of stems

2 cups cherry tomatoes, halved

1½ tablespoons clear rice vinegar

½ teaspoon kosher salt

Heat the oil in the wok over medium-high heat until a piece of a chile sizzles when added to the oil but doesn't turn black. Drop in the chiles and garlic, remove from the heat, and let cool to room temperature.

In a large salad bowl, combine the mint and tomatoes. Toss in the cooled chili oil, rice vinegar, and salt and mix until all the leaves and tomatoes are evenly coated. Add more salt to taste and serve.

WILD MUSHROOM SALAD · 云南凉拌山珍

Hiking in the hills around the ancient city of Lijiang in the northwest of Yunnan, I came upon a Naxi woman adding plump mushrooms to two large baskets already filled to their brims. I stooped to pick a mushroom from the patch, but the woman waved her hand, yelling *"Du!"* or "Poisonous!" She handed me another one with a yellow cap and ridges and said it was okay. Whew, close one! The Naxi people know their mushrooms. They put the edible fungi in stir-fries and stews and stuff them with meat. In this delicious salad recipe, the mushrooms are cooked crispy and then tossed with beans, basil, watercress, and a spicy black bean dressing.

Yunnan has one of the world's most abundant wild edible mushroom crops. More than 600 varieties of wild mushrooms grow within the province, which is responsible for more than 70 percent of China's entire mushroom export trade. Most local farmer's markets and specialty grocery stores carry wild mushrooms, but it is a good idea to know that the seller is an expert. Poisonous ones can grow anywhere. If you can't purchase wild ones, substitute fresh white button mushrooms.

SERVES 4

Heat the vegetable oil in a wok over high heat. Drop in the mushrooms, garlic, and soy sauce and stir-fry for about 3 minutes, removing any liquid that accumulates in the pan as you stir-fry. When the mushrooms are cooked through and browned, use a slotted spoon to transfer the mushrooms and garlic to paper towels to drain and cool.

If the edamame beans are not cooked already, bring a small pot of water to a boil, blanch them for 3 minutes, and then drain and set aside to cool.

Whisk together the sesame oil, chili bean sauce, rice vinegar, sugar, and salt in a small bowl.

Toss the watercress, basil, and green onions in a large salad bowl. Then toss in the mushrooms and garlic, edamame beans, kidney beans, and chickpeas. Drizzle the dressing over the salad and toss lightly so that everything is evenly coated. Serve immediately.

2 tablespoons vegetable oil

4 cups thinly sliced assorted wild mushrooms (such as chanterelles, oyster, and/or cremini)

6 cloves garlic, thinly sliced

2 tablespoons light soy sauce

½ cup edamame beans

2 tablespoons toasted sesame oil

1 tablespoon chili bean sauce

1 tablespoon clear rice vinegar

1 teaspoon sugar

¼ teaspoon salt

2 cups firmly packed watercress, ends trimmed

1 cup loosely packed fresh basil, leaves and tender parts of stems

3 green onions, green parts only, cut into 1½-inch lengths

½ cup canned kidney beans, drained

½ cup canned chickpeas, drained

ELEPHANT TRACKS AND TEA LEAVES

Our first trekking adventure in Yunnan turned Nate and me into adrenaline junkies. When we returned one recent summer, I had a plan. Going around Jinghong, the capital of Xishuangbanna, I asked several locals the same question. "Where can we go in the mountains to camp with elephants in the wild? No guide. Danger, no problem. We're professionals." I admit, the professional part was a little bit of an exaggeration, especially since our good friend Laura was visiting us from Vanderbilt University in Tennessee and this was her first trip to China and also her first time camping. Laura said she was sure she was up for anything, but this attitude only lasted two days, until she realized our goal of coming face-to-face with a herd of ten-foot-tall, 10,000-pound raging wild animals.

A day into our trek, I looked down to see huge four-toed craters between my feet. "Are these elephant tracks?" I asked Du Li, a water buffalo herder whom we had met along the way. Du Li lowered his machete and nodded. "Yes, they are." He pointed at the uprooted trees and trampled bamboo stalks that blazed our path down the side of the mountain. "And this here is where they walked." *Score*, I thought, *we're that much closer.*

An hour later two men in a coughing, three-wheeled, chain-operated tractor came upon us. "The elephants are coming. Climb aboard," said the driver. I explained that indeed that was why we had come, "to see the elephants." Spit sprayed from his mouth as he screamed at me, "No. They will kill you!" There was no further discussion on our part; we just climbed aboard. Nate stared at me wide-eyed, and I tried to act normal. We did not offer a translation for Laura.

After a night under mosquito nets in the safety of a bamboo hut lifted on stilts, we set out again—still seeking thrills, but less so than the day before. Eventually our long fight through thick underbrush ended and we found our feet on a worn path, winding through miles of tea plantations to a village situated in the valley below.

Here we were invited to set our packs down and eat with the Kun family on their porch. Tea leaves brewed in our cups. Salted pork and crispy green beans filled our plates. Curious neighbors joined our table and in their own words told us about the wild elephant conservation program in their area—an effort fraught with complication and danger. It's one thing to hear about this situation but entirely another to live it. When the wild elephant population dwindled in the Sanchahe Nature Reserve, the Chinese government took away people's guns. Now their only protection comes from fireworks and sticks. Government crop reimbursements are rare and promised safety fences had yet to be built at the time we visited. Mr. Kun

told me that he and his family hide when the "angry elephants come right up and lean into the side of our house and trample our crops." Here we were in a small land region where Mr. Kun said elephants had killed thirteen people and injured handfuls more in the past year. Many of the Dai Minority people in the region actually worship elephants. Still, they must do what they can to protect themselves.

When we got up to continue on our journey, Laura piped up to inform Nate and me that no, she still didn't speak Chinese, but that she could read faces and body language and held no desire to see the angry elephants. She most definitely wouldn't be climbing over that next mountain even if she could "carry that machete." She had hiked her last mile and wanted to return to

Jinghong right then, and furthermore had been ready to do so ever since that feral dog had chased her and me, gnashing its teeth inches from our ankles, during our toilet run in the middle of the previous night.

We agreed and left Xishuangbanna and the nature reserve, hitching on the back of motorcycles. Mr. Kun was my ride, and I spoke up so he could hear me over the hum of the bike. "I am afraid of the elephants," I said. For a moment he didn't answer. Then he slowed down and turned to me, saying, "*Wo ye hen pa* [I am also afraid]." I looked out at the burned fields and chopped trees on one side of the road ahead of me and the elephant-trampled forest on the other—where man and nature clash—and I knew I was content just to have seen their tracks.

DAI BANANA LEAF FISH · 香蕉叶烤鱼

Peeking out from below the rickshaw canopy, I see a blur of reds and yellows and shades of green—hibiscus and orchids, palm trees and flowers I've never seen before. The road is lined with tall banana trees heavy with their fruit, and below, the Mekong River rushes by on its way to the South China Sea. Yunnan banana trees, the tallest variety in the world, are plentiful in Xishuangbanna, and Dai cooks make use of their large leaves by wrapping them around everything from fish fillets to mushrooms to pig brains. They stuff the packets full of fresh herbs like mint or cilantro and then grill them over hot coals. The leaves seal in the juices and insulate the contents from the heat of the grill.

If banana leaves are available in your area (they can usually be found frozen at Asian or Latin grocery stores), wrap each of these fish fillets in a leaf and bake in the oven to create a succulent, tasty fish. Served right in the leaves, the fillets look undeniably cool. Otherwise, wrap the fish in aluminum foil for similar results. This goes great with Pineapple Rice (page 169).

SERVES 4

3 fresh small red chiles, seeded and thinly sliced

2 cloves garlic, minced

1 tablespoon minced fresh ginger

1 teaspoon kosher salt

1 cup loosely packed fresh cilantro, coarsely chopped

¾ cup loosely packed fresh basil, coarsely chopped

1 tablespoon vegetable oil

¼ cup white wine

4 (6-ounce) fillets white fish, such as tilapia or halibut

4 banana leaves or 12-inch pieces heavy-duty aluminum foil

Preheat the oven to 450°F. Use a mortar and pestle to mash the chiles, garlic, ginger, salt, cilantro, and basil into a chunky paste. Whisk in the oil and wine until blended well.

Place a fish fillet to the right of center on a banana leaf or a piece of foil. Place one-quarter of the cilantro paste on the fish and smear it around so the fish is covered. Fold the left side of the banana leaf or foil in half over the fish. Fold each of the three open sides inward several times to make a packet with a tight seal. If you're using a banana leaf, use toothpicks to secure the folded edges. Place the packets seam side up on a baking pan and bake for 10 to 12 minutes, until the fish is white and cooked through.

Serve right in the banana leaf (or on a fresh one), or remove the fish from the foil and place on a plate with all the juices.

LEMONGRASS CHICKEN WINGS · 香草烤翼

At the foot of the Jinghong suspension bridge that spans the muddy Mekong River, an outdoor food market comes alive at dusk. Locals crowd the narrow walkways between stalls laden with piles of skewered meats and vegetables ready to be grilled or boiled and then eaten standing up. The choices are overwhelming and sometimes a little scary: barbecued eels, river moss, pig kidneys, pine needles, river minnows, and chunks of honeycomb complete with lingering honeybees. We tried a few of the oddities (river moss—not so bad, grilled giant larvae—not fans), but our clear favorite was these amazing chicken wings. Back home in New York, we make them for parties because they're excellent finger food. After chopping up the tender lower portion of the lemongrass for the sweet and tangy marinade, tie the leaves around the wings to add flavor and flair.

MAKES ABOUT 20 WINGS

3 stalks lemongrass, tender sections only, minced
4 cloves garlic, minced
1 tablespoon minced fresh ginger
¼ teaspoon kosher salt
Zest and juice of 1 large lemon
1 teaspoon toasted sesame oil
¼ cup sugar
2 tablespoons Asian fish sauce
2 pounds chicken wings (about 20), tips removed
20 leaves peeled from lemongrass stalks

Preheat the oven to 400°F and line a baking sheet with parchment paper or aluminum foil. Use a mortar and pestle to mash the minced lemongrass, garlic, ginger, salt, and lemon zest into a coarse paste.

Whisk the lemon juice, sesame oil, sugar, Asian fish sauce, and lemongrass paste in a small bowl. Place the chicken wings in a large resealable plastic bag with the marinade and toss them well so they're all coated. Place the bag in the refrigerator and marinate for 3 to 4 hours.

Remove from the refrigerator and wrap a lemongrass leaf around each wing a couple of times, tying the ends together in a knot. Place the wings on the prepared baking sheet and bake for 30 minutes, or until cooked through. Serve warm.

CROSSING THE BRIDGE NOODLES · 过桥米线

We couldn't get enough of this healthy, do-it-yourself noodle soup while eating our way through Kunming, the capital city of Yunnan. The ingredients are brought to the table raw and set next to a bowl filled with a steaming, light, savory broth: small plates of paper-thin chicken slices, squid, shrimp, spinach, Yunnan ham, mushrooms. We added the ingredients to our liking and they cooked right in the bowl.

The story behind Crossing the Bridge Noodles goes something like this: There once was a scholar who, while studying for an important exam, isolated himself in a cottage away from distractions. Every night his wife crossed a long bamboo bridge to bring him noodles and by the time she reached his table they had become cold. Being somewhat smarter than her scholar husband, the wife devised a plan. She poured a layer of chicken fat on top of the broth to insulate the noodles from the cold air and to keep them hot until she arrived at her husband's cottage. When he was ready to eat, she dropped the raw ingredients into the bowl to cook right there. And yes, the scholar passed his exam.

SERVES 4

Soak the mushrooms in hot water for 20 minutes to rehydrate them. Drain the mushrooms, thinly slice them, and set aside.

Prepare the rice noodles according to their package instructions or boil until al dente. Drain and set aside.

In a large covered pot, bring the stock, oil, rice wine, green onions, and ginger to a boil, then decrease the heat and simmer for 10 minutes. Season with salt to taste.

Submerge 4 large soup bowls in the sink under hot tap water until they are very warm, then dry them. Divide the cooked noodles between the bowls. Arrange the calamari, shrimp, chicken, mushrooms, spinach, prosciutto, and cilantro leaves on a large serving platter.

Return the pot of soup broth to a boil and then pour the broth over the cooked noodles. Serve the bowls of noodles and soup immediately, while still very hot, and instruct your guests to add meats and vegetables from the serving platter to their bowls. The ingredients will cook in seconds in the hot broth. If you are concerned that you will not be able to serve the broth hot enough at the table for the ingredients to cook through, you can blanch the calamari, shrimp, and chicken in boiling water for 20 seconds ahead of time.

4 dried Chinese black mushrooms

8 ounces dried rice noodles

4 cups Chicken Stock (page 262) or low-sodium chicken broth

3 tablespoons vegetable oil

1 tablespoon Shaoxing rice wine or dry sherry

3 green onions, green and white parts, chopped

1 slice ginger, smashed with the side of a knife

Salt

6 ounces calamari tubes, cleaned and sliced into ¼-inch-thick rings

4 ounces medium shrimp, peeled, deveined, and sliced lengthwise

1 (4-ounce) boneless, skinless chicken breast, sliced paper-thin

2 cups firmly packed spinach

4 ounces prosciutto, thinly sliced

Handful of fresh cilantro leaves

THE LAND OF ETERNAL SPRING

Kunming, the capital of Yunnan, has an appropriate nickname: "The Land of Eternal Spring." It's a beautiful day. The cab stops and we step out into a park that surrounds a 1,300-year-old pagoda. The sunlight shines through the trees in patterns on the bamboo tables below. A group of middle-aged women sit with tea mugs and tea cookies, passing mah-jongg tiles back and forth. A crowd of men circle around a chessboard on the sidewalk while their pet birds hang in cages from tree limbs above. I wish I'd brought my camera.

Someone touches my arm, and I turn to face a woman with gray hair curling around her eyes and a knobby cane bowing under her weight. "Can I tell you a story?" she asks in English. Odd as it sounds, I decide to grab a cup of tea and listen. What she tells me is in fact her story. As a young ambitious woman in the city of Shanghai, Wang Xin Yao studied to become a doctor. This was during the late 1960s, when a drastic turn took place in

the Cultural Revolution. Chairman Mao decided that the more education one had (this often meant exposure to Western thought and ideologies), the more "bourgeois corrupted" and "politically unreliable" one was. A campaign resounded by drum and gong throughout the country, a call for "educated youths" to go to the faraway countryside "to be reeducated by the lower and middle-poor peasants." Some went willingly, thrilled to volunteer for the greater good, while others like Xin Yao were forced to leave their studies in Shanghai and relocate to the southernmost region of Yunnan, Xishuangbanna. For the next twenty years she braved the dangerous rain forest and jungles there to provide remote villagers with medical care. She worked without electricity or knowledge of the languages of those she helped.

When the vast relocation movement was abandoned at the end of the Cultural Revolution, she stayed in Yunnan, having already made her family

there and fearing she wouldn't know the people she had left; she had changed so much.

"What is Shanghai like today?" she begged to know. She had never been back. I described it as best I could. For the unmarried reeducated youths who did return (married youths were not permitted to return), their jobs were systematically assigned to them by the Office of Educated Youths in Shanghai. Neither education nor interests played any part in their decisions for the applicants.

I look down into my teacup at the small jasmine flowers swirling in the water. "You have spent your life doing something worthwhile," I said. "I hope to do the same."

This is not an unusual story; more than 1 million youths from Shanghai and 15 million youths from China's other urban cities hopped aboard trucks and relocated to labor camps in rural areas across the country. Some went as far as the Russian frontier to work in the frozen wastelands of Heilongjiang Province, while others journeyed to sunny southern Yunnan to sweat in the fields for seventy cents a day, all singing the upbeat songs of the Party:

Go to the countryside,
Go to the frontier,
Go where our motherland needs us the most!

JUNGLE PASSION FRUIT SMOOTHIE ▪ 百香果沙冰

The voluptuous taste of passion fruit transports me to a tropical paradise where I'm wearing a fabulous swimsuit and working on my tan. Fresh passion fruit is best for this smoothie, but if you can't find it, substitute frozen passion fruit pulp or passion fruit juice. A paper cocktail umbrella is recommended.

SERVES 2

In a blender, combine the passion fruit, mangoes, banana, yogurt, honey, ice cubes, and ginger and blend until smooth. Divide the smoothie between 2 chilled glasses and garnish with the mint sprigs.

1 cup passion fruit pulp (fresh or frozen) or passion fruit juice
2 cups peeled and diced ripe mangoes
1 banana
½ cup plain yogurt
2 tablespoons honey
2 cups ice cubes
1 teaspoon grated fresh ginger
2 sprigs mint, for garnish

FRIED BANANAS ▪ 炸香蕉

These are oh-so-easy to make. Sweet bananas are battered and fried to crispy perfection and drizzled with honey. We like to go a little untraditional and serve the fried bananas with a scoop of vanilla ice cream.

SERVES 4

Whisk together the milk and eggs in a medium mixing bowl. Add the flour, baking powder, and salt and whisk until the batter is smooth and lump-free. Peel the bananas, cut them in half, and then slice them lengthwise (if using mini bananas, just slice lengthwise).

Heat 1 inch of oil in a wok over medium heat until a drop of batter turns golden brown in 30 seconds. Coat 4 banana pieces with batter and place them in the wok. Fry until all sides are golden brown, making sure to turn them over once. Use a strainer to transfer to paper towels to drain. Repeat with the remaining bananas, working in batches.

Pile a few fried bananas on each serving plate. Generously drizzle the honey over the bananas and garnish with the mint sprigs. Serve immediately.

½ cup whole milk
2 large eggs
1 cup glutinous rice flour
1 teaspoon baking powder
½ teaspoon salt
4 ripe bananas, or 8 ripe mini bananas
Oil, for deep-frying
Honey, for drizzling
4 sprigs mint, for garnish

PINEAPPLE RICE · 菠萝饭

In southern Yunnan, fresh fruit is available year-round, and Dai cooks find inventive ways to incorporate it into their food. Pineapple sticky rice is a perfect example of this and has become a favorite in Yunnan restaurants all over China. The combination of sweet pineapple and starchy rice creates a dish that can be eaten as a side dish or as a dessert. If you're feeling creative, serve the rice inside a hollowed-out pineapple.

SERVES 4

1/3 cup pineapple juice
2 tablespoons sugar
2 tablespoons vegetable oil
3 cups cooked short-grain white rice, chilled (see page 257)
½ cup minced fresh pineapple

Combine the pineapple juice and sugar in a small bowl and stir until the sugar is dissolved.

Heat the oil in a wok over medium heat. Add the rice and stir-fry for 1 minute. Add the pineapple and pineapple juice mixture and stir for 2 minutes, or until the rice becomes sticky and clumpy. Serve hot.

HAM AND CHEESE BUNDLES WITH HONEY-PEAR SAUCE · 火腿夹乳饼

People who say cheese tastes good on anything are forgetting Chinese food. Sweet and sour shrimp with melted cheese, anyone? Dairy is not a regular part of the Chinese diet despite government campaigns to promote it. This may be because a large percentage of the population is thought to be lactose intolerant. There is, however, one exception. The Sani and Bai minorities in Yunnan make a firm goat's milk cheese called *ru bing* (乳饼). Unlike most cheeses that melt when heated, *ru bing* can be fried or even grilled without losing its shape. Thin slices of deep-fried and sugared *ru bing* are spun around bamboo sticks like cotton candy. *Ru bing* is also served pan fried alone or with slices of cured Yunnan ham. This recipe uses easy-to-find Greek halloumi cheese. It tastes and behaves similarly to the impossible-to-find *ru bing*.

SERVES 4 TO 6

1 tablespoon plus 2 teaspoons vegetable oil
1 clove garlic, minced
1 large ripe pear, peeled and minced
½ cup water
2 tablespoons honey
1 teaspoon clear rice vinegar
1 (8-ounce) block Greek halloumi cheese, cut into ¼-inch-thick slices
4 ounces prosciutto, thinly sliced
Freshly cracked black pepper

Heat 1 tablespoon of the oil in a small saucepan over high heat. Add the garlic and stir-fry for 10 seconds. Add the pear, water, honey, and rice vinegar and stir continuously until it reduces down to 1/3 cup sauce. Set aside to cool.

Heat the remaining 2 teaspoons of oil in a nonstick skillet over medium-high heat. Fry the cheese slices for 1 minute on each side, or until they are golden brown and crusty.

Arrange the cheese slices on a serving plate. Top each slice with the prosciutto and a spoonful of the pear sauce. Sprinkle with the cracked black pepper and serve.

POTATO BALLS WITH SPICY DIPPING SAUCE ▪ 傣味香辣土豆球

These potato balls are like a Yunnan version of Tater Tots—crunchy on the outside and mashed potato–soft on the inside. Paired with a tangy dipping sauce infused with fresh red chile slices, they are addictive.

MAKES ABOUT 40 BALLS

To make the dipping sauce, combine the chiles, garlic, sugar, lime juice, water, and Asian fish sauce in a saucepan and bring to a boil. Decrease the heat and simmer for 5 minutes. Remove from the heat and let cool to room temperature.

Place the potatoes in a saucepan and add enough water to cover them. Bring to a boil and cook for 20 minutes, or until the potatoes are cooked through and fork-tender. Drain the potatoes well and place them in a large mixing bowl. Use a potato masher to mash the potatoes until smooth. Slowly stir in the butter, water, flour, egg, and salt and mix until smooth.

Heat up the potato mixture in a large saucepan or wok over medium heat. Stir constantly for about 3 minutes or until the dough begins to clump, and then remove from the heat and let cool. Grease your hands with a little oil and form a tablespoon of the potato dough into a ball. Repeat with the remaining potato dough.

Heat 2 inches of oil in a wok over medium heat until a small piece of potato dough turns golden brown in 30 seconds. Fry about 10 of the balls for about 2 minutes, or until they are golden brown and crispy. Make sure to turn the balls over while cooking so that they brown on all sides. Use a wire strainer to transfer the balls to paper towels to drain. Repeat with the remaining balls. Serve the piping-hot potato balls with a side of the dipping sauce.

DIPPING SAUCE

6 fresh small red chiles, seeded and
   thinly sliced
3 cloves garlic, minced
¼ cup sugar
Juice of 1 lime
½ cup water
¼ cup Asian fish sauce

POTATO BALLS

1½ pounds baking potatoes, peeled
   and cubed
2 tablespoons unsalted butter, at
   room temperature
¼ cup water
¼ cup all-purpose flour
1 large egg
½ teaspoon salt

Oil, for deep-frying

TIBET
西藏

TIBET: EATING WITH MONKS 西藏

A lanky teenage monk rushed out from the shadows of an ancient wooden doorway just as we let our heavy packs slip from our shoulders. "You cannot stay here. Women are not allowed in the monastery overnight," he said. Mary Kate and I looked at each other and then back over our shoulders at the sun vanishing behind the rugged red rock mountains of Tibet that we had just traversed. There was no way we could find the next village before nightfall. "Where else can we go?" I asked, and without giving an answer, the eager boy gathered up his red robes and disappeared behind the monastery gate.

"I told you we should have brought a tent. I knew this wouldn't work," Mary Kate complained.

"Oh no, I'm the one who wanted to buy the Terra Nova Hyperspace!" I said. "You said we couldn't afford it!"

"Excuse me for not wanting to drop our last six hundred dollars on a top-of-the-line tent with titanium poles!" Mary Kate fired back. I was about to argue when our mysterious friend returned, bounding over the square toward us with an excited smile. His lama, or spiritual leader of the temple, would make an exception.

"Po Po," he said, patting his chest as we introduced ourselves. We followed him through the austere hallways of the Buddhist monastery and into a small musty room. Incense smoke hung in the air and wax drippings clung to the soles of our shoes, layered on the floor from years of burning yak butter candles. We sat down on the edge of a cot piled high with thick yak wool blankets, and an audience of curious monks gathered one by one at the threshold of our door. I invited them in, and an old man with finely chiseled lines on his face sat beside me, adjusting his glasses and peering at my face; others, many much younger, crowded around. Their faces slid in and out of sight in the dim candlelight as we watched and listened to them talk among themselves in the singsong melody of the Tibetan language. With the language barrier, our conversation turned into a game of charades. Mary Kate motioned like a plane with her arms to show how we had arrived in Tibet, and when the conversation lulled even more, I plugged my iPod into my small battery-operated speaker. Radiohead, I thought, would be something they would like. It was the closest music I could think of that related to the moody, otherworldly sounds I had heard from Tibetan temple choir ensembles.

Po Po brought his hands to his mouth as though drinking from a cup. We nodded thankfully, and he passed us bowls filled with a milky, buttery tea. "*Ni e ma?* [Are you hungry?]" he asked in basic Mandarin after we drained our bowls. Adding a handful of barley flour to the empty bowls, he tilted in more warm yak butter tea from a kettle. Learning from watching his hands, we kneaded the mixture in our own bowls, swirling in more butter tea as necessary, until its consistency became akin to a grainy cookie dough. Po Po had surely done this countless times before. Many monks eat only *tsampa*, or roasted barley flour, their entire lives. After some practice, we scooped up a handful of our sand-colored dough, squeezing it in our hands so that it took the shape of our closed palms and knuckles. Tearing off pieces of the *pa*, we ate.

It occurred to me that the extremely basic food of Tibet isn't necessarily something to write home about. The yak butter flavor in *tsampa* can sometimes taste rancid, and monks, who once made up one-sixth of the population, use only a few ingredients to prepare meals: barley flour, yak butter, yak yogurt, salt, and tea. Add the meat of yak to that list, for non-monks and non-vegetarians, and that is the extent of the traditional Tibetan diet. This simple diet was born out of the limitations of the region's harsh environment. The Tibetan Plateau is 14,000 feet above sea level, and many Tibetans live at mountainous elevations even higher than that on the alpine tundra, where trees and most crops cannot survive. At these altitudes the golden fields of hearty barley plants seem to thrive, and barley grains are roasted and ground by hand into flour to make *tsampa*, the Tibetan staple food. The grains can also be fermented with yeast to make *chhaang*, Tibetan barley beer. With little wood for fire, yak meat is air-dried jerky-style, and Tibetans boil water using a large concave mirror, which reflects the sun's intense rays onto a metal kettle. The boiling water is mixed with yak butter and steeped with dried black tea leaves, an import from China, to make yak butter tea.

The rural countryside of Tibet as it is today, vast and empty and untouched by man, will not be around much longer. The Chinese government is rapidly modernizing this Autonomous Region and enforcing an assimilation agenda. Good or bad, the Qinghai-Tibet Railway now connecting Tibet to the rest of China is ushering in a new era of a more accessible and open Tibet. In Lhasa and other Tibetan cities, more and more drab gray structures replace magnificent, centuries-old traditional Tibetan stucco buildings, yet they are housing much-needed schools, roads, banks, and modern hospitals. Ethnically Han Chinese people are changing the face of the region as well by taking advantage of government-sponsored financial incentives to relocate and work in the high-altitude province.

With the railway and opening of the region, Tibetan food is increasingly being influenced by India, Nepal, and China. Curries, tandooris, and fried noodles are now found on Tibetan restaurant menus. Western tourists looking for a taste of home in the capital city of Lhasa can visit the Hard Yak Café and bite into a yak burger with ketchup and pickles. Though the food may not be the most provocative, exciting fare in the world, it is hearty and healthy and certainly a fascinating window into the lifestyle and culture of a widely misunderstood people whose history is shrouded in mystique and whose future is turbulent and unsure at best.

TIBETAN BUTTER TEA ▪ བོད་ཇ།

"He [drink]," Tenzin said, handing me a chipped ceramic bowl filled with warm butter tea, called *pocha*. I was tired and sore from days of trekking in the high mountains, and the buttery tea soothed my parched throat and the bowl warmed my cold hands. Tibetans drink dozens of cups of this restorative butter tea a day. Not only does it quench thirst but it is also a satisfying drink packed with energy to sustain people throughout the day.

SERVES 4

Combine the water and tea in a medium saucepan, bring to a boil, and then turn off the heat and let steep for 5 minutes. Use a fine mesh strainer or cheesecloth to strain the liquid over a large bowl; discard the tea leaves. Transfer the liquid back to the saucepan and bring to a boil, then decrease the heat to a simmer. Add the salt, sugar, butter, and half-and-half and whisk until the butter has completely dissolved and a little foam forms on the surface. Serve the tea in small bowls.

4 cups water
1 heaping tablespoon loose black tea
½ teaspoon salt
1 teaspoon sugar
1 tablespoon unsalted butter
2/3 cup half-and-half

TSAMPA WITH TOMATO CHUTNEY SAUCE ▪ ཙམ་པ།

Tsampa, or roasted barley flour, holds an important place in Tibetan culture. Thrown into the air during marriages and celebrations, *tsampa* flour is a mark of joy, and thrown at funerals, it releases the departed soul. *Tsampa* is also the Tibetan staple food, most commonly eaten after being kneaded by hand with warm butter tea to make a smooth, nutty dough. Tibetan monks who adhere to strict Buddhist vegetarianism eat a steady daily diet of *tsampa*.

Tibetan cooks often jazz up the otherwise plain-tasting *tsampa* dough with a variety of zesty dipping sauces, like this recipe for Tomato Chutney. For a breakfast version, forgo the chutney and dunk the dough instead into a bowl of thick Greek yogurt swirled with honey. To make this recipe you will need a coffee grinder or a spice grinder to grind the roasted barley grains into a floury powder. We like to make *tsampa* in the traditional way by instructing each of our guests to form the dough in small batches by hand in their own individual bowl, but you can also make it in one large batch ahead of time.

SERVES 4 TO 6

To make the *tsampa*, heat a large skillet over medium heat. Add the barley and dry-roast for about 4 minutes, using a wooden spoon to move the grains around so they roast evenly. When the grains turn a very light golden color (take care that the grains don't turn too dark), remove them from the skillet and let cool. Using a coffee grinder, grind the roasted barley in batches until it is a fine, floury powder.

If you or your guests want to form the *tsampa* in the traditional way—in small batches by hand—place 1/3 cup of roasted barley flour in a small bowl. Add 5 tablespoons of warm butter tea and use your index finger to mix the dough in a circular motion until the dough clumps. Add more flour or tea as necessary. Next, use your hand to knead the dough until it is the consistency of cookie dough. Tear off a small piece of the dough (about 1½ tablespoons) and squeeze it in the palm of your hand so it takes the shape of your palm. Repeat with the remaining dough.

If you want to form all the *tsampa* at once, combine 1½ cups of the roasted barley flour with 1½ cups of the tea in a large mixing bowl. Use your hands to knead the dough until it is the consistency of cookie dough. Add more flour or tea as necessary. Tear off a small piece of the dough (about 1½ tablespoons) and squeeze it in the palm of your hand so it takes the shape of your palm. Repeat with the remaining dough.

To make the chutney, heat the oil in a medium saucepan over medium heat. Add the onion and sauté for about 8 minutes, or until it starts to caramelize. Add the bell pepper and sauté for an additional 5 minutes. Add the tomatoes with their juice, raisins, ginger, brown sugar, cumin, cinnamon, chili powder, and clear rice vinegar to the saucepan. Bring to a gentle simmer and cook for 8 minutes. Remove the chutney from the heat and let cool. In a food processor or blender, blend the chutney until smooth. Serve the *tsampa* with a side of the chutney for dipping. Extra chutney can keep in the refrigerator for up to 3 days and is a great condiment for eggs, sandwiches, and tortilla chips.

TSAMPA
2 cups organic hulled barley
Tibetan Butter Tea (page 180)

TOMATO CHUTNEY
2 tablespoons vegetable oil
1 medium onion, chopped
1 red bell pepper, seeded and chopped
1 (15-ounce) can peeled tomatoes with juice, chopped
½ cup golden raisins
½ teaspoon minced fresh ginger
2 tablespoons firmly packed brown sugar
¼ teaspoon ground cumin
¼ teaspoon ground cinnamon
¼ teaspoon Asian chili powder
2 tablespoons clear rice vinegar
Salt

YAKITY YAK YAK YAK

Mary Kate sidled up next to the grunting, pawing beast. The yak's broad, buffalo-like humped shoulders heaved next to her under a massive, black-and-white shaggy coat.

"Why are you doing this again?" I hollered from a comfortable, safe distance behind my zoom lens.

"Shh . . . don't take it yet!" She yelled back through her teeth, tiptoeing ever closer with that mischievous smile she gets when she's about to get herself killed for a picture. "I need just a little closer," she said. I rolled my eyes and then watched the smelly, 500-pound creature turn to face Mary Kate, visions of her being impaled by its 2-foot curved horns flashing through my mind. "Ready!" she said.

I snapped the picture and Mary Kate raced back to see the digital proof of just how near she got. She studied it for a second. "Oh, it's not good. My eyes are closed. One more time," she said. "No way," I said; that would have to do.

We continued our trek along the Tibetan alpine tundra and through a valley where fifty or so more yaks roamed under the guidance of their herder. Yaks are hearty, ox-like creatures and grow in the wild to stand six feet at their withers and to weigh nearly one ton. They have a unique ability to brave freezing temperatures and to live at high altitudes where most other animals cannot. For thousands of years, yaks have been vital to the survival of the Tibetan people. Without them, people may never have been able to inhabit the harsh landscape of the Tibetan Plateau.

Still today, 90 percent of Tibetans live in the countryside, and yaks are central to their way of life. Their fur is used to decorate spiritual prayer flagpoles and their milk is churned into butter to use as an offering to the gods. The soft butter is sculpted into statues of deities, mixed with clay to make bricks for building monasteries, and molded into candles that burn by the hundred in monasteries across Tibet.

Climbing over a mountain pass, we descended upon a small clay-brick house, where a man working out front caught sight of us. His wiry black hair stuck out from beneath a yak hide fedora, and he kindly invited us to follow him into his home for a rest. As we neared, we noticed that the walls of his house were dotted with softball-size clumps of yak dung. Mary Kate pointed curiously, and the man motioned to a fire pit nearby. He sticks the yak manure on the sides of his house to dry in the sun and whenever his family needs a fire, he scrapes some off to burn it. Yak dung is an important source of fuel for Tibetans because the Tibetan Plateau is largely treeless, and so lumber for firewood must be carried over great distances on the backs of yaks. For this reason yak meat is rarely cooked over a fire; instead it is air-dried in strips like jerky.

The man's wife served us bowls of yak butter tea from a tin kettle near where we sat on the floor and offered us tangy yak yogurt that she had made herself from milk. I couldn't imagine her milking the giant yaks, though she surely had. Then she went back to weaving a shawl out of—what else?—yak wool, with yarns dyed in green, yellow, and navy blue.

BARLEY BEER BEEF SOUP · རྩམ་ཐང་།

The tractor crawled to a stop next to a strip of barley crops, their golden stalks the only color in the pale green valley. Our driver motioned for us to follow him as he joined a group of Tibetan men and women sitting cross-legged not far off, laughing and singing. The soft grass comforted my sore bum, which had been mercilessly vibrating on the back of the tractor for the past hour, and a Tibetan man with rosy cheeks and disheveled black hair inched closer to me and produced a plastic bottle from under his coat. He poured its contents—a cloudy liquid not unlike dirty dishwater—into a dented tin cup and pushed it my way. I pressed the cup to my lips and took the smallest of sips. Then I polished it off, welcoming its crisp, refreshing taste and sweet smell. This was my first taste of Tibetan barley beer, called *chhaang*. Brown flecks of barley hull hovered in the cup to prove the beer's homemade origin.

This recipe calls for simmering beef, barley, and vegetables with just a touch of beer. Eating it always transports me back to the Himalayan foothills where I sat for a time passing around a dented tin cup with ten other Tibetans. Serve this hearty soup with bottles of Lhasa brand barley beer if you can find it, or else any pale lager will do.

SERVES 6

Season the meat generously with salt and pepper. Heat 2 tablespoons of the oil in a large soup pot over medium-high heat. Brown the beef for about 4 minutes, or until it is seared on all sides, then remove it from the pot.

Heat the remaining 1 tablespoon of oil in the pot over medium heat and sauté the carrot and onion for about 10 minutes, or until the onion turns slightly translucent. Add the water, beer, soy sauce, and beef to the pot. Bring to a boil, then decrease the heat and simmer gently, covered, for 1½ hours. Add the tomatoes with their juice, the barley, butter, and mushrooms to the pot and cook for an additional 30 minutes, or until the barley is tender. Season with salt to taste and stir in the cilantro just before serving.

1 pound beef shin or beef brisket, cut into 1½-inch cubes
Salt and freshly ground black pepper
3 tablespoons vegetable oil
1 large carrot, peeled and diced
1 small onion, diced
6 cups water
½ cup pale lager-style beer
2 teaspoons soy sauce
1 (14-ounce) can diced tomatoes with juice
¾ cup pearl barley
2 tablespoons unsalted butter
2 cups stemmed and quartered button mushrooms
2 tablespoons minced fresh cilantro

TIBETAN NOODLE SOUP · ཐུག་པ།

Tibetan Noodle Soup in its most basic form is a simmering broth with hand-torn dough noodles and bits of vegetables or yak thrown in—a combination of whatever ingredients home cooks have on hand. In the cities, where cooks have access to a broader range of ingredients, it becomes a wonderfully soothing and warming vegetable soup.

SERVES 4

Heat the oil in a wok or large saucepan over medium heat. Add the garlic, ginger, chiles, and cumin seeds and stir-fry for 20 seconds. Toss in the carrot and onion and sauté for about 8 minutes, or until the onion turns slightly translucent. Add the vegetable broth, water, turmeric, black pepper, and soy sauce and bring to a boil, then decrease the heat and simmer for 15 minutes. Add the Hand-Torn Noodles and cook for 8 to 10 minutes, or until they are tender. (If you are using egg noodles, cook until al dente.) Stir in the spinach and cook for 1 minute. Season with salt to taste. Sprinkle the cilantro leaves over the soup just before serving.

2 tablespoons vegetable oil
2 cloves garlic, minced
1 tablespoon minced fresh ginger
2 dried red chiles, seeded and minced
1 teaspoon cumin seeds
1 large carrot, peeled and thinly sliced
1 small onion, chopped
3 cups vegetable broth
3 cups water
½ teaspoon ground turmeric
½ teaspoon freshly ground black
    pepper
1 tablespoon soy sauce
4 ounces Hand-Torn Noodles (page
    261), or fresh wide egg noodles,
    chopped into 2-inch lengths
1 cup firmly packed spinach leaves,
    coarsely chopped
Salt
Handful of fresh cilantro leaves

BORN FOR THE SKY

Our dad retired recently from thirty years in the Air Force, and he wanted a relaxing vacation visiting his kids during our culinary tour in China. "Something, you know, near the beach," he volunteered, "and I want to eat a lot too." Nate thought it would be a better idea to take him on what we knew would be our most intrepid leg of the trip, returning to Tibet. "No one should retire from life," Nate told him. "You need to get in shape before you get here," he said.

Well, when we picked our dad up at the airport in Chengdu, Sichuan Province, a launching point for trips to Tibet, it was apparent that our dad had grown a little soft around the edges in retirement. He was obviously (to me, anyway) not going to be able to trek for two weeks through the Tibetan Himalayas.

"Maybe we should just take him around Sichuan?" I asked Nate. Again, Nate thought he had a better idea. We would build up our dad's endurance. So that first day we took him to climb Mount Emeishan in Sichuan Province and the next day to climb another nearby peak, Leshan Mountain. By the third day, when we flew to Lhasa, the capital of Tibet, our dad was dehydrated, exhausted, and pissed off.

For the first two days, he stayed in the hotel complaining about his back and a headache while Nate complained that he was exaggerating. This seemed to be some kind of father-son karma for all the times our dad made us get up early on vacations and go to museums we didn't care to see. This allowed me endless opportunities to play the good child. "Here, Dad, I've brought you some *momo* dumplings," or "Can I get you a pillow for your back?" However, that second night Nate began to worry too. Our dad couldn't keep any food down, and he started talking about the TV in his room—but there was no TV in his room.

Then his words slurred and he lost consciousness.

We half-carried our dad down the street to the Xizang Junqu Zongyiyuan military hospital while he slipped in and out of a daze. Inside a waiting room, a nurse inspected him and immediately transferred him to the intensive-care wing, where a Chinese doctor poked and prodded him with medieval-looking medical tools. I asked again and again if the needle the doctor was using was clean, not trusting their assurance that it was sanitized, but we had no other options. Our dad was hooked up to an IV drip on the already blood-stained bedsheets—stains compliments of some previous patient—and the doctor took us aside to discuss the situation. Nate's and my medical vocabulary was extremely limited. All we understood was that he had "water pressing on the brain" and that his condition was "very severe, indeed."

High-altitude cerebral edema (HACE), or "water pressing on the brain," is a serious matter. One tourist dies a year in Tibet, on average, from various forms of altitude sickness. He would need to stay in the hospital for the rest of the week and then leave immediately for Chengdu. We visited him often, but he insisted we didn't need to stay. Although the two other patients in the room had passed on, he said the flies were keeping him company. When he introduced us to a few flies he'd named, we stopped worrying. At least his humor was back.

Known as the Roof of the World, Tibet is one of the highest inhabited places on earth and home to the world's highest mountain range, which includes Mount Everest, or Chomolungma, "mother of the Earth," as it is called by the Tibetans. Many Tibetan natives live at higher elevations than 14,000 feet, roughly the height of Pikes Peak in Colorado, and live on 40 percent less oxygen than people at sea level. It is a mystery why Tibetans seem to thrive in these high altitudes, with the intense sun exposure and winds that accompany them. Some studies suggest the reason is because Tibetans take more breaths per minute than people who live at sea level and that their blood vessels are correspondingly wider, which makes them more efficient at delivering oxygen to tissue around the body.

After our dad left the hospital and spent another week traveling with us in Sichuan Province, he flew straight from China to Florida, where he met up with our mom and extended family for our annual beach vacation that we missed that year. When we called to check on him, he put us on speakerphone for the whole family to hear. "You kids tried to kill me, but everyone is impressed with the twenty pounds I lost at my Tibetan spa." We heard a few little nervous laughs, and then our grandmother asked what we knew everyone was thinking: "Oh my word, what are ya'll doing over there? What kind of cookbook is this?"

VEGETABLE MOMO DUMPLINGS
WITH CILANTRO-YOGURT DIPPING SAUCE ▪ མོག་མོག

Momo dumpling wrappers are a little thicker than traditional dumpling wrappers, and they are sometimes made with whole wheat flour. You can make your own with the recipe for Whole Wheat Momo Dumpling Wrappers on page 259 or use store-bought dumpling wrappers, especially wheat ones. Freeze any dumplings you don't cook for later. See Dumpling Folding Tips on page 255 and Dumpling Freezing Tips on page 256.

MAKES ABOUT 30 DUMPLINGS

To make the dipping sauce, combine the cilantro, chiles, yogurt, garlic, salt, and oil in a blender and blend until smooth. Set aside.

To make the dumplings, place the potatoes in a saucepan and add enough water to cover them. Bring to a boil and cook for 20 minutes, or until the potatoes are cooked through and fork-tender. Drain the potatoes and place in a bowl. Use a potato masher to mash the potatoes until they are smooth.

Heat the oil in a large saucepan over medium heat. Add the onion and cook for about 6 minutes, or until translucent. Add the mushrooms and cook for 1 minute, then remove the pot from the heat and let cool. When cool, mix in the mashed potatoes, cheese, green onions, cumin, salt, and soy sauce until thoroughly blended.

Fill a small bowl with water. To form the dumplings, hold a wrapper in the palm of your hand and place 1 tablespoon of filling in the center. Dip your finger in the water and run it around the edge to help make a good seal. Lightly fold the wrapper over on itself, but don't touch the edges together. Starting at one end, use your fingers to make a small pleat on the side of the wrapper closest to you, then press the pleat into the other side and pinch together firmly. Keep making pleats down the dumpling opening in this way until completely sealed. Repeat this process with the remaining wrappers and filling.

Spray a steamer tray with the nonstick vegetable spray to prevent sticking. Arrange several of the dumplings on the tray with about 1 inch of space between them. Insert the steamer tray into the pot, cover, and steam the dumplings for 10 minutes (see How to Steam on page 254). Repeat with the remaining dumplings. Serve warm with the dipping sauce.

CILANTRO-YOGURT DIPPING SAUCE
1½ cups firmly packed fresh cilantro
2 Anaheim green chiles, seeded and coarsely chopped
¾ cup plain Greek yogurt
2 cloves garlic
¼ teaspoon salt
1 tablespoon vegetable oil

DUMPLINGS
1 pound baking potatoes, peeled and diced
1 tablespoon vegetable oil
½ medium onion, chopped
½ cup chopped fresh shiitake mushrooms
¼ cup grated yak cheese or Parmesan cheese
2 green onions, green and white parts, chopped
¼ teaspoon ground cumin
¼ teaspoon salt
½ tablespoon light soy sauce
30 round Whole Wheat Momo Dumpling Wrappers (purchased premade, or see page 259)
Nonstick vegetable cooking spray, for the steamer

SHANGRI-LA

I traveled to Tibet for the first time as a study-abroad student in Beijing knowing little more than what I had learned from a Tibetan Freedom Concert featuring the Beastie Boys and R.E.M. that came through my high-school city. Stepping off the plane in Lhasa for the first time felt dreamlike, like stepping into a heavenly Monet sky. This may have had something to do with my lightheadedness from entering the high-altitude capital city of Tibet, as I later fainted from lack of oxygen. However, I'm not alone in thinking of the expansive Tibetan sky—the clearest cerulean blue—as otherworldly, ethereal even. Legends like that of the Shangri-La, a utopia on earth where people live forever, were born from its splendor.

When I felt up to it, I trotted around the city, not able to get enough of the people and the sights. In the center of Lhasa, the seventeenth-century Buddhist Potala Palace rises, cliff-like, from the foot of the Himalayas in a heavenly sheen of clay and timber and a shimmering crown of gilded turrets. A proud rickshaw driver told me that the gods made the palace from the earth itself in a fortnight, but I had already seen the magic of this place before anyone told me.

Strolling the flagstone streets that circle the Jokhang Temple, I watched pilgrims prostrate themselves in an act of devotion to deities, and monks and nuns twirl golden prayer wheels and chant deep, eerie incantations, their long maroon robes flapping around their ankles as they walked. Stunning women with high cheekbones and ruddy complexions wore Lhasa-style headdresses of red wool woven with turquoise stones, orange coral beads, and gold medallions. At the Bakhor market, Tibetans from the countryside sold huge blocks of yellow yak butter, dried milk chips, wooden bowls, and antique silver trinkets. These people looked like characters right out of the pages of *National Geographic* to me, but they were real and here and happy to talk with me.

Throughout our research and travel in Tibet, Mary Kate and I have been shocked to discover the layers of complexity of the political situation there; the more we learn, the less we know. On the whole, I don't think the Han Chinese people in the rest of China are aware of and educated about how

the government's policies have affected the Tibetans. For one thing, the Communist Party's official line is that the People's Republic of China "liberated" Tibet. Also, to help promote tourism to the out-of-the-way province among Chinese tourists, China's government-owned media has painted Tibet as an idealized Shangri-La and the Tibetans as a surreal, almost magical folk.

The American and foreign press (and Hollywood) also have their own agendas and typically offer only the one-sided point of view of the Tibetan government-in-exile, which is based in India and was first established by the Dalai Lama in 1959 after China took control of Tibet and exiled him from his own country. Since Tibet's "liberation," the Tibetan government-in-exile estimates that 1.2 million Tibetans have died as the "direct result of China's invasion and occupation of Tibet" and that many others have been persecuted or imprisoned for their political and/or religious views. Even so, the Tibetans' struggle did not begin here. During the years 1913 to 1951, when Tibet had its freedom from Chinese rule, the country was a feudal theocracy with a small ruling class and a strict caste system that was brutally enforced by Tibetan guards. The people, many falling into the category of serfs or slaves, the land, and the animals in Tibet were lorded over by lamas, or spiritual priests, and ultimately by the Dalai Lama himself from his 1,000-room, thirteen-story Potala Palace.

The most contemplative observations that I have uncovered about Tibet have come from the Tibetans and Chinese citizens themselves. Typically these ideas do not fall on one side or the other of the political argument but rest somewhere in the murky gray in-between. One observation in particular sticks in my mind, made by the Chinese author Ma Jian in his book *Stick Out Your Tongue*. He points out that the Tibetans are real people, with real appetites and ambitions and flaws and hopes. "To idealize them," Ma Jian writes, "is to deny them their humanity." Ma Jian's book was banned in China for its controversial viewpoint, and he now lives in Britain.

Whether you come to Tibet to seek adventure in its intrepid mountains, to meet the Tibetans for yourself, or for a kind of spiritual journey to learn from a rapidly disappearing culture, you will not be disappointed. The sky alone is worth the trip.

TIBETAN CURRY POTATOES · ཞོག་གོ་ཁ་ཚ།

The group of young monks didn't see me enter the softly lit room of the temple. Hunched over a wooden board, they sat intently concentrating on their *dul tson kyil khor,* or literally "mandala of colored powders." Each monk held a *chak pur,* or metal funnel, in his hands and, using a small rod to cause the funnel to vibrate, poured millions of grains of dyed sands—vibrant reds, yellows, greens, blues—within a large circle drawn with chalk on the wood. Working in a radial pattern, they painted an exquisite and detailed geometric shape to represent the universe and a window into enlightenment. Their meticulous work went on for days in the room, and when the beautiful mandala was complete, the monks swept up the sand and carried it to a stream, where they released it into the waters.

The impermanence of life is a tenet of Tibetan Buddhism, and the lesson of the *dul tson kyil khor* is to teach us to prepare for and to face life's impermanence. In art school I was taught to make drawings on acid-free archival-quality paper that does not yellow and to use materials and paints that will hold up for years. It was shocking and powerful for me to see an artist experience his work and then let it go.

Turmeric—that divine golden yellow powder that gives curry its bright yellow color and is an important part of this Tibetan dish—reminds me of the vibrant colors used to make the sand mandalas in Tibet.

SERVES 4

Place the potatoes in a large pot, cover with water, and boil for 15 minutes, or until they are fork-tender but still firm. Drain the potatoes, and when they are cool enough to handle, slice them into ¼-inch-thick circles. Set aside.

In a small skillet over medium heat, dry-roast the Sichuan peppercorns for a few seconds, until they are fragrant, and then remove from the skillet and repeat with the cumin seeds. Be careful not to burn the spices. Combine the peppercorns and cumin seeds in a mortar and pestle or coffee grinder and grind into a coarse powder.

In a small saucepan over low heat, bring the butter to a gentle simmer. When a layer of white foam appears on the surface of the melted butter, remove the saucepan from the heat. Strain the butter through cheesecloth or a coffee filter to remove the foamy white solids.

Heat the clarified butter in a large skillet over medium heat. Add the garlic and ginger and stir-fry for 30 seconds. Add the onion and sauté for 6 minutes, or until translucent. Stir in the ground spice mixture, the turmeric, salt, chile, and soy sauce and cook for 1 minute. Toss in the potatoes and stir so that they are all coated with the sauce. Cook for 8 more minutes, or until the potatoes are soft and everything gets a little brown and crunchy. Stir in the green onions and serve when they are wilted.

1½ pounds Yukon Gold potatoes, peeled
½ teaspoon Sichuan peppercorns
1 teaspoon cumin seeds
½ cup (1 stick) unsalted butter
4 cloves garlic, minced
1 tablespoon minced fresh ginger
1 small onion, chopped
1 teaspoon ground turmeric
½ teaspoon salt
1 dried red chile, seeded and minced
1 tablespoon light soy sauce
2 green onions, green parts only, chopped

NEPALESE CHICKEN TARKARI ▪ བལ་ཡུལ་བུ་ཤ

While grabbing breakfast at a restaurant facing Lhasa's Bakhor market, I met a twenty-nine-year-old Nepalese cook named Bibek. He had been working in the city for the past seven years, ever since his brother told him about opportunities in Tibet. Bibek said I couldn't write about Tibetan food without mentioning Nepalese food. Nepal and India border Tibet's western side, and the countries' flavors have influenced Tibetan menus. Curries, tandooris, flatbreads, and dals have jumped the border and are now served at restaurants next to more traditional Tibetan fare. The countries also share a deeper bond: There are more than 100,000 Tibetans, including the Dalai Lama, living in exile in India and Nepal.

SERVES 4

Wearing rubber kitchen gloves so the turmeric doesn't stain your hands, rub the turmeric, black pepper, and salt all over the chicken and let marinate in the refrigerator, covered, for 30 minutes.

In a small skillet over medium heat, dry-roast the mustard seeds for a few seconds, or until they are fragrant, and then remove from the skillet and repeat with the fenugreek seeds. Be careful not to burn the spices. Combine the mustard seeds and fenugreek seeds in a mortar and pestle or coffee grinder and grind into a coarse powder.

Heat the oil in a wok or large saucepan over medium-high heat. Add the garlic, ginger, ground spice mixture, cumin, chiles, and bay leaves and stir-fry for 20 seconds. Add the onion and sauté for about 6 minutes, or until slightly translucent. Drop in the marinated chicken and stir-fry for 4 minutes, then add the stock and tomatoes. Bring to a boil, then decrease the heat and simmer gently for 35 minutes. Sprinkle with the chopped cilantro and serve with the rice.

1 teaspoon ground turmeric
1 teaspoon freshly ground black pepper
¼ teaspoon salt
4 boneless, skinless chicken breasts, cubed
1 teaspoon mustard seeds
1 teaspoon fenugreek seeds
3 tablespoons vegetable oil
2 cloves garlic, minced
1 tablespoon minced fresh ginger
1 teaspoon ground cumin
4 dried red chiles, seeded and minced
2 bay leaves
1 large onion, chopped
2 cups Chicken Stock (page 262) or low-sodium chicken broth
2 large tomatoes, chopped
Handful of fresh cilantro leaves, coarsely chopped
2 cups cooked white rice, for serving (see page 257)

SICHUAN

四川

SICHUAN: MOUTH-NUMBINGLY SPICY 四川

I tangled my fingers in my horse's matted mane, bracing for a bumpy ride, as her front hooves stepped into the stream—my dad's horse and Nate's horse flanking me in the water crossing. Midway through the knee-high water, my mare slipped, and before she was able to regain her footing on the rocky ground, a saddlebag filled with pots and pans fell, clattering and splashing in the water. My dad's horse was spooked at the sound and bucked him off into the icy stream. "Cold!" he screamed. Then Nate's skittish horse freaked and bolted across the mountain pass ahead of us. I caught a last glimpse of him as he disappeared into the trees, his arm flailing like a rodeo star.

Our two guides acted fast, pouncing on my dad and the cooking supplies. I pointed to the trees. "Should someone go after him?" I asked. Fabio, the taller of the two with a low-buttoned shirt and pretty long hair that he constantly flipped in the wind (he'd asked me to give him an English name and I couldn't resist), took off after Nate. I kicked the sides of my horse to follow. As I listened to Nate's faint voice in the distance yelling out *"Ting! Ting!"* ("Stop! Stop!" in Chinese) with several English obscenities mixed in, I recalled a summer afternoon ten years earlier. I was tossing hay in my horse's stall when the front gates of the barn by our house in Ohio burst open and Nate's horse charged through with a missing rider and a broken bridle. A neighborhood search ensued. Hours later we found Nate lying in a field with a nasty gash on his head and no memory of how he got there. At the time I had been jealous of his black and purple battle wounds and amnesia and all the school he got to miss by being in the hospital, but all these years later, out here on a four-day horseback riding trip in the remote mountains of Sichuan Province, I didn't feel envious in the least.

Nate's horse finally entered a clearing and stopped as abruptly as he'd begun, plunging his nose into a thick patch of green grass. Fabio and I trotted up next to him, and my mare jerked the reins out of my hands and buried her face in the grass too. "Did you guys see that? I almost died!" Nate said, leaping off his horse. "Yeah, that was like . . . whoa, look at that!" I said, distracted. A tall poppy flower with large pink, velvety petals was growing a few yards in front of where our horses grazed. "Whoa, that looks like the opium kind of poppy," Nate said. We counted another two of the beautiful straight-stemmed flowers nearby. Today the few poppies that grow wild like this in the mountains of Sichuan are a small reminder of a debilitating drug epidemic that once gripped the nation and sparked two wars involving Britain (the Opium Wars). It is hard for me to believe that not even that long ago in recent history, China was the world's foremost opium producer and home to millions of addicts. At the turn of the twentieth century, Sichuan Province alone was responsible for 40 percent of the country's opium-producing cash crop. The red, white, yellow, and pink poppies took well to the terraced mountains of Sichuan, thriving next to beans and potatoes. This high-altitude region of Songpan where we were riding our horses was one of the last places in the country to be eradicated of the euphoria-inducing plant during Mao Zedong's anti-drug and anti-narcotics campaign in the 1950s.

The three of us wrestled our horses away from the grass and led them down into the valley where our other guide, Pei Yun, was setting up our night's campsite. The view around us was breathtaking—a leafy collage of greens and stark pine trees silhouetted against the clear blue sky. As far as I could see, giant green steps cascaded down the terraced mountain slopes where farmers had cut into their steep sides to create flat rings of farmable land. Nowadays in Sichuan, the province known as "the Land of Plenty" for

its crisscrossing rivers and vast fertile land, farmers harvest more than 10 percent of all of China's grains, corn, soybeans, and other food crops.

Unsaddling our horses to join the others, we carried our saddlebags toward the tent and the campfire Pei Yun had already set up. Our dad caught our attention from atop a flat rock where he was waiting for us, arms folded. He had a Tibetan-style yak wool blanket wrapped around his waist like a skirt, and his only pair of pants and underwear hung dripping wet on a stick near the campfire. "I'll be in the tent. Tell me when dinner's ready," he said, limping off and slamming the flap shut behind him. It was clear that his two-week "vacation" visiting his kids in China was not turning out as he had imagined. At least this horseback-riding adventure was an improvement from his stay in a Tibetan hospital the previous week (see page 187 for more on that).

Fabio got to work on dinner, dropping a bushel of green bean stalks between Nate and I and instructing us to separate the pods. While we did this, he withdrew a drawstring canvas pouch from his saddlebag and spread out several plastic bottles and jars of seasonings and spices on the ground. Heating some oil in a blackened pot, he tossed in some garlic, minced ginger, Sichuan peppercorns, and ground dried chiles and waited until it all sizzled over the crackling fire. Two heaping handfuls of the green beans dropped

into the pot and a few minutes later, Fabio was scraping the cooked spicy beans into a chipped enamel bowl. For the campfire noodle soup, he balanced a deep pot of river water over the coals and kneaded some flour and water in a bowl to make a springy dough. When the pot began bubbling, he tore off thumb-size bits of the dough and chucked them in to boil along with cabbage leaves and chopped tomatoes. Last, he added even more ground dried chiles and a handful of Sichuan peppercorns; this was definitely going to be a spicy meal. "Oh, can you eat spicy? A lot of foreigners can't," he asked, a little late.

By now our dad had joined us to dry off by the fire, and tin bowls and steaming tea mugs were set out for us under a tarp propped up by sticks. Pei Yun broke twigs from a tree and whittled the bark off the tips for us to use as chopsticks. I imagined this was how chopsticks were invented in China 3,500 years ago: first made from twigs as rudimentary on-the-go cutlery, then later crafted out of bamboo, silver, jade, ivory, and porcelain. We took turns reaching for the beans with our chopsticks and dishing out the noodle soup. After a few minutes, our dad pushed his bowl away in the dirt and spit out a mouthful of green beans. "Nathan. What did Fabio put in this?" he asked. "I can't feel my tongue. My lips are swelling!"

Nate turned to me. "You mean you didn't warn him?" he said, winking and feigning alarm.

"Don't listen to him, Dad," I said. "It's supposed to taste like that. It's part of the flavor." Sichuan peppercorns, which Fabio had generously added, are curious little berry pods from the prickly ash tree that have a citrusy, piney aroma and a numbing ability. They grow wild in the cool, high-altitude regions near the Himalayas, and Sichuan cooks have been cooking with them for generations. The peppercorns zap your tongue and set your mouth abuzzing and, when combined with red chile peppers, create *ma la*, or "mouth-numbing spicy," the flavor most identified with Sichuan cuisine. *Ma la* provides the "zing" factor in dishes such as Kung Pao Chicken (page 213), Sichuan Hot Pot (page 210), and Mapo Tofu (page 211). For more about Sichuan peppercorns and *ma la*, see Hot Stuff on page 208.

After realizing that the numbing sensation wasn't caused by some poisonous wild mushroom he had just eaten, our dad warmed up to the spice. "Here's another one," he said, pinching another peppercorn between his chopsticks. I knew how he was feeling; the sensation is strangely addictive. The tingling starts on the tip of your tongue and spreads to your lips and eventually envelops your mouth with a lingering heady spiciness that leaves you craving more.

SPICY SICHUAN GREEN BEANS · 干煸四季豆

Spicy Sichuan Green Beans (*gan bian si ji dou*) are addicting. The outside of the beans fries crinkly and crispy—like French fries—and the chiles and Sichuan peppercorns burst with flavor in my mouth. I've never had leftovers to speak of at the end of a meal.

This dish traditionally uses the long, spindly green beans called yard-long green beans *(lü jiang dou*, 绿豇豆*)*. The monster-size beans can reach a length of more than three feet, and they hang down from vines growing on trellises rather than on small plants close to the ground like most beans. Other than being incredibly long, the beans taste almost identical to the fresh green beans you can find at the nearest grocery store.

SERVES 4

Make sure the green beans are dry, with no water clinging to them. Heat 1 inch of oil in a wok over high heat until little bubbles appear around a bean dropped in the oil. Add the green beans and fry for 8 to 10 minutes, stirring occasionally. The bean skins should look crinkly with brown spots. Using a perforated strainer, transfer the beans to paper towels to drain.

Drain all but 1 tablespoon of oil from the wok and reheat over medium-high heat. Add the Sichuan peppercorns and stir-fry for 10 seconds. Drop in the garlic, ginger, chiles, and green onions and stir-fry for 20 seconds (be careful not to burn the spices). Add the pork and stir-fry for 1 minute, or until all the meat is browned. Toss in the green beans, soy sauce, and chicken powder, if using, and stir-fry for 1 more minute. Season with salt to taste and serve.

1 pound fresh green beans, ends trimmed and cut into 3-inch lengths

Oil, for deep-frying

½ tablespoon Sichuan peppercorns

3 cloves garlic, minced

1 teaspoon minced fresh ginger

6 to 10 dried red chiles, seeded and chopped

3 green onions, white parts only, chopped

4 ounces ground pork

2 tablespoons light soy sauce

1 teaspoon chicken powder (optional)

Salt

DAN DAN NOODLES · 担担面

Sichuan noodle vendors used to carry these noodles with a pole over their shoulders called a *dan* (担). Each end of the pole dangled with a bucket filled with noodles and broth. Dan Dan Noodles take their name from this mobile food setup and are still a quick and delicious snack served up on Chengdu streets. I like to make a batch of Dan Dan Noodles and keep them in the fridge for eating later in the week. I keep the sauce in a separate covered container and toss the noodles with a little sesame oil to keep them moist. Then when I'm ready to eat, I combine the noodles and sauce and zap a bowl in the microwave for a meal in no time. Make sure you rinse the Chinese pickled mustard greens well, as they can be quite salty.

SERVES 4

Combine the beef, 1 tablespoon of the soy sauce, the hoisin sauce, and rice wine in a small bowl. Heat a wok over medium heat and dry-roast the Sichuan peppercorns for about 20 seconds, or until fragrant. Then remove the wok from the heat and lightly crush the Sichuan peppercorns in a mortar and pestle or in a bowl with the side of a wooden spoon. Set aside.

Heat the vegetable oil in the wok over medium-high heat and add the garlic, ginger, the white parts of the green onions, and chile and stir-fry for 30 seconds. Add the beef mixture, pickled mustard greens, and crushed Sichuan peppercorns to the wok and stir-fry until the meat is cooked through, about 2 minutes. Transfer the contents of the wok to a bowl and set aside.

Bring a large saucepan of water to a boil. Blanch the bok choy in the water for 1 minute, or until it turns bright green. Remove the bok choy with a slotted spoon and set aside. Replace the water in the pot and bring to a boil again. Cook the noodles in the pot according to their package instructions or boil until al dente. Drain, then divide the noodles among 4 serving bowls.

Wipe out the wok and set it over high heat. Add the stock, sesame oil, chili oil, black rice vinegar, sugar, the green parts of the green onions, and the remaining 2 tablespoons of soy sauce. Bring to a boil, then decrease the heat to a simmer for 3 minutes.

Top each bowl of noodles with the meat mixture and the bok choy. Ladle over the hot broth and serve.

5 ounces ground beef

3 tablespoons light soy sauce

1 teaspoon hoisin sauce

1 tablespoon Shaoxing rice wine or dry sherry

1 teaspoon Sichuan peppercorns

1 tablespoon vegetable oil

2 cloves garlic, minced

2 teaspoons minced fresh ginger

2 green onions, green and white parts kept separate, chopped

1 dried red chile, seeded and minced

2 tablespoons minced Chinese pickled mustard greens, rinsed very well

4 heads baby bok choy, ends trimmed and quartered

11 ounces fresh round egg noodles or Japanese udon noodles

4 cups Chicken Stock (page 262) or low-sodium chicken broth

1 teaspoon toasted sesame oil

1 tablespoon Chili Oil (page 257)

1 tablespoon Chinese black rice vinegar

1 teaspoon sugar

BANG BANG CHICKEN · 棒棒鸡

Bang Bang Chicken gets its funny name from a heavy stick called a *bang* that Chinese cooks use to pound the chicken, shredding and tenderizing it. The noodles, chicken, cucumbers, and herbs are tossed in a smooth, nutty sesame dressing, and then everything is spiked with a jolt of Sichuan pepper.

SERVES 4

Bring a pot of water to a boil. Boil the chicken in the water for 10 minutes, or until the chicken is cooked through. Drain the chicken and let rest until it is cool enough to handle. Shred the chicken by pounding it a few times with a rolling pin and then pulling it apart into shreds with your fingers. Dry-roast the Sichuan peppercorns in a wok over high heat for 20 seconds, or until fragrant. Transfer the Sichuan peppercorns to a mortar and pestle or a small bowl with a wooden spoon and crush them into a coarse powder. Set aside.

Soak the noodles in a bowl of hot tap water for 10 minutes, then drain and use scissors to cut them into 3-inch lengths. Bring a small pot of water to a boil. Blanch the noodles in the water for 3 minutes, then drain and rinse under cool water. Drain the noodles again.

In a large salad bowl, whisk together the ginger, garlic, sesame paste, sesame oil, soy sauce, clear rice vinegar, sugar, and water until well blended and the sugar is dissolved. Toss in the noodles, chicken, cucumber, green onions, and cilantro and toss until everything is evenly coated. Divide the mixture among 4 bowls and sprinkle with the ground Sichuan peppercorns and sesame seeds before serving.

12 ounces boneless, skinless chicken breasts
1 tablespoon Sichuan peppercorns
2 ounces bean thread noodles
1 tablespoon minced fresh ginger
4 cloves garlic, minced
1/3 cup Asian sesame paste
1 tablespoon toasted sesame oil
2 tablespoons light soy sauce
2 tablespoons clear rice vinegar
1 tablespoon sugar
1/3 cup water
1 small English cucumber, peeled and thinly sliced
5 green onions, green and white parts, diagonally chopped
1 cup coarsely chopped fresh cilantro
1 tablespoon sesame seeds

A fiery red broth bubbles away in the kitchen sink–size pot set in the center of our sidewalk restaurant table, swirling with mouth-numbing Sichuan peppercorns and no less than a hundred spicy red chile peppers. Through the steam billowing out from our fire-breathing hot pot and those on the tables around us, I watch people of all ages dabbing beads of sweat from their necks and brows with tissues. Some of the men have their shirts off, and I've taken to fanning myself with the menu to deal with the sweltering summer heat and the fire in my mouth. Nate and I use our chopsticks to dip our spread of raw sliced meats, skinned frogs, fish balls, dumplings, pulled noodles, and greens into the gas-heated pot, and in seconds we are fishing out our flash-cooked food and dunking it in a cooling sesame dipping sauce. In my experience, eating doesn't get hotter or better than a meal of Sichuan hot pot in Chengdu, the capital city of China's spiciest province, a place where people pride themselves on dishing up and indulging in food so spicy that it literally numbs your mouth.

I didn't always love hot stuff. My first visit to Sichuan, in high school, was a harrowing experience during which I survived solely on rice and crackers. Spicy for me was a bag of chips and a jar of mild salsa, and to my horror, Sichuan cooks put chiles by the shovelful in everything, even dishes that aren't normally

prepared in a spicy manner in the rest of China. "*Shi zai zhongguo, wei zai sichuan* [China is the place to eat, but Sichuan is the place for flavor]" goes the popular Chinese saying. Flavor here refers to spicy, blazing hot, scorching, or incendiary.

However, for all its love of spice, China has only been cooking with chile peppers for a few hundred years. The Aztecs, Incas, and other natives of South America were the first to eat chile peppers, and the rest of the world didn't get its first taste of the curiously fiery fruits until Christopher Columbus discovered the New World. Up until this time, garlic cloves and black peppercorns were the spiciest foods Europeans had yet to encounter. Spanish and Portuguese traders were quick to embark around the globe with their new culinary treasure. Soon chile peppers were peppering dishes in Africa, India, and China, particularly in Sichuan Province.

Before the chile pepper made its way to Asia, cooks in Sichuan had already long been seasoning dishes with Sichuan peppercorns, or *hua jiao* (flower peppers), the reddish-brown outer husks of tiny berries plucked from native Sichuan prickly ash trees. The unusual nature of Sichuan pepper (also called Chinese prickly ash) is that it is not piquant or spicy; rather, it is numbing. The peppercorns have a mild, citrusy flavor and contain an alkaloid that temporarily numbs your tongue. They are one of the spices that are ground to make Chinese five-spice powder.

When chile peppers arrived in Sichuan, cooks threw them into their woks along with Sichuan peppercorns, and Sichuan's world-famous flavor *ma la*, or "mouth-numbing spicy," was born. *Ma la* flavoring can bring a simple dish to another level—the numbing sensation created by the peppercorns soothes the heat of the peppers in your mouth and intensifies their flavor.

After living in Texas and China, I've come to love the flavor and excitement of spicy food, and one summer Nate and I went on a mission to find out just how hot was hot in Sichuan. We found ourselves in the southern city of Chongqing, rumored to be the province's spiciest city, and a few locals pointed us in the direction of the restaurant serving the spiciest fare in town. "You are not afraid of spicy?" said the waitress, gazing up from her notebook when I ordered "*zui la de huo guo* [the spiciest hot-pot broth you've got]." I shrugged her off. Of course we weren't afraid. I should have been. The meal was so spicy that after I had plucked two chile-doused bites of meat from our pot, I could eat no more. Nate fared worse than me after catching a pepper in his throat, and while he ran to the bathroom with a napkin over his mouth, I sat silently weeping behind a handful of tissues. We paid our bill and left.

There's a more scientific way of determining hotness than pain. The Scoville scale measures the amount of capsaicin (the alkaloid responsible for heat) present in chile peppers. A bell pepper has zero Scoville Heat Units (SHU), and a jalapeño pepper has an SHU range of between 3,000 and 8,000. The red chiles popular in China range anywhere between 40,000 and 60,000 SHU. Most commonly eaten dried in China, the chile peppers, set out to air-dry on bamboo trays all over town, fittingly look like firecrackers.

SICHUAN HOT POT · 四川火锅

At outdoor hot-pot restaurants in Chengdu, spicy red chiles are added with a heavy hand to the bubbling fondue pots in the center of the tables, and handfuls of Sichuan peppercorns float on the broth surface, ready to tingle on the tongue. Beer flows freely (probably responsible for the rowdy atmosphere), and waiters bring an endless supply of vegetables and paper-thin meats to cook in the broth. Sichuan Hot Pot is meant to be eaten with a group of friends. Serve your guests the raw ingredients and let them drop what they want to eat in the hot pot. Seconds later, they'll fish the cooked food out with chopsticks and dunk it in bowls of Sesame Dipping Sauce. You can easily add more servings to this recipe by adding more ingredients to the spread. In addition to a few essentials, see our suggestions that follow for other ingredients to add, or take this opportunity to try any or all of those strange-looking Asian vegetables that you've had your eye on but have never known how to use.

It is important to slice the meat paper-thin so that it cooks quickly in the broth. You can ask your butcher to slice it for you, or partially freeze it before slicing with a sharp knife. We recommend serving this recipe with a side of 2 cups cooked white rice (page 257).

SERVES 4 TO 6

To make the broth, heat the vegetable oil in a large fondue pot or an electric wok (see Essential Cooking Equipment on page 252) on high heat. Add the Sichuan peppercorns, chiles, and chili bean sauce and stir-fry for 1 minute, or until fragrant. Add the ginger, garlic, stock, cumin, green onion, dark soy sauce, chili oil, dried tangerine peel, if using, star anise, and Chinese black mushrooms and bring to a boil, then decrease the heat to a gentle simmer.

Arrange the beef, cabbage, potatoes, tofu, and any other ingredients on separate serving dishes around the fondue pot.

Give each guest a small bowl of the dipping sauce topped with cilantro and a bowl of white rice. Raise the fondue pot's heat so it's bubbling in the center of the table. Instruct your guests to add ingredients to the pot with their chopsticks. When the ingredients are cooked (usually after a few short minutes), pluck the food from the broth using chopsticks (or a slotted spoon) and dunk in the dipping sauce before eating. Add boiling water from a kettle to the hot pot whenever the level of liquid dips too low.

BROTH

3 tablespoons vegetable oil

½ cup Sichuan peppercorns

10 to 20 dried red chiles

3 tablespoons chili bean sauce

4 slices ginger

4 cloves garlic, sliced

8 cups Chicken Stock (page 262) or low-sodium chicken broth

1 teaspoon ground cumin

1 green onion, halved crosswise

1 tablespoon dark soy sauce

1 tablespoon Chili Oil (page 257)

2 (about 2-inch-square) pieces dried tangerine peel (optional)

2 star anise

3 dried Chinese black mushrooms

DIPPING INGREDIENTS

2 to 3 pounds flank steak, sliced paper-thin and against the grain

8 ounces napa cabbage leaves, halved

3 medium potatoes, peeled and thinly sliced

8 ounces firm tofu, cubed

Select a handful of 3 or 4 of the following ingredients: thinly sliced lotus root; frozen dumplings; peeled and cubed winter melon, squash, or pumpkin; straw mushrooms; fresh egg noodles; thinly sliced zucchini; fried tofu; calamari rings; watercress or bok choy; mung bean sprouts

Sesame Dipping Sauce (see page 31)

Handful of fresh cilantro leaves, coarsely chopped

MAPO TOFU · 麻婆豆腐

The town of Leshan, in southern Sichuan, is famous for its silky tofu and one humongous stone Buddha. Carved into the side of Mount Lingyun at the intersection of the Dadu, Minjiang, and Qingyi rivers, the 232-foot-high Leshan Giant Buddha *(le shan da fo)* sits majestically on his throne, protecting the city from floods and fishermen from dangerous currents. The Giant Buddha was carved by monks in the Tang Dynasty, and although he is sprouting some leaves behind his ears and around his ankles, he looks pretty good for his 1,200 years. Nate and I slowly climbed down the steep stairs carved directly into the mountain that led down to the Buddha's feet to get a better look. It was truly impressive. His big toe could have held a table and an entire dinner party of ten people!

The other attraction in Leshan is *xiba* tofu, which is made with cool river water pulled from the local rivers that roll by the Buddha's feet. Sichuan cooks use protein and nutrient-rich tofu *(doufu, 豆腐)* in all kinds of dishes. On its own, tofu has a pretty bland taste, but it acts like a sponge when cooked with other foods, soaking up flavor and spices. Mapo Tofu is a classic Sichuan dish made with soft tofu cubes swimming in a fiery broth of spicy chili bean sauce, ginger, and garlic. Serve with a side of white rice.

SERVES 4

Dry-roast the Sichuan peppercorns in a wok over high heat for 20 seconds, or until fragrant. Transfer the Sichuan peppercorns to a mortar and pestle or a small bowl with a wooden spoon and crush them into a coarse powder. Set aside.

Combine the meat and sesame oil in a medium bowl. Heat the vegetable oil in a wok over high heat. Add the meat and stir-fry for 5 minutes. Add the rice wine, soy sauce, ginger, garlic, green onions, and chili bean sauce and stir-fry for 30 seconds. Add the stock and tofu, but do not stir or the tofu will break apart. Bring to a boil, then decrease the heat and simmer for 5 minutes. Add the cornstarch slurry and simmer for 1 more minute to thicken the sauce. Sprinkle with the crushed Sichuan peppercorns and serve.

1 tablespoon Sichuan peppercorns
8 ounces ground pork or beef
1 teaspoon toasted sesame oil
1 tablespoon vegetable oil
2 tablespoons Shaoxing rice wine or dry sherry
2 tablespoons light soy sauce
1 tablespoon minced fresh ginger
2 cloves garlic, minced
2 green onions, green and white parts, minced
2 tablespoons chili bean sauce
1¼ cups Chicken Stock (page 262)
1½ pounds soft tofu, drained and cut into ¾-inch cubes
1 tablespoon cornstarch, mixed with 2 tablespoons cold water

KUNG PAO CHICKEN · 宫保鸡丁

To give you an idea of just how popular Kung Pao Chicken is with expats living in China, a clothing shop in Beijing called Plastered does brisk business selling T-shirts to foreigners emblazoned with the dish's Chinese name, *gong bao ji ding* (宫保鸡丁). I wear my T-shirt proudly. This authentic version of the recipe tastes nothing like the globby gunk served at many Chinese restaurants in the West. Loads of peanuts are stir-fried with chunks of succulent chicken served in a sweet and spicy sauce.

SERVES 4

To make the marinade, combine the rice wine, soy sauce, and cornstarch in a shallow dish and stir until dissolved. Toss in the chicken and marinate, covered, in the refrigerator for 20 minutes.

To make the stir-fry, heat 1 tablespoon of the oil in a wok over medium-high heat. Add the chicken and stir-fry until cooked through but still moist and succulent. Transfer the chicken to a bowl and wipe out the wok.

In a small bowl, mix together the soy sauce, black rice vinegar, cornstarch slurry, and sugar and stir until the sugar is dissolved.

Heat the remaining 2 tablespoons of oil in the wok over medium heat until a piece of a chile sizzles when added to the oil but doesn't turn black. Add the chiles, ginger, garlic, Sichuan peppercorns, and green onions and stir-fry for 30 seconds, or until the spices become really fragrant. Add the sauce mixture, chicken, and peanuts and stir a few times so the sauce thickens. Serve warm.

MARINADE
2 teaspoons Shaoxing rice wine or dry sherry
2 teaspoons light soy sauce
1½ teaspoons cornstarch
1 pound boneless, skinless chicken breasts, cut into ¾-inch cubes

STIR-FRY
3 tablespoons vegetable oil
2 teaspoons light soy sauce
1½ tablespoons Chinese black rice vinegar
1 teaspoon cornstarch, dissolved in 1 tablespoon water
1 tablespoon sugar
2/3 cup roasted peanuts
5 to 10 dried red chiles, seeded and chopped
1 tablespoon minced fresh ginger
4 cloves garlic, thinly sliced
1 teaspoon Sichuan peppercorns
6 green onions, white parts only, chopped

STRAWBERRY-CHILE COCKTAIL · 辣味草莓鸡尾酒

Throw Chengdu's reputation as a laid-back town of sleepy tea drinkers out the window. Our nights out on the town inspired this Strawberry-Chile Cocktail—a blend of spicy red chiles, strawberries, and vodka. It's Sichuan Province in a martini glass.

SERVES 2

Bring the water to a boil in a small saucepan and stir in the sugar. Once the sugar is completely dissolved, remove from the heat and let cool to room temperature.

In a blender, combine the strawberries, seeded chile, and the sugar syrup and process until well blended and smooth, about 40 seconds.

Fill a cocktail shaker with the ice cubes, and add the strawberry puree, vodka, and grenadine. Give the cocktail shaker a few good shakes, and then strain evenly into 2 martini glasses. Make a small cut in the side of the 2 whole chiles and perch one on the rim of each glass as a garnish. Serve immediately.

¼ cup water
¼ cup sugar
1 cup fresh strawberries, tops removed
¼ fresh small red chile, seeded
Ice cubes
½ cup premium vodka or rum
1½ teaspoons grenadine
2 whole small fresh chiles, for garnish

SICHUAN SPICY FISH · 水煮鱼

Tender fish fillets swirling in a bright red sheen of chili oil and floating red chiles—this dish looks a lot spicier than it actually is. Pinch the fish out of the pot with chopsticks; just don't drink the broth.

SERVES 4

Combine the egg white, cornstarch, rice wine, and salt in a large mixing bowl.

Slice the fish fillets into thin pieces by holding your knife parallel to the cutting surface and slicing the fillets into 1/3-inch-thick slices. Then cut them into 3-inch squares. Toss the fish in the cornstarch mixture and marinate, covered, in the refrigerator for 20 minutes.

In a wok over high heat, combine 10 of the chiles, 1 tablespoon of the Sichuan peppercorns, the water, stock, chili bean sauce, black pepper, ginger, garlic, and green onions and bring to a boil. Lower the heat and let simmer, covered, for 5 minutes. Remove the marinated fish from the refrigerator. Slide the fish pieces into the simmering liquid, but do not stir. Cook until the fish is white and cooked through, about 1 minute, then turn off the heat.

Place the fish and cooking liquid in a soup tureen or serving bowl. Sprinkle the cilantro over the top of the soup. In a clean wok or saucepan, heat the oil over medium heat until a piece of a chile sizzles when added to the oil but doesn't turn black. Add the remaining chiles and the remaining 1 tablespoon Sichuan peppercorns and fry for 1 minute. Then pour the hot oil and chiles over the soup and serve immediately.

1 egg white

3 tablespoons cornstarch

2 teaspoons Shaoxing rice wine or dry sherry

½ teaspoon salt

1 pound white fish fillets (such as tilapia or halibut)

20 to 30 dried red chiles

2 tablespoons Sichuan peppercorns

2 cups water

2 cups Chicken Stock (page 262) or low-sodium chicken broth

2 tablespoons chili bean sauce

¼ teaspoon freshly ground black pepper

4 slices ginger, smashed with the flat side of a knife

3 cloves garlic, minced

4 green onions, white parts only, chopped

2 tablespoons coarsely chopped fresh cilantro

½ cup vegetable oil

FISH FRAGRANT EGGPLANT · 鱼香茄子

Here's a dish that gets lost in translation. The sauce, known as *yu xiang* or "fragrant fish sauce," is an aromatic and tasty ensemble of spices traditionally used in the cooking of fish in Sichuan Province. It doesn't actually have fish in it (or even smell like it!). Some versions of this dish use ground pork, but we like the eggplant stewed alone in the tangy sweet and sour sauce. This expat-favorite dish is made with narrow Asian eggplants, which are available at farmer's markets and specialty grocery stores. They have fewer bitter seeds and thinner skins than their Western oblong counterparts.

SERVES 4

Trim the ends of the eggplants, peel them, and slice lengthwise into 3-inch-long by ¾-inch-thick strips. Place the strips in a bowl, toss them with the salt, and set aside for 30 minutes to draw out excess water. Rinse the strips well under cool water, drain, and pat them dry with paper towels.

In a small bowl, combine the soy sauce, garlic, ginger, sugar, sesame oil, chili bean sauce, and clear rice vinegar.

Heat the vegetable oil in a wok over high heat. Add the eggplant strips and stir-fry for 3 minutes. Add the soy sauce mixture and stock to the wok. Bring to a boil, then decrease the heat and simmer for 20 minutes, covered. Stir in the cornstarch slurry and simmer for 1 additional minute so that the sauce thickens a bit. Sprinkle in the green onion and when it is just wilted, serve.

1½ pounds narrow Asian eggplants
1 teaspoon salt
1 teaspoon light soy sauce
3 cloves garlic, minced
1 tablespoon minced fresh ginger
2 teaspoons sugar
1 teaspoon toasted sesame oil
1 tablespoon chili bean sauce
1 tablespoon clear rice vinegar
3 tablespoons vegetable oil
¾ cup Chicken Stock (page 262) or
    low-sodium chicken broth
1 teaspoon cornstarch, dissolved in
    1 tablespoon cold water
1 green onion, green parts only,
    minced

Shi Shi lounged back on her log sofa seemingly without a care in the world. Her furry legs lay about, casually sprawled over its edge, and her nose, black as a truffle, softly grunted and wrinkled as she munched away on a hunk of bamboo clutched in her paws. Using her curious panda's thumb, an elongated wrist bone that acts as an opposable thumb, she stripped the hard bark off the outside of the bamboo stalk and chewed away at the tender insides with her mouth open, revealing sharp white teeth. Bits of bamboo tumbled from her lips onto her belly, and every once in a while she reached for a piece of the fallen food, as if her big belly were a plate.

At the Chengdu Panda Breeding and Research Center, where scientists are hard at work breeding the endangered "national treasure" of China, Nate and I found the giant pandas, known as *da xiong mao* (big bear cats) in Chinese, so disarming with their cute little round ears, fuzzy black and white bodies, and lazy lumbering nature that we had to remind ourselves that they were not teddy bears, but actual bears that can grow as large as five feet tall and weigh as much as 300 pounds. "I am going to jump over the railing and give her a big hug," Nate remarked loudly, raising a few eyebrows among the ten or so other English-speaking tourists, as we stood outside Shi Shi's pen. Giant pandas in captivity are mostly docile and a huge tourism draw for China, yet they are still capable of being as dangerous as other bears.

In the back area of the research center, we fawned over the panda cubs in the nursery, who were squeaking like little puppies as they tried to stand on their back paws to roll a soccer ball. However, we found the center's short video of the birthing of a cub in captivity disturbing, to say the least. In the video, a mother gives birth to a hairless and helpless pink newborn roughly the size of a sushi roll and weighing in at only half a pound. She appears to show no natural

maternal instincts and clearly wants nothing to do with the pipsqueak. The lack of reproductive instincts of giant pandas in captivity is a main limiting factor in conservation efforts.

In the wild, there are only about 1,500 giant pandas left, and most of them live in the rainy and cool bamboo forests in the mountain ranges of Sichuan. Pandas eat almost exclusively bamboo, which is very low in nutrients and highly indigestible by the bears, so they have to eat as much as eighty pounds of it each day to keep up their cuddly physique. The pandas have been known to eat fruits, insects, and even some rodents in the wild; in captivity they also enjoy snacking on carrots, apples, and sugarcane. With the world's attention focused on the survival of the panda, the Chinese government offers huge rewards to peasants in the countryside who save a starving wild panda, and there is no leniency for poachers, who face public execution.

I still remember seeing my first giant pandas, when I was seven, at the National Zoo in Washington, DC. Ling-Ling and Hsing-Hsing, the bear pals who first arrived at the zoo in 1972, were instant celebrities. Americans came by the thousands to ogle the rare species that had previously been banned from entering the country in the 1950s as "a product of Communist China." A plaque hung on the front of the National Zoo's panda home reading "mammal of mystery," and newspapers touted their arrival as "panda-monium." Chou Enlai, then the Premier of China, had gifted the pandas to the United States after President Nixon's goodwill visit to China, and Mrs. Nixon was the first to visit the two new Chinese ambassadors at the zoo. "They give you an extra dimension of joy," she said. "I think everyone would like to cuddle them." The United States reciprocated by sending two Alaskan musk oxen (not nearly as huggable creatures) to the Beijing Zoo.

Nixon called his visit to China "the week that changed the world," and it ushered in a new era in Chinese international relations. After Ling-Ling and Hsing-Hsing, China successfully gifted twenty-three pandas to other countries in what became known as "panda diplomacy." The endearing giant creatures helped to restore China's public image around the world and to reestablish their relations with countries they had ignored or shunned during the years of Chairman Mao's isolationist policies.

Giant pandas have since captured the imagination of the world and have come to symbolize China. The World Wildlife Federation uses a stylized panda as its logo and Panda Express, the most prolific Chinese restaurant chain in the United States, is easily identifiable as Chinese by just its name. In 2008, pandas entered Hollywood in the DreamWorks movie *Kung Fu Panda*. The movie's main character, Po, is a slacker panda who learns martial arts to defend his Sichuan village against a treacherous snow leopard. Louis Vuitton, the fancy designer label, even got on the panda bandwagon when a line of spring handbags debuted on the catwalks decorated with cute panda character illustrations.

I hope that someday I'll be able to live my lifelong dream of keeping a giant panda as a pet, but until then I'll have to make do with the little stuffed animal that I bought in the Chengdu breeding center gift shop.

STIR-FRY BEAN SPROUTS · 炒豆芽

My shopping satchel swells when I stroll through the produce section of a Chinese market. A myriad of vegetables and greens greet me and I never know which one to pick: Bok choy, slender purple eggplants, water spinach, bamboo shoots, lotus roots, or hearty napa cabbage are piled high in bins. I usually end up buying five or more different vegetables. Though the names and flavors may be confusing, I know that any one I stir-fry will make a dish packed full of healthy nutrients. There is a reason why Chinese food has earned a reputation as one of the healthiest cuisines in the world.

Whenever I crave a quick and healthy vegetable stir-fry, I reach for mung bean sprouts. These sprouts are considered "superfoods" and are low in fat and high in protein, vitamins K and C, and manganese.

SERVES 4

Make sure the sprouts are dry, with no water clinging to them. Heat the oil in a wok over high heat. Add the green onions and ginger and stir-fry for 20 seconds. Add the bean sprouts to the wok and stir-fry for 2 minutes. Toss in the salt and soy sauce and stir-fry for an additional 30 seconds. Remove the ginger slices and serve.

- 1 pound fresh mung bean sprouts or fresh soybean sprouts
- 2 tablespoons vegetable oil
- 3 green onions, green and white parts, diagonally sliced
- 2 slices ginger
- ½ teaspoon salt
- 2 teaspoons light soy sauce

COOL CUCUMBER-PEAR SALAD · 梨拌黄瓜

The Chinese words for "eating vinegar" (*chi cu*) are slang for "jealousy." Calling someone a "jar of vinegar" (*cu guan zi*) means he or she is quick to get jealous. Vinegar's bad rap probably has something to do with the tart, crisp taste of clear rice vinegar that makes your mouth pucker.

Sichuan cooks make use of clear rice vinegar by tossing it with chopped vegetables to make small pickled salads. We love the taste of this one. The cool cucumbers and sweet pear slivers are tossed in a sweet and tangy ginger dressing that is spiked with chili oil.

SERVES 4

In a bowl, toss the cucumbers with the salt and let sit for 30 minutes to draw out excess moisture. Rinse the cucumbers under water, drain well, and pat dry. Combine the sugar and vinegar in a small bowl and stir until the sugar is dissolved.

Heat the sesame oil in a wok over medium heat until a piece of a chile sizzles when added to the oil but doesn't turn black. Add the chiles and stir-fry for 10 seconds, then remove the wok from the heat and let cool. Combine the cucumbers, pear, garlic, bell pepper, and ginger in a large bowl. Pour the sesame oil and chiles over the bowl, then the vinegar mixture, and toss until everything is evenly coated. Refrigerate for 6 hours or overnight before serving.

- 1 pound English cucumbers, peeled, quartered, and cut into 3-inch lengths
- 1 teaspoon salt
- 2 tablespoons sugar
- ¼ cup clear rice vinegar
- ¼ cup toasted sesame oil
- 5 to 10 dried red chiles, seeded and chopped
- 1 large pear, peeled, cored, and slivered
- 2 cloves garlic, minced
- ½ red bell pepper, seeded and thinly sliced
- 1 (2-inch) piece ginger, peeled and sliced into matchsticks

TANGERINE BEEF · 陈皮牛肉

I stepped up on a cinder block to enter the open kitchen and realized then just how short the cook was; he flicked on the burner and the flame shot up as high as his chin. His broom closet–size kitchen swelled with heat and even with my average height, I towered over him awkwardly as he wielded the wok with beef and soy sauce. "You must play basketball!" he suggested.

On his kitchen wall and out of reach of the blazing flame, plastic bags of spices hung from low-set rusty hooks, and his windowsill nearby lay scattered with tangerine peels set out to dry in the sun. Cooks in China are in the habit of keeping the peels of the tangerines they eat and spreading them out to dry in the sun for later use. Then they just rehydrate a few pieces whenever they want to add a nutty, slightly bitter note to a stir-fry or stew. Tangerine Beef is a Sichuan specialty and tall on flavor.

SERVES 4

Soak the tangerine peel in warm water for 1 hour to rehydrate, then drain. Peel the orange and use a spoon to scrape away as much of the white pith as possible. Reserve the fruit for another use. Bring a small pot of water to a boil. Blanch the orange peel in the water for 6 minutes to get rid of any bitterness, and then slice into slivers. Dissolve the cornstarch in a large bowl with the light soy sauce, dark soy sauce, 1 tablespoon of the rice wine, and ginger. Add the beef and toss so that all the strips are coated, then marinate, covered, in the fridge for 20 minutes.

Heat 2 tablespoons of the oil in a wok over high heat. Tip the contents of the beef bowl into the wok and stir-fry for about 1 minute, or until the beef is browned but still slightly pink inside. Take care not to overcook the beef or it will get tough. Remove the beef and any liquid from the wok.

Add the remaining 1 tablespoon of oil to the wok and when it is hot, add the Sichuan peppercorns, chile, the white parts of the green onions, the tangerine peel, and orange peel, and stir-fry for 45 seconds. Add the remaining 1 table-spoon of rice wine, the hoisin sauce, chili bean sauce, and sugar and stir for a few seconds. Toss in the beef and the green parts of the green onions and stir until the onions start to wilt. Serve hot.

5 (about 1-inch-square) pieces dried tangerine peel

1 orange

1 teaspoon cornstarch

1 tablespoon light soy sauce

1 tablespoon dark soy sauce

2 tablespoons Shaoxing rice wine or dry sherry

1 tablespoon minced fresh ginger

1 pound beef flank steak, thinly sliced against the grain into 2-inch-long strips

3 tablespoons vegetable oil

½ teaspoon Sichuan peppercorns

1 dried red chile, seeded and chopped

3 green onions, green and white parts kept separate, chopped into ½-inch segments

2 teaspoons hoisin sauce

1 teaspoon chili bean sauce

1 teaspoon sugar

GREEN TEA SHORTBREAD COOKIES · 抹茶酥

Teahouses are social gathering places in Sichuan, and our favorite is the tea garden in the People's Park in Chengdu. Locals come to sit in bamboo chairs beside the lake under the drooping willow tree branches and sip tea. People play cards, catch up on their reading, nibble cookies, and . . . get their ears cleaned. Professional ear cleaners come around to the tables and, if you want, they will clean your ears. Using a thin metal rod with a piece of clean cotton attached to the end, the ear cleaner swabs out your ear and then, using a device resembling a tuning fork, he vibrates the rod to massage your ear canal. I've tried it, and while my ears did feel cleaner, I think I'm a Q-tip kind of guy.

These cookies are our favorite accompaniment for tea. They are dusted with sugar and Sichuan peppercorn powder, and the green tea in them gives the cookies a mild fresh flavor and colors them green. Matcha green tea powder is a high-quality Japanese green tea powder and will make the cookies a very bright green color. You can find it at tea shops and at online tea stores. However, if you can't locate it, drop Chinese green tea leaves into a coffee grinder and grind them into a powder.

MAKES 30 COOKIES

Preheat the oven to 375°F and line 2 baking sheets with parchment paper. Place the flour, confectioners' sugar, green tea powder, and salt in a food processor and process until well combined. Add the butter and vanilla to the food processor and pulse until a dough forms. Roll the dough into a 2-inch diameter cylinder and then cover with plastic wrap. Chill the dough in the refrigerator for 30 minutes.

In a shallow dish, mix the granulated sugar and ground Sichuan peppercorns together. Use a sharp knife to slice the dough cylinder into 1/3-inch-thick rounds. Place each round in the sugar mixture and then flip it over so that both sides are evenly coated with the mixture. Place the cookies on the prepared baking sheets, spacing them 1½ inches apart. Bake for 12 minutes, or until the edges are firm but not brown. Let cool completely on wire racks before serving.

2 cups all-purpose flour

¾ cup confectioners' sugar

1½ tablespoons matcha green tea powder

½ teaspoon salt

1 cup (2 sticks) unsalted butter, at room temperature, cubed

1 teaspoon vanilla extract

½ cup granulated sugar

1½ tablespoons ground Sichuan peppercorns

XINJIANG
新疆

XINJIANG: LAMB KEBABS AND BREAD ON THE TAKLIMAKAN DESERT 新疆

I grab the kicking animal by its fatty butt with one hand and slip my other under its curly-haired belly, hoisting it into my arms. I am now the proud owner of a very angry, smelly little lamb whom I have named Xiao Fei ("Little Fatty" in Chinese). In the distance—200 yards off—Mary Kate's purple Nike T-shirt bobs toward me through a sea of a bazillion men in white Muslim skullcaps and countless more moving furry waves of livestock. She left me earlier to go try to test-drive the camels and horses up for auction on the other side of this expansive open-air livestock market while I stayed here squeezing sheep rumps.

The strange sheep bred here in the deserts of Xinjiang Province have humongous butts! They look as if they had two camel humps that migrated to their behinds. This fatty tissue, like camel humps, boosts the animals' metabolism and ability to go without water in this arid region, where temperatures can soar north of 120°F. They have another purpose, however—the plumper, the fatter the cheeks, the higher the value of the sheep. I procured Xiao Fei by joining the men around me in the intense and exciting fray of bartering and haggling for the animals. "How much? We are old friends, give me a good deal!" I yelled, only to realize my Chinese was little help to my cause. The traders spoke Arab languages—Uighur, Kazakh, Persian, and Kyrgyz—and they spoke at best only a little

Chinese. I did, however, learn one word that day from the local Uighur language: *"Boish boish!"* It means turn around. Like, now. A donkey cart or whole herd of cattle might be on your heels.

Mary Kate's back.

"Hey," I say. "How was it over there?"

No answer. Her eyes narrow in on my arms. "What in the heck are we going to do with that?" she asks.

Xinjiang, or as it literally translates, "New Frontier," is a predominantly Muslim-populated region that composes the northwest corner of China and is smack dab in the middle of the Taklimakan Desert, one of the world's largest, hottest, and most unforgiving deserts. Just so caravan merchants and travelers are warned ahead of time, the name Taklimakan translates as "You go in, you don't come out." Xinjiang rests atop 30 percent of China's oil reserves and is larger in land than Alaska, with mineral-rich deposits including gold. It also strategically borders no less than eight countries, including Russia, Pakistan, and India. We are in Xinjiang's far-flung western city of Kashgar at the largest, most famous bazaar in Asia, located just 170 miles from the Chinese-Afghanistan border; I feel like we're on the other side. The Uighurs (pronounced *WEE-gurs*), a Central Asian people with a Turkic language and of Middle Eastern descent, claim Xinjiang as their ancestral home. They

have very little in common with the Chinese, ethnically or culturally. Some have blue eyes and sandy hair, thick beards and strong, Arab features.

Today is Sunday, the day 50,000-plus traders flood the city from surrounding territories to hawk their goods and livestock that they bring in on the back of donkey carts. This is a 2,000-year-old trading center that was once the epicenter of the fabled Silk Road caravan route that helped develop the modern world. Starting in eastern China and ending in the Mediterranean Sea, the Silk Road linked the Far East with India, the Roman Empire, and the world, spreading ideas and technology, foods, spices, religion, and yes, silk.

Xiao Fei turns out to be scrawnier than I thought, and Mary Kate is not on board with my hope of learning how to roast a whole lamb, a famous and impressive Uighur dish served at banquets. This is probably for the best, but I can't take him home with me either, so I fuzz up the little guy's hair to make him look bigger and Mary Kate parades around him as if she were Vanna White and desperately in need of selling a vowel. "The greatest lamb that ever was!" she says, drawing more annoyance than interest from the men

around us. Finally Xiao Fei sells for a tough loss to a trader who I gather is Kyrgyz, and Mary Kate and I take a donkey cart taxi a few miles north on roads recently paved by the Chinese government as a part of their campaign to modernize Kashgar. Vertical poplar and aspen trees scrape the sky along the sides of the boulevard, and we soon reach the other section of the Kashgar giant outdoor bazaar: the goods. Stall after stall is filled from top to bottom with fur hats, inexpensive gold jewelry, bolts of silk fabric, and bins of Middle Eastern spices like cardamom and turmeric. Fruits and nuts grown in the desert oasis of Turpan tempt shoppers from heaping wicker baskets. Garlic cloves woven together into five-foot-long braids wrap around the seat and frame of a boy's bike. "I give you cheap!" he yells to me.

Toward the afternoon Mary Kate and I go on the prowl for some eats from one of the many outdoor eateries on the colorfully alive streets of Kashgar. Down a street behind the Id Kah Mosque, a cook pulls and flings dough in the air to stretch long noodles before serving *laghman* up in a bowl with green bell peppers and a tomato-red sauce. Smoke from cumin-crusted lamb kebabs grilling on a nearby hardwood grill fills my nostrils. Lamb in every form is the main event in Xinjiang. Uighurs are Muslim and their food is *halal*, which means it is prepared according to Islamic law. Pork and alcohol are never consumed.

"How about that stand?" I say, pointing to a roadside vendor selling *apke* soup, floating lamb heads stewing in a cauldron.

Mary Kate winces. "We'll have to try that later. It's a little too real for me right now," she says.

Instead we try a restaurant that serves us on the sidewalk, where we sit on the edge of a blue wooden bed frame covered with an Asian handwoven rug. A waitress sets teacups and a teapot filled with cinnamon tea on a stand in the center of the bed, and Mary Kate dumps out the contents of her shopping bag. She's bought an armful of exotic spices and strange hocus-pocus trinkets at the market, like dried and splayed sand lizards that she just couldn't live without. Picking up the rough, curled skin of a snake she bought from a medicine man, she says, "There has to be a way to get this home on the plane."

We order pastries folded with mutton and onion called *samsa* and also naan, a Frisbee-size flatbread stamped with a spiral design and sprinkled with onion flecks, roasted sesame seeds, and whole cumin. Not too far from where we sit is the restaurant's outdoor dome oven where these are baked. Nearly as large as my entire kitchen back in New York City, the oven is lit from below, where glowing firewood heats the clay walls to ridiculously high temperatures. I watch as the baker reaches down past his shoulder into the manhole-size opening at the top and slaps the dough on the side of the oven, where it sticks to a salt patina. The hot walls of the oven bake the bread crispy on the bottom but leave it soft in the center. About fifteen minutes later he retrieves the golden

brown bread with a long steel rod and adds it to a stack on a table.

Yesterday Mary Kate and I got a lesson from a Uighur baker who has been baking breads in these ovens for thirty years. He had scars on his hands and arms from accidentally touching the sides, and the hair on his forearms was permanently singed. "You're doing what no one else has done, you know," he told me, excited to teach us how to make naan for this cookbook. When we explained that in America we don't have clay ovens like his and we'd have to come up with a workaround like using a pizza stone or quarry tiles to create a surface hot enough to bake the naan, he was shocked.

"How do you still not have one yet?" he asked. "We've already been using these for 5,000 years!"

GRILLED LAMB KEBABS WITH YOGURT · 羊肉串和酸奶

The secret to good kebabs is to first toss the meat cubes in egg and cornstarch. This makes the mix of freshly ground spices stick to the lamb and forms a crusty layer when grilled. The meat's center stays tender and juicy.

Xinjiang cooks roast spices whole to intensify their flavor and give them a fuller character. To roast spices at home, toast them in a dry pan over medium heat until you just start to smell their fragrance. Make sure to keep an eye on them—spices are unforgiving once they burn, with no way to rescue them. When the spices cool, grind them into a powder in a mortar and pestle or a spice or coffee grinder.

These kebabs go well with Naan Flatbread (page 234) and a side of Kashgar Onion Salad (page 239). If you are using bamboo skewers, soak them in water for 1 hour before using.

MAKES ABOUT 18 SKEWERS

Beat the egg with the cornstarch in a large bowl. Toss in the lamb so that all the cubes are coated, and refrigerate for 1 hour.

Prepare a medium fire in a charcoal or gas grill and oil the grill grates. Dry-roast the cumin and coriander seeds in a skillet over medium heat just until you smell the spices' aroma; be careful not to let them burn. Then immediately remove the skillet from the heat and let cool. In a mortar and pestle or a coffee grinder, grind the seeds into a coarse powder. Mix the powder with the salt and chili powder until well combined.

Thread 5 cubes of lamb onto each skewer and rub the spice mixture all over the meat. Brush the tops of the skewers with the oil. Grill the skewers until they are crusty and brown on the outside and medium-rare on the inside. Serve the kebabs with a side of yogurt for dipping.

1 large egg

2 tablespoons cornstarch

2 pounds boneless lamb or beef, cut into ¾-inch cubes

3 tablespoons cumin seeds

3 tablespoons coriander seeds

1 teaspoon salt

1 teaspoon Asian chili powder

3 tablespoons vegetable oil

1½ cups plain Greek yogurt

NAAN FLATBREAD · 馕

Naan Flatbread is traditionally baked in large outdoor dome ovens called *tan-doors*. The hot clay walls of the oven bake the bread crispy on the bottom but leave it soft in the center. You can re-create this cooking method in your oven at home by using a pizza stone. This is a flat piece of earthenware that heats up to very high temperatures and helps to distribute the heat evenly across the bottom of the bread to give it a crunchy crust. If you don't want to spring for a new pizza stone, you can use a few clay quarry tiles that can easily be found at your local home improvement center—a method pioneered by Julia Child in her recipe for authentic French bread. Be sure to purchase unglazed quarry tiles that are lead-free, and it's a good idea as well to ask a knowledgeable salesperson which tiles would be best (and safe) to cook with. Before preheating the oven, place the pizza stone or quarry tiles on the oven rack with at least 1 inch of space around the edges to allow the hot air to circulate.

MAKES 5 BREAD ROUNDS

Combine the yeast and warm water in the work bowl of a mixer or a large bowl and let rest for 5 minutes.

To make the dough in a mixer, slowly mix the flour and 2 teaspoons of the salt into the yeast mixture and mix with a dough hook to form a dough. Transfer the dough to a lightly floured work surface and knead for an additional 5 minutes by hand, until it is soft and elastic.

Alternatively, to knead the dough by hand, slowly stir 3 cups of the flour and 2 teaspoons of the salt into the yeast mixture with a wooden spoon. Keep adding more flour until the dough is too thick to continue stirring. Spread out the remaining flour on a work surface. Knead the dough on top of the flour for 10 minutes, incorporating the flour into the dough so that it becomes soft and elastic.

When you're done kneading the dough using either method, place it in a lightly oiled bowl, cover with a damp kitchen towel, and then place in a warm, dry place for 2 hours, or until the dough doubles in size.

On a lightly floured work surface, punch the dough down and then divide it into 6 balls. Flatten the balls into 5-inch disks, and keep covered with the kitchen towel when you are not working with it.

2 teaspoons active dry yeast

2½ cups warm water

6 cups unbleached all-purpose flour

2 teaspoons kosher salt, plus more for sprinkling

2 green onions, white parts only, minced

1½ teaspoons cumin seeds

2 tablespoons sesame seeds

With lightly floured hands, use your fingers to press each dough disk from the center outward to form 9- to 10-inch rounds with a small lip around the edge. If the dough is very elastic and shrinks in size, alternate between the dough disks to allow time for the gluten molecules to stretch. Use a fork to prick the dough's surface in a pattern of a ring of 7 large circles, with each circle just touching the other. Then, prick several smaller concentric circles within each of the larger circles. The overall effect should look like 7 exploding fireworks on the dough's surface. This technique is not just for aesthetics, as it prevents the dough from bubbling when baking.

Just before baking, splash the center of the dough with a little water. Bake the bread in batches, using a pizza paddle or a lightly floured rimless baking sheet to slide the dough onto the hot baking stone or quarry tiles. Bake until the bread turns golden brown, 8 to 10 minutes. Remove the bread from the oven. Mist each bread round with water and sprinkle with salt, a scattering of green onions, a pinch of cumin seeds, and 1 teaspoon of sesame seeds. Slide the bread back in the oven and bake for about 30 seconds or until the green onions start to turn brown and are heated through.

UIGHUR ROAST CHICKEN · 新疆烤鸡

Uighur cooks are masters of the art of grilling and roasting. They skewer splayed whole fish with sticks stuck in desert sand next to flaming wood coals, grill whole lambs in *tandoor* ovens, and on special occasions they roast an entire camel (called *kao luo tuo*), which involves lowering the camel into a giant clay oven using a system of ropes, pulleys, and wooden cranes.

For this Uighur Roast Chicken, truss the chicken with kitchen twine before roasting it to help the meat cook evenly and stay moist and succulent. To truss a chicken, place the two chicken leg knuckles over the middle of a 3-foot-long piece of twine, and then tie the legs together with a half-knot. Then take the two ends of the twine and crisscross them around the body of the chicken once, tying the ends snugly together underneath the neck opening. Trim any extra twine.

When I asked a Uighur cook for a recipe for whole-roasted camel, he told me that the process is similar to this roast chicken recipe. I'm sure that trussing the 600-pound camel would be a different thing entirely.

SERVES 4

1 (3-pound) chicken
1 tablespoon kosher salt
2 teaspoons ground cumin
½ teaspoon paprika
½ teaspoon freshly ground black
    pepper
1 large lemon, halved

Preheat the oven to 450°F. Rinse the chicken and dry it very well inside and out. Rub the salt all over the outside and inside of the chicken. In a small bowl, mix together the cumin, paprika, and black pepper and set aside.

Truss the chicken with kitchen twine. Place the chicken in a roasting pan and bake for 20 minutes. Remove the chicken from the oven, dab the spice mixture all over the chicken, and then return to the oven. Bake for an additional 25 to 30 minutes, until the meat is cooked through. You can test it by sticking a chopstick into the thickest part of the meat; if the juices run clear, not pink, the chicken is done. Remove the chicken from the oven, squeeze the lemon over the chicken, and let it rest for 10 minutes before carving and serving.

KASHGAR ONION SALAD ▪ 洋葱沙拉

The sharp taste of onions makes this salad ideal for eating with grilled lamb kebabs or roasted meats. Stick it in the refrigerator for a few hours to let the flavors meld and the onions and tomatoes soak up the spicy dressing.

SERVES 4

Whisk together the vegetable oil, clear rice vinegar, chili oil, salt, and sugar in a small bowl. Put the onion, tomato, and cilantro in a salad bowl and toss with the dressing until everything is coated. Chill in the refrigerator for at least 3 hours before serving.

1 tablespoon vegetable oil
1 tablespoon clear rice vinegar
½ teaspoon Chili Oil (page 257)
¼ teaspoon salt
½ teaspoon sugar
1 onion, thinly sliced into half-moons
½ medium tomato, coarsely chopped
1 cup lightly packed fresh cilantro, coarsely chopped

POLO CARROT RICE ▪ 手抓饭

Similar rice dishes can be found in other Central Asian countries with names like *pilaf, plov,* and *pilau.* In this Uighur version, short-grain rice, carrots, and raisins are simmered with mutton joints to create a flavorful and very moist rice dish.

SERVES 6

Heat the oil in a large pot over high heat. Add the lamb shanks and cook until they are browned on all sides, about 3 minutes per side. Remove the lamb from the pot. Reduce the heat to medium and add the onion and carrots to the pot. Stir for about 10 minutes, or until the onion becomes translucent. Add the lamb, rice, garlic, cumin, and salt to the pot and stir until all the grains of rice are coated with oil. Pour the water into the pot. Bring to a boil, then decrease the heat and simmer, covered, for 25 minutes.

Turn off the heat and stir in the almonds and raisins. Replace the cover and let stand for 15 minutes before serving.

1/3 cup vegetable oil
1½ pounds lamb shanks
1 large onion, sliced into half-moons
3 large carrots, peeled and slivered
3 cups short-grain white rice
3 cloves garlic, peeled
½ teaspoon ground cumin
1 teaspoon salt
3½ cups water
3 tablespoons slivered almonds
¾ cup golden raisins

NOODLE ANXIETY

I rolled up the sleeves of my white chef's jacket and wrapped the five-foot noodle around my wrist. Hoping against hope that I looked like I knew what I was doing, I shuffled up to the edge of the forty-gallon steaming cauldron. The three Uighur cooks next to me whom I was imitating with what I hoped appeared to be ease and grace began pulling and tearing off thumb-size bits of the long noodles with their fingers and flinging the bits into the boiling water with machine gun–like speed and precision. I smiled weakly and fired away myself. I did not get off to a good start. My first three torn noodles missed the pot completely and went *splat* on the floor. Sweat began to run down my red cheeks—the restaurant was slammed with the lunch rush—so I put aside my pride and began frantically

tearing the noodles as fast as my inept fingers could, hurling one misshapen noodle after another into the pot, occasionally piping up with a *"dui bu qi* [sorry]!" or, more often, "shit!" and kicking the noodles that I dropped on the floor under the stove when the other cooks left to reload with more dough from the counter.

The head chef stopped to look over my shoulder in the midst of making his rounds of the other forty line cooks in the kitchen. "No, like this! Faster, faster!" he screamed. Whatever he could see past my hair, which had grown into a frizzy poof in the sweltering humidity of the kitchen, was not to his liking. "I was under the impression you were a cook, yes or no?" he accused.

This took some explaining. The night before, Nate and I had eaten a fantastic version of *da pan ji* (大盘鸡), or literally "big plate o' chicken," spiked with chiles, green peppers, and potatoes, at this same large Xinjiang restaurant. After paying the bill, Nate had pleaded our way into the kitchen to see how they made the dish firsthand. Just as a nice waiter was showing us back in the kitchen, the head chef got word and stormed in, throwing us out of his restaurant in a theatrical rage, only to change his mind and call after us when we were halfway down the street. "Come back tomorrow morning. Be ready," he shouted.

When we arrived early the next morning, before the restaurant opened, it was clear that we were not there for a quick lesson on how to make Big Plate o' Chicken

but rather were to be used as two new line cooks for the busy kitchen. A manager met us at the door with folded chef's whites and escorted us into separate rooms in the employee dormitory above the restaurant, where we were told to change into the uniforms. As Nate and I walked through the swinging doors into the kitchen, our eyes briefly met, and I knew he was thinking, like me, that we were in over our heads. Although we knew Chinese food, Xinjiang food with its folded dough pastries, lamb butchering, noodle stretching, and huge fire-breathing clay ovens was a whole different beast.

Nate was given the easy job of prepping vegetables, and he set about chopping the piles of tomatoes, onions, and carrots next to him on the counter. My job, on the other hand, was to make *laghman* (لەغمەن) or, as it is called in Chinese, *la mian* (拉面), literally "pulled noodles." I watched the young cook next to me as he worked the dough, folding it over on itself several times to align the proteins and form a dough that was elastic and springy but not tough. He stretched and tugged it between his two outstretched hands over and over again, like an accordion player. In between pulls, he wrapped the ever-lengthening noodle around his fingers, dipping it into flour to keep the strands separate. It ended up basically turning into one giant long noodle—probably twenty feet long!

Noodles are a staple of northern China and Xinjiang, much like rice is in southern China. In the West we usually use a noodle press to squeeze dough into spaghetti and fettuccine, but in China, noodles are stretched by hand into different shapes and sizes. At a popular restaurant in Beijing called Noodle Loft, the cooks fling *la mian* tableside like noodle acrobats—sometimes slinging a long noodle at a guest's face and yanking it back just before it makes contact.

After some embarrassing attempts at making *la mian*, it was pretty clear that this was not my calling, and I was happily demoted. My new post was making the easier *mian pian* noodles, flat wheat noodles that are stretched only once and then torn into bite-size pieces before being parboiled.

Some say Marco Polo smuggled the recipe for *la mian* out of China in his camel saddlebag and brought it back to Italy, where it became known the world over as "pasta." But no one really knows. One thing is for certain: China has been making noodles for a very, very long time. In 2005, a team of Beijing archaeologists discovered a 4,000-year-old bowl of noodles stuck in the dirt of the Yellow River in Xinjiang's neighboring province, Qinghai. Their guess is that they were hand pulled.

CINNAMON SPICE TEA · 新疆茶

We are at once in a maze of shadowed narrow lanes winding between ancient mud houses and mosques. These houses in Kashgar's Old Town have stood here for centuries, and I feel like I've gone back in time to biblical days. The sounds of artisans hammering knives and carving wood spill out from the shops that line the way. I pass a group of women wearing burqas, their faces completely hidden behind the dark brown cloth. Toddlers laugh and play with a soccer ball at their ankles.

We follow Musa, our guide and Uighur translator, through a well-worn poplar door, and I'm surprised to see a small courtyard flooded with sunlight. Pots of red and pink roses sit next to a miniature orange tree. I look up to my left and see a two-story mansion made of mud bricks and a Uighur woman standing in the doorway. She has been waiting for us.

Inside the house we are invited to sit on Persian rugs around a low dining table. The table is covered corner to corner with a sprawling spread of food: candy jars filled with sweets, walnuts and pistachios, pastries piled high on painted trays, and all kinds of dried fruits. Our host pours cups of cinnamon tea, and we drink.

SERVES 4

Bring the water to a boil in a large pot or kettle and add the tea, cardamom, cinnamon, clove, and saffron. Simmer for 5 to 6 minutes, until the tea turns a rich amber color. Strain the tea through a fine mesh strainer, and then serve with sugar, if using, to sweeten to taste.

5 cups water
4 teaspoons loose green tea leaves
4 green cardamom pods, lightly crushed with the flat side of a knife
1 cinnamon stick
1 whole clove
3 strands saffron
Sugar, for serving (optional)

BIG PLATE O' CHICKEN · 大盘鸡

Big Plate o' Chicken, or *da pan ji*, is easily the most popular Xinjiang dish among expats in China. Its name is not an exaggeration; the dish arrives at the table on a huge serving platter and is piled high with chicken pieces, chopped bell peppers, and thick chunks of potato. Our favorite recipe uses a can of beer to give an extra bite to the zesty, savory broth.

SERVES 4

Heat 2 tablespoons of the oil in a wok over medium-high heat. Fry the chicken pieces, in batches if necessary, for about 12 minutes, or until all the sides are browned. Remove the chicken and wipe out the wok.

Heat the remaining 2 tablespoons of the oil in the wok over medium heat. Add the Sichuan peppercorns, chiles, cumin, star anise, garlic, and ginger and stir-fry for 20 seconds. Add the potatoes, chile peppers, bell pepper, and green onions and stir-fry for 1 minute. Add the beer, water, chili bean sauce, soy sauce, and sugar, then decrease the heat and simmer for 15 minutes, or until the potatoes are fork-tender. Serve hot.

¼ cup vegetable oil

1½ pounds bone-in, skin-on chicken breasts, legs, and thighs, chopped into 1½-inch pieces (use a heavy cleaver, or ask your butcher to chop them for you)

1 teaspoon Sichuan peppercorns, lightly crushed

6 to 10 dried red chiles, seeded

1 teaspoon cumin seeds

2 star anise

4 cloves garlic, sliced

1 (1-inch) piece ginger, sliced

1½ pounds potatoes, peeled and sliced into ¼-inch-thick disks

2 Anaheim chile peppers, seeded and chopped into 1½-inch squares

1 small red bell pepper, seeded and chopped into 1½-inch squares

3 green onions, white parts only, coarsely chopped

1 (12-ounce) can pale lager-style beer

½ cup water

3 tablespoons chili bean sauce

1 tablespoon light soy sauce

1 tablespoon sugar

LAGHMAN NOODLES WITH TOMATO SAUCE · 新疆拉面

In the reflection of the cracked mirror hanging in a blue tiled frame on the wall, the shop clerk flutters about the room behind me lightly picking up silk scarves—deep reds, cheery eggplant, ice blue, golden hues, and patterns as varied as camouflage and polka dots. She returns, this time with a light brown scarf that she assures me is in fashion this summer. Wrapping my head and tying a knot below my chin, she looks at my reflection in the mirror with me. "You look like very Uighur girl," she says, smiling.

Most Uighur women in the conservative Muslim city of Kashgar wear head coverings. While in town, I wore one too, and Nate and I with our Western features actually blended in. Some people even mistook us for locals and started up conversations with us in Uighur. This was a first in our travels in China. We slipped into noodle shops unnoticed at lunchtime and dinnertime, as everyday folks just coming to eat.

The ubiquitous Xinjiang *laghman* noodles that we ate in these shops are topped with stewed tomatoes and peppers swimming in a wonderful tomato sauce. Traditionally, the noodles in this dish are hand pulled and extremely difficult to make, involving stretching dough by hand into long cords. We recommend using the much easier Hand-Torn Noodles (page 261) or buying fresh round noodles, which have a similar taste.

SERVES 4

Heat the oil in a wok over medium heat. Drop in the garlic, onion, lamb, and 1 teaspoon of the salt and stir-fry for about 8 minutes, or until the onion is translucent. Add the tomatoes and their juice, the peppers, green onions, and chili oil. Bring to a simmer and cook for 15 minutes, or until the peppers are tender.

Meanwhile, bring a large pot of water to a boil, add the remaining ½ teaspoon salt. Add the Hand-Torn Noodles and cook for 8 to 10 minutes or until they are tender. If using fresh round noodles, cook until al dente. Drain well and divide them among 4 serving plates. Top the noodles with the sauce, scatter with the cilantro leaves, and serve.

3 tablespoons vegetable oil

5 cloves garlic, thinly sliced

1 medium onion, thinly sliced into half-moons

8 ounces boneless lamb, cubed

1½ teaspoons salt

1 (28-ounce) can peeled tomatoes with juice, coarsely chopped

2 green bell peppers, seeded and chopped into 1½-inch squares

5 green onions, white parts only, chopped into 1-inch lengths

1 tablespoon Chili Oil (page 257)

1 pound Hand-Torn Noodles (page 261) or fresh round noodles

Handful of fresh cilantro leaves

TANGY CHICKPEA SALAD · 鹰嘴豆沙拉

Chickpeas—those smooth, meaty-tasting little yellow beans packed with protein and nutrients like iron and vitamin B—are (in our humble opinion) greatly underused in Western cooking. During our last visit to Kashgar, we returned again and again to the same food booth at the Id Kah Square market to eat more of this tasty, tangy salad. From beneath a large multicolored umbrella, the woman scooped the salad into ceramic bowls and heaped them with piles of fresh herbs.

SERVES 4

Use a mortar and pestle or a wooden spoon against the side of a medium bowl to mash the garlic, cumin, salt, and chile flakes together. Whisk in the clear rice vinegar, oil, and egg yolk.

Place the chickpeas, carrots, and green onions in a large salad bowl. Pour the vinegar mixture over and toss until everything is evenly coated. Cover the bowl and chill in the refrigerator for 1 hour.

Before serving, toss the salad with the cilantro and mint leaves and sprinkle with the cracked black pepper to taste.

1 clove garlic, minced
1 teaspoon ground cumin
½ teaspoon kosher salt
½ teaspoon crushed red chile flakes
2 tablespoons clear rice vinegar
3 tablespoons vegetable oil
1 egg yolk
2 (15-ounce) cans chickpeas, rinsed and drained
2 large carrots, peeled and slivered
3 green onions, green and white parts, chopped
Handful of fresh cilantro leaves, coarsely chopped
Handful of fresh mint leaves, coarsely chopped
Freshly cracked black pepper

RAISIN-WALNUT PASTRIES · 葡萄干核桃酥

Grapes growing in the oasis town of Turpan are dried by the ton. Raisins then are donkey carted to Xinjiang's capital city of Urumqi, where they are a main event at the lively Wuyi night market. Raisins heaped in baskets, raisins in polo fried rice, raisins in pastries. A Uighur vendor fills buttery dough balls with a mixture of plumped-up raisins, walnuts, cinnamon, and sugar. Then he fries the morsels golden on a dimpled griddle. We've adapted the recipe to use store-bought pastry dough and to bake in a home oven.

Vendors also sell homemade vanilla ice cream made from huge blocks of ice. The blocks are cut from frozen lakes in nearby mountains and then carted into town to be churned in large metal drums to make the ice cream. A scoop of vanilla ice cream is the perfect accompaniment to these pastries.

MAKES 6 PASTRIES

½ cup golden raisins
½ cup water
½ teaspoon ground cinnamon
¼ cup sugar
1 (9-ounce) sheet frozen puff pastry, thawed but still cold
½ cup walnuts, coarsely chopped
1 large egg, beaten
French vanilla ice cream, for serving

Preheat the oven to 400°F and lightly grease a baking sheet. In a small saucepan, combine the raisins with the water and bring to a boil, then remove from the heat and let stand for 5 minutes. Drain the raisins well. In a small bowl, mix together the cinnamon and 2 tablespoons of the sugar.

On a clean work surface, cut the cold puff pastry dough lengthwise into 3 strips, then cut the strips in half to create six 4 by 6-inch pieces. Place 1 heaping tablespoon of the raisins on the lower center of each piece of dough. Top each pile of raisins with the walnuts and 1 heaping teaspoon of the sugar mixture. Brush the egg around the edges of the dough, fold the pastry over the filling, and use the tines of a fork to press the edges together to form a seal. Brush the tops of the pastry pockets with the remaining egg and sprinkle with the remaining 2 tablespoons of the sugar.

Place the pastries on the prepared baking sheet and bake for 15 to 20 minutes, until they are golden brown. Serve each pastry with a scoop of vanilla ice cream.

BASICS

ESSENTIAL COOKING EQUIPMENT

Cooking great Chinese food doesn't require fancy kitchen gadgets and a lot of special equipment. However, there are a few essential kitchen items that you will need:

Wok

A wok is the single most important piece of cooking equipment used in Chinese kitchens. Cooks have devised methods to cook just about everything in the rounded pots: stir-frying, braising, deep-frying, steaming, smoking, making soups. We recommend purchasing a 14-inch flat-bottomed wok made of carbon steel with a single wooden handle. If it does not come with a lid, buy one that fits snugly on top. Before using a new wok, you must season it to prevent food from sticking and to keep it from rusting (see How to Season a Wok on page 253). Make sure not to get a wok with a nonstick coating, as this coating will not allow you to season it properly.

Wooden Spatula

A flat wooden or bamboo spatula used to stir ingredients in the wok while stir-frying. A wooden spoon will also work.

Perforated Strainer

A strainer allows you to scoop ingredients out of a wok when blanching or deep-frying. Traditional ones are made out of woven copper or steel wire with a long bamboo handle, but those made out of perforated stainless steel work equally well.

Wire Strainer

A fine-mesh steel strainer is useful for straining small particles out of liquids such as soup stocks. Cheesecloth is often an acceptable substitute.

Cleaver

A cleaver is the only knife most Chinese cooks use in the kitchen. It is not a large, heavy butcher's cleaver but rather a smaller lightweight cleaver that is used to adeptly chop vegetables and cut through hunks of meat and bone. When selecting a cleaver, buy one with a forged carbon steel blade, which will hold its edge the longest. A chef's knife is an acceptable substitute.

Scissors

Scissors cut soaked noodles and come in handy when seeding dried red chiles. Just snip off the stem ends of the chiles and shake out the seeds.

Mortar and Pestle

This tool, consisting of a small bowl and a blunt stick, usually made out of stone or wood, is used to grind spices and herbs. This is a very handy piece of equipment to have around the kitchen, and we highly recommend buying one. However, a coffee grinder can be used as an alternative to grind dry spices, and a wooden spoon can be used to pulverize fresh herbs in a small bowl.

Steamer

This is a bamboo or metal tray that fits in a pot over boiling water. When a lid is placed on the steamer tray or pot, the steam from the water below cooks the food inside. If you don't have a steamer, you can improvise with items you already have in your kitchen (see How to Steam on page 254).

Chopsticks

These are, of course, the primary eating utensils in China, but Chinese cooks also make use of chopsticks for a multitude of uses while cooking, including adding and removing ingredients from the wok, beating eggs, and mixing. We think bamboo or wooden chopsticks are easier to hold than plastic ones, which can feel slippery in your fingers. For a visual guide to using chopsticks, see How to Use Chopsticks on page 254.

Mini Rolling Pin

A small wooden rolling pin, about 1 inch in diameter and 8 inches in length, is useful for making dumpling wrappers. Its small size allows you to roll the wrappers with one hand while turning the dough in a circular motion with the other. If you don't have one, you can improvise with a wooden dowel or a regular large rolling pin.

Hot Pot

A large pot with an inside heating element is placed in the center of the dining table to serve fondue-like hot-pot dishes. Traditional hot pots are heated with coal, but nowadays people use gas or electric hot pots. We use an electric pot that we purchased at Wal-Mart, but an electric wok, a large fondue pot, or a tabletop gas burner will also work. If using an electric hot pot, take care to secure the cord so that no one trips over it.

HOW TO SEASON A WOK

Contrary to what you might think, a shiny new wok is not a good thing. Similar to a cast-iron skillet, a carbon steel wok should be seasoned with a patina of blackened cooking oil to prevent food from sticking to it. A wok will naturally accumulate this coating over time with use, but if you have recently bought a new wok or have been a little too thorough when cleaning yours, you can easily season it.

First clean the wok by scrubbing it with soap to remove any coating of oil from the manufacturer. Place the wok on the stove over high heat, and when it is heated and completely dry, pour about 3 tablespoons of sesame oil into the wok. Heat until the oil is smoking. Fold a piece of paper towel into about a 3-inch square and use a pair of kitchen tongs or chopsticks to rub the oil all around the interior of the wok with the paper towel. You will notice the surface of the wok begins to darken. Continue rubbing the oil into the wok until the entire inside of the wok is blackened. When washing the wok after future uses, do not use steel wool or an abrasive sponge, because this will remove the seasoning and you will have to repeat the process.

HOW TO STIR-FRY

Stir-frying, or *chao* (炒), is a catchall term for the various techniques Chinese cooks use to quickly fry vegetables and meat (or tofu) in a small amount of oil in a wok over high heat. When stir-frying, a wooden spatula or spoon is used to constantly stir the food so that it cooks evenly and doesn't burn. The process preserves the crunchy texture of the vegetables and locks in flavors and healthy antioxidants. Stir-frying at home is quick and easy, and by following these three steps you can improvise your own stir-fry using ingredients of your choosing.

Step 1: Prep the ingredients.

The first thing you want to do before turning your stove on is to prep all the ingredients. Once you start stir-frying, ingredients are added in quick succession to the wok and there is no time to measure and chop. Rinse the ingredients (both meat and vegetables) and use paper towels (for meat) or a clean kitchen towel to get them good and dry, or otherwise when you throw them into the wok the moisture will make them steam rather than fry.

When you cut up the vegetables, consider how long the vegetable pieces will take to cook and slice them accordingly. For instance, hearty vegetables like carrots or lotus root take longer to cook than less hearty vegetables like mushrooms and bean sprouts. If you stir-fry large pieces of carrots and mushrooms together, by the time the carrots are cooked through, the mushrooms will be soggy and overcooked. To remedy this, you can either thinly slice the carrots so that they also cook quickly, or you can start cooking the carrots first and then throw in the mushrooms toward the end.

When the recipe calls for dry and liquid ingredients to be added to the wok at the same time, combine them ahead of time. For example, salt, soy sauce, and oyster sauce can be whisked together beforehand so that they can be added together in one whoosh to the wok.

Step 2: Cook the protein.

Heat the wok first over medium-high heat and add 1 to 2 tablespoons of oil. Use an oil with a relatively high smoking point that won't break down under the heat (this is not the time to use olive oil). Peanut oil, soybean oil, and most vegetable oils work well. Pick up the wok by the handle and swirl the oil around so that the wok is coated. Throw your chopped spices like garlic, ginger, and chiles into the wok and stir for 10 to 20 seconds, just until the spices become fragrant and they flavor the oil; be careful not to let them burn. Immediately add your protein (poultry, meat, or tofu) to the wok and use a wooden spatula or spoon to stir the meat constantly until it is browned on all sides and cooked through. Remove the protein from the wok and set aside. If there is any burnt residue in the wok, wipe it out.

Step 3: Cook the vegetables.

Heat a little more oil in the wok over high heat and then toss in your vegetables. Stir them continuously so that they cook evenly. When they are almost cooked through, add any sauces and liquids to the wok and stir. If you are adding a cornstarch slurry to thicken the sauce, add it now. Once the sauce has thickened and the vegetables are cooked through but still a little crunchy, stir back in the cooked protein. When everything is heated through, serve immediately.

HOW TO USE CHOPSTICKS

1. Rest the upper third of one chopstick in the space between your thumb and index finger. Use the side of your thumb to apply pressure and smash the chopstick against the end of your ring finger.

2. Grasp the upper third of the other chopstick between your thumb, index, and middle finger.

3. Move the top chopstick independently while the lower one stays stationary.

HOW TO STEAM

Steaming is a healthy way to cook vegetables, meat, fish, and dumplings without using any oil. This method also makes a bread that is light and moist. To steam food, pour 2 inches of water into the base pot of a steamer and bring to a boil. Follow the recipe's instructions on whether to place the food in a shallow dish or directly on the steamer tray, and then put the tray in place. Cover the tray and steam for the amount of time specified in the recipe. If you don't have a steamer, you can make one by placing coffee mugs upside down in a large pot and resting an aluminum pie pan on the mugs to act as a tray. Use a pencil to poke holes all over the pie pan to allow steam to circulate. For recipes that require food to be steamed in a shallow dish, rest a large heatproof plate directly on top of the mugs. Then add 2 inches of water to the pot and bring to a boil. Place the food on the tray or plate and cover the pot.

CHINESE TEA 101

The Chinese discovered tea thousands of years ago, and today there is no other beverage more popular in China. It is common to see a glass jar full of green tea tucked beside the seat of a taxi driver or a mug of green tea resting on the desk of an office worker.

All tea leaves come from the same plant species, but the way that the leaves are processed changes their color and flavor. Freshly picked tea leaves can be dried immediately to produce green or white tea. They can also be allowed to ferment for a period of time to produce other varieties of tea, such as black tea, with varying intensities of flavor and color. Appreciating tea is like appreciating fine wine. High-quality tea has layers of complex flavors, and its taste is influenced by the soil and climate where the tea was grown. We visited a tea plantation in Xishuangbanna, an area in China's Yunnan Province famous for growing pu'er tea. We saw mountain after mountain there ringed with tiny tea shrubs. The tea smelled and tasted earthy and mossy with a hint of sweetness—reminiscent of the jungle around us.

When making most Chinese teas, you don't need to keep the tea leaves separate in a tea infuser or filter them out before serving. Simply add the tea leaves to the boiled water in a teapot or directly in a teacup. When the leaves are done steeping, they will sink to the bottom of the pot or cup. Chinese people generally drink their tea plain, without milk, sugar, or other additives. Exceptions include Hong Kong Milk Tea (page 101), Tibetan Butter Tea (page 180), and chrysanthemum tea.

White tea (bái chá) 白茶

This is made with very young leaves, picked before they fully open, and is the least processed form of tea. The leaves are pale green in color, have a subtle, light flavor, and contain the least amount of caffeine. The most popular white tea is silver needle tea (bái háo yín zhēn, 白毫银针) from Fujian Province.

Green tea (lù chá) 绿茶

Green tea leaves have been dried or steamed after picking to halt the fermentation process. When brewed, the tea is golden in color and has a light, grassy flavor.

Oolong tea (wū lóng chá) 乌龙茶

These tea leaves have been only partially fermented. When brewed, the tea has an earthy flavor and is golden in color.

Black tea (hóng chá) 红茶

Called "red tea" in Chinese, black teas have been allowed to ferment until the leaves turn a black color. This is the type of tea most people drink in the West and includes varieties like English Breakfast tea and Earl Grey tea. It is not very popular in China except in Hong Kong, where it is used to make Hong Kong Milk Tea (page 101).

Pu'er tea (pǔ ěr chá) 普洱茶

This type of tea is made of black or green tea leaves that have been aged to acquire a faintly musty, hay-like flavor. It is produced exclusively in Yunnan Province and is often sold in compressed round disks called "bricks" to make it easier to store and transport.

Flower tea (hūa chá) 花茶

These types of teas are made by adding flower petals or whole flower heads to a base of green or black tea leaves. Flower teas have a sweet flavor and wonderful floral aroma. Two types are particularly important to the Chinese:

Jasmine tea *mò lì hūa chá* 茉莉花茶
A very popular type of flower tea is made with jasmine flowers. It has a strong floral taste and smell. Whenever I drink jasmine tea while back home in New York, the flavor transports me back to China.

Chrysanthemum tea *jú huā chá* 菊花茶
This is a type of flower tea made from the whole heads of the white chrysanthemum flower. It is thought to help digestion and is usually drunk with rock sugar.

DUMPLING FOLDING TIPS

Truth is, it's hard to make a bad dumpling. Sure, your dumpling may not win any beauty contests, but as long as it stays closed while cooking, it will taste just as lip-smackingly scrumptious as those that do. If you're making Jiaozi Dumplings (page 12), Guotie Pot Stickers (page 42), or Vegetable Momo Dumplings (page 190), use the crimped edge fold method. However, if you don't want to attempt the traditional crimped edge fold, simply use the half-moon fold method by folding the dumpling wrapper in half over the filling to make a half-moon shape. For Shanghai Soup Dumplings (page 51), use the pomegranate fold. Homemade dumpling wrappers do not need water to make a seal.

Crimped Edge Fold

1. Hold a dumpling wrapper in the palm of your hand and place the filling in the center. Dip your finger in a bowl of water and run it around the edge to help make a good seal.

2. Lightly fold the wrapper over on itself, but don't touch the edges together. Starting at one end, use your fingers to make a small pleat on the side of the wrapper closest to you.

3. Press the pleat into the other side and pinch together firmly.

4. Keep making pleats down the dumpling opening in this way until completely sealed.

Half-Moon Fold

1. Hold a dumpling wrapper in the palm of your hand and place the filling in the center. Dip your finger in a bowl of water and run it around the edge to help make a good seal.

2. Lightly fold the wrapper over on itself, and then press the edges together to make a seal.

Pomegranate Fold

1. Place a dumpling wrapper on a work surface and then place the filling in the center of the wrapper.

2. Use your fingers to make a series of small pleats around the edge of the wrapper until all the pleats come together at the dumpling's top.

3. Twist the pleats shut to seal the dumpling.

DUMPLING FREEZING TIPS

Once you're on a roll folding dumplings, it's a good idea to make more than you will actually eat and freeze the extra for later. We always find ourselves reaching for frozen dumplings when we need to put a meal together quickly. However, if you throw all the freshly made dumplings into a plastic bag, they will freeze stuck together into one giant block of dumplings. To avoid this, first spread out the uncooked dumplings on a lightly greased baking sheet, taking care that they do not touch each other. Place the sheet in the freezer for about 30 minutes. Then throw all the dumplings into a large resealable plastic bag and store in the freezer. When you are ready to eat them, do not defrost the dumplings, but cook them frozen exactly like you would fresh dumplings—just add 3 minutes to the cooking time.

HOW TO MAKE RICE

When people eat white rice in China, they usually eat the short-grain variety. Short-grain rice contains more starch than long-grain rice, which makes it clump more and consequently easier to pick up with chopsticks. Long-grain rice, which doesn't clump, is better suited for fried-rice dishes. We encourage you to invest in a rice cooker, which makes the rice come out perfectly every time. However, if you don't have a rice cooker, you can easily cook rice on the stovetop with this recipe.

MAKES 2 CUPS

1 cup short-grain or long-grain white rice
1 cup water for short-grain rice, or 1⅔ cups water for long-grain rice

Combine the rice and water in a medium saucepan over high heat. Bring to a boil, stir a few times, and then decrease the heat to a gentle simmer and cook, covered, for 18 minutes. Do not lift the lid.

Remove the saucepan from the burner and let rest, covered, for 15 minutes. Remove the lid and fluff the rice with chopsticks or a fork before serving.

CHILI OIL 辣椒油

Chili oil is an ingredient that gives a jolt of heat to many Chinese dishes. Cooks add it to soups, stir-fries, and it is often a condiment on restaurant tabletops. You can buy it bottled at Asian grocery stores or easily make your own.

MAKES 1 CUP

1 cup peanut oil or vegetable oil
3 tablespoons toasted sesame oil
4 tablespoons crushed red chile flakes

Heat the peanut oil and sesame oil in a wok over medium heat until a piece of a chile sizzles when added to the oil but doesn't turn black. Remove the wok from the heat and stir in the chile flakes. Let the oil cool to room temperature, and then strain through a wire strainer or cheesecloth. The oil will keep in a sealed container in the refrigerator for up to 3 months.

DUMPLING WRAPPERS · 饺子皮

You can buy premade Chinese dumpling wrappers from any Asian grocery store, and in most cases they work as well and taste as good as homemade wrappers. However, Shanghai Soup Dumplings (page 51) should be made with homemade wrappers or they will not hold their soup when steaming. If you are making wrappers for Shanghai Soup Dumplings, try to keep the center of the wrappers thicker than the edges when rolling the dough disks.

MAKES 52 WRAPPERS

3 cups all-purpose flour
1 cup boiling water
3 tablespoons cold water

To make the dough in an electric mixer, place the flour in the work bowl of the mixer and slowly mix in the boiling water with a dough hook and then add the cold water to form a dough. Transfer the dough to a lightly floured work surface and knead for an additional 5 minutes by hand, or until it is soft and smooth. Divide the dough in half and then roll into 2 cylinders (about 1 inch in diameter). Cover the cylinders with plastic wrap and let rest for 30 minutes.

Alternatively, to make the dough by hand, place the flour in a large bowl and slowly stir in the boiling water. Then add the cold water and mix until well combined. Turn out the dough onto a lightly floured work surface and knead for 10 minutes, or until the dough is soft and smooth. Divide the dough in half and then roll into 2 cylinders (about 1 inch in diameter). Cover the cylinders with plastic wrap and let rest for 30 minutes.

Use a sharp knife to cut each of the cylinders into 26 rounds, and cover the rounds with plastic wrap when not working with them so that they don't dry out. Roll each round into a ball. Then on a lightly floured work surface, flatten each ball into a 3-inch-wide disk, first with the palm of your hand and then using a mini rolling pin and working in a circular motion. The wrappers will keep in the refrigerator wrapped in plastic wrap for up to 2 days.

WHOLE WHEAT MOMO DUMPLING WRAPPERS · 西藏饺子皮

These whole-wheat wrappers are healthy and tasty. They are used to wrap Tibetan Momo Dumplings (page 190) and they are a little thicker and more filling than traditional dumpling wrappers.

MAKES 48 WRAPPERS

1 cup whole wheat flour
2 cups all-purpose flour
1 cup boiling water
¼ cup cold water

To make the dough in an electric mixer, combine the whole-wheat flour and all-purpose flour in the work bowl of the mixer and slowly mix in the boiling water with a dough hook and then add the cold water to form a dough. Transfer the dough to a lightly floured work surface and knead for an additional 5 minutes by hand, or until it is soft and smooth. Divide the dough in half and then roll into 2 cylinders (about 1 inch in diameter). Cover the cylinders with plastic wrap and let rest for 30 minutes.

Alternatively, to knead the dough by hand, sift the whole wheat flour and all-purpose flour together in a large mixing bowl and slowly stir in the boiling water. Then add the cold water and mix until well combined. Turn out the dough onto a lightly floured work surface and knead for 10 minutes, or until the dough is soft and smooth. Divide the dough in half and then roll into 2 cylinders (about 1 inch in diameter). Cover the cylinders with plastic wrap and let rest for 30 minutes.

Use a sharp knife to cut each of the cylinders into 24 rounds, and cover the rounds with plastic wrap when not working with them so that they don't dry out. Roll each round into a ball. Then on a lightly floured work surface, flatten each ball into a 3-inch-wide disk first with the palm of your hand and then using a mini rolling pin and working in a circular motion. The wrappers will keep in the refrigerator wrapped in plastic wrap for up to 2 days.

MANDARIN PANCAKES 北京烤鸭面饼

These are the thin crêpes used to wrap up Peking Duck (page 11). We recommend buying them frozen at an Asian grocery store, but if you cannot find them you can easily make them at home with this recipe.

MAKES 12 PANCAKES

1¾ cups all-purpose flour
¾ cup boiling water
½ teaspoon vegetable oil
2 tablespoons toasted sesame oil

To make the dough in a mixer, place the flour in the work bowl of an electric mixer and slowly mix in the boiling water and vegetable oil with a dough hook to form a dough. Transfer the dough to a lightly floured work surface and knead for an additional 5 minutes by hand, or until it is soft and smooth. Cover the dough with plastic wrap and let rest for 30 minutes.

Alternatively, to knead the dough by hand, place the flour in a large mixing bowl and slowly stir in the water and vegetable oil until well incorporated. Turn out the dough onto a lightly floured surface and knead for about 10 minutes, or until smooth. Cover the dough with plastic wrap and let rest for 30 minutes.

Roll the dough out into a 12-inch-long cylinder and use a sharp knife to cut the cylinder into 12 rounds. Smash each round into a 2-inch-wide disk using the palm of your hand. Brush the tops of the disks with the sesame oil and stack the disks in 6 pairs, placing the oiled sides together. On a floured work surface and using a floured rolling pin, roll each of the pairs into thin 7-inch disks.

Heat a dry nonstick skillet over medium-high heat and cook a pancake for about 1 minute, or until it begins to bubble. Flip the pancake and cook for another 30 seconds. Remove the hot pancake from the heat and use your hands to peel it apart into 2 Mandarin pancakes. Repeat this process with the remaining dough disks, stacking the thin pancakes on top of one another as they are completed. Serve warm.

You can make these pancakes ahead of time and freeze them for up to 3 months. Before serving, thaw the pancakes and then warm the individual pancakes in a dry skillet over high heat.

HAND-TORN NOODLES · 面片

These noodles are easy to make and form. You can make the dough up to 3 hours ahead of time, just make sure to keep them covered with plastic wrap so they don't dry out. When you are ready to cook them, tear the dough into small pieces and throw them directly into a pot of boiling water or soup to cook.

MAKES 1 POUND

1 cup cake flour
1 cup all-purpose flour
½ teaspoon salt
¾ cup warm water
1 teaspoon vegetable oil

In a large bowl, sift together the cake flour, all-purpose flour, and salt. Slowly stir in the water until well incorporated. Turn out the dough onto a lightly floured surface and knead for 10 minutes, or until the dough is very smooth and elastic. Use a knife to divide the dough into 6 equal pieces. Roll each piece into a 7-inch-long cylinder, and then use the palm of your hand to lightly flatten the cylinders into strips. Brush both sides of the strips with oil, cover with plastic wrap, and let rest for 30 minutes.

To cook the noodles, hold a dough strip between your hands. Gently pull the dough into a 4-foot-long strip by gently swinging the center of the dough up and down as it stretches between your hands. Wrap one end of the dough strip loosely around your wrist and hold the other end between your thumb and index finger of the same hand. Use your thumb and index finger to advance the dough; pinch flat and tear off 1-inch pieces of the dough with your other hand. Throw the pieces into a pot of boiling water or soup. Cook the noodles for 8 to 10 minutes, or until they are tender.

CHICKEN STOCK · 鸡汤

Chicken stock serves as the base for most Chinese soups, and it is used to add a depth of flavor to many sauces. You can buy it fresh from specialty grocery stores or make your own with this recipe. Fresh stock tastes far superior to canned broth or bouillon, but if you don't have the time or patience to make your own, substitute canned low-sodium chicken broth. We like to freeze stock in ice cube trays and then place the frozen cubes in a large freezer bag. Whenever a recipe calls for stock, we just grab a few cubes from the freezer.

MAKES ABOUT 14 CUPS

Rinse the chicken parts and trim any excess fat. Place the chicken parts, garlic, green onions, ginger, onion, salt, and water in a large stockpot. Bring to a boil over high heat, and then immediately lower the heat to a simmer and cook uncovered for 2 hours. Use a ladle to skim any foam, fat, or scum off of the surface as often as necessary.

Strain the stock through a wire strainer or cheesecloth. When the stock cools, skim off any fat that has solidified on the surface. The stock will keep in a sealed container in the refrigerator for up to 3 days and in the freezer for up to 3 months.

4½ pounds raw chicken bones (wings, backs, necks, legs, or a mixture)

8 cloves garlic, smashed with the side of a knife

4 green onions, green and white parts, halved

1 (2-inch) piece ginger, sliced

1 medium onion, coarsely chopped

1 teaspoon salt

6 quarts cold water

BEEF STOCK · 牛肉汤

Chinese cooks make beef stock by simmering beef bones with spices like cinnamon, star anise, and ginger, which gives the stock a rich, spiced flavor. Just like with chicken stock, we like to freeze stock in ice cube trays and then place the frozen cubes in a large freezer bag. Whenever a recipe calls for stock, we just grab a few frozen cubes.

MAKES ABOUT 8 CUPS

Blanch the bones in a large stockpot of boiling water for 2 minutes. Then drain the bones by pouring the contents of the stockpot through a colander set in the sink. Place the bones back in the stockpot and add the cold water. Bring to a boil over high heat, and then immediately lower the heat to a simmer, skimming with a ladle to remove any foam, fat, or scum that floats to the surface. Add the star anise, cinnamon, ginger, onion, white pepper, and salt and simmer uncovered for 4 hours, skimming when necessary.

Strain the stock through a wire strainer or cheesecloth. When the stock cools, skim off any fat that has solidified on the surface. The stock will keep in a sealed container in the refrigerator for up to 3 days and in the freezer for up to 3 months.

6 pounds meaty beef soup bones, cut into 2-inch pieces (ask the butcher to do this for you)

5 quarts cold water

3 star anise

1 cinnamon stick

1 (3-inch) piece ginger, sliced

1 medium onion, coarsely chopped

¼ teaspoon freshly ground white pepper

½ teaspoon salt

SAMPLE MENUS

Chinese food is the perfect food for dinner parties. Some of the dishes, like hot pot and dumplings, lend themselves to making with your guests (start a dumpling assembly line!). Also, most Chinese dishes are served family style in the center of the table, which encourages everyone to interact. Give guests an empty plate and chopsticks and instruct them to go for it.

To add a little pizzazz to the table setting, we like to cover the dining table with Chinese newspaper, which you can buy in Chinatown or at an Asian grocery store. The pictures and words on the newspaper are a conversation starter, and the newspaper catches any stray drips and pieces of food dropped by first-time chopstick users. Here are a few sample menus that we like to cook for friends.

EASY LUNCH
Bang Bang Chicken p. 207
Jungle Passion Fruit Smoothie p. 168

BACKYARD BARBECUE
Naan Flatbread p. 234
Grilled Lamb Kebabs with Yogurt p. 232
Kashgar Onion Salad p. 239
Mango Pudding p. 110
Dragon Fruit Sangria p. 134

IMPRESS YOUR FRIENDS DINNER PARTY
Hot and Sour Soup p. 6
Peking Duck p. 11
Stir-Fry Baby Bok Choy p. 112
Sweet and Sour Shrimp p. 112
Bread Bun Dessert p. 7
Strawberry-Chile Cocktail p. 213

INFORMAL DINNER PARTY
Wild Mushroom Salad p. 158
Pineapple Rice p. 169
Dai Banana Leaf Fish p. 163
Fried Bananas p. 168
Lychee Martini p. 20

CLASSIC CHINESE MEAL
Guotie Pot Stickers p. 42
Kung Pao Chicken p. 213
Stir-Fry Sugar Snap Peas p. 93
White rice p. 257
Jasmine tea p. 255

EVERYBODY JOIN IN
Sichuan Hot Pot p. 210
Sesame Dipping Sauce p. 31
Chocolate Sesame Balls p. 21
Hong Kong Milk Tea p. 101

THIS IS CHINESE FOOD?
Dai Tomato-Mint Salad p. 155
African Chicken p. 130
Macanese Fried Rice p. 143
Danta Vanilla Custard Tarts p. 132
The Shanghai Lil Cocktail p. 41

GLOSSARY

Try showing the sales clerk this book and pointing to the Chinese names that follow if you have trouble finding an ingredient on the shelves of an Asian grocery store. Also check our Web site (www.feedingthedragon.com) for pictures of ingredients and more information.

If you have yet to feel the thrifty rush that comes from shopping at an Asian grocery store, we recommend you do so. Not only are the Asian spices and sauces much, much cheaper than the ones you will find elsewhere but Western spices and produce are comparatively inexpensive as well.

Alum 明矾 (*míng fán*): Powdered alum (crystallized potassium aluminum sulfate) is a white powder used in pickling to help vegetables keep their crispness. It is also used when making Chinese Youtiao Fried Dough Sticks (page 63) to give them a crispy outside. You can buy alum in the spice section of a specialty grocery store or at online spice Web sites. Note: Alum is toxic for humans if more than 1 ounce is consumed.

Asian chili powder 辣椒粉 (*là jiāo fěn*): Find this spice made of pure ground dried red chiles in the spice section, or make your own by grinding dried red chiles into a fine powder using a coffee grinder or mortar and pestle. This spice is different than regular chili powder which is often a mixture of many different spices.

Asian chili sauce 辣椒汁 (*là jiāo jiàng*): Chinese people like their food spicy. Chili sauce is a condiment that can be used to add a little heat to anything: seafood, noodles, or stir-fry dishes. It is usually made from ground chiles, vinegar, sugar, and salt. We like Tuong Ot brand sriracha sauce (the clear bottle with the bright green lid and a picture of a rooster on the label), but any Asian chili sauce or Asian hot sauce will do.

Asian eggplant 长茄子 (*cháng qié zi*): These purple eggplants are long and slender. They have less bitter seeds than their Western oblong counterparts and their skins are thinner. Find them at specialty or Asian grocery stores. They are sometimes called Chinese eggplants. Substitute any purple variety of eggplant.

Asian sesame paste 芝麻汁 (*zhī ma jiàng*): This brown paste made from ground roasted sesame seeds looks and tastes similar to peanut butter, but it has a richer, rounder flavor. It should not be confused with Mediterranean tahini, which is made with unroasted sesame seeds and tastes very different. Make sure you stir the paste before using it, because it often separates into a layer of oil and solid paste when left on the shelf for a while. Substitute creamy peanut butter.

Baby corn 玉米笋 (*yù mǐ sǔn*): Small, immature ears of corn are harvested when the ears reach 3 to 4 inches. Their flavor is not as sweet as that of mature corn, and the whole vegetable is eaten, including the cob. Baby corn is often added to Chinese stir-fries to add a crunchy texture. Find it canned in water at the supermarket or Asian grocery stores.

***Bai jiu* liquor** 白酒 (*bái jiǔ*): *Bai jiu* is a clear Chinese spirit distilled from sorghum. The taste is similar to vodka but it has a more flowery aftertaste. Some varieties have been lovingly described by expats living in China as tasting like paint thinner. *Bai jiu* has an extremely high alcohol content (between 80 and 150 proof) and is usually drunk from small ceramic cups during banquets in China by guests toasting one another. One of the most popular brands of *bai jiu* is *Erguotou* (二锅头), which comes in a distinctive green glass bottle with a red, white, and blue label. Find *bai jiu* at specialty liquor stores or at any liquor store in a Chinatown. Substitute brandy if necessary.

Bamboo shoots 竹笋 (*zhú sǔn*): Bamboo shoots are the young sprouts of an edible variety of bamboo. They are harvested just after the shoots peek above the ground and before they reach 1 foot in length. They are usually a light yellow color and are a good source of fiber and potassium. They taste like a cross between asparagus and artichoke hearts and can be found canned in water at most supermarkets.

Banana leaves 香蕉叶 (*xiāng jiāo yè*): The large green leaves of the banana tree. They are used to wrap meats and seafood for grilling or steaming. The leaves add a hint of flavor and allow steam to penetrate the inside of the packet. After cooking, the packet is brought to the table and opened for a beautiful presentation, though the leaves are not eaten. Find fresh or frozen banana leaves at Asian or Latin grocery stores. Unused leaves can be refrozen. Substitute aluminum foil if you can't find them.

Barley 大麦 (*dà mài*): Barley is a hearty, light brown grain that has been used by cooks for thousands of years. It is an extremely adaptable crop and grows well in the harsh climate of Tibet. Tibetans grind it into a flour to make *tsampa*, the Tibetan staple food, and ferment it to brew chhaang, Tibetan barley beer. There are two main types of barley used in cooking. Hulled barley has had only the outer husk removed and still retains its bran and germ, which makes it very nutritious. Pearl barley has had the outer husk and bran removed, but it has also been steamed and polished so that it is less chewy and cooks faster. You can find both types of barley at health food stores and larger supermarkets.

Bean thread noodles 粉丝 (*fěn sī*): These are not really noodles but are long, clear strands of starch, usually made from mung beans or sweet potatoes. They are sometimes referred to as cellophane noodles and can be found dried at any Asian grocery store.

Black pickled rutabaga 玫瑰大头菜 (*méi guì dà tóu cài*): A pickled root similar to a turnip, it is usually finely chopped in dishes and used as a flavoring agent instead of a main ingredient. It is extremely salty, so rinse it well before cooking with it. It can be bought fresh or vacuum packed at Asian grocery stores. You may substitute Chinese pickled mustard greens.

Black rice vinegar 黑米醋 (*hēi mǐ cù*): A dark-colored vinegar made from fermented black glutinous rice, it has a sweet-smoky flavor and is often used as a dipping sauce for dumplings. Find it at Asian grocery stores. If you can't locate it, substitute balsamic vinegar.

Black tree ear fungus 黑木耳 (*hēi mù ěr*): A variety of fungus also known as cloud ear fungus, black fungus, and hairy wood ear fungus, but don't let the name scare you. It is actually mostly tasteless and is used primarily in cooking for its velvety texture. It is normally sold dried and resembles pieces of brown coral. According to traditional Chinese medicine, black fungus improves blood circulation and heart health. You may substitute sliced Chinese black mushrooms or shiitake mushrooms.

Bok choy 小油菜 (*xiǎo yóu cài*): A type of cabbage with thick pale green stalks and bright green leaves, it resembles a bunch of celery. The leaves, which have a slightly sweet flavor, can be steamed, blanched, or stir-fried. Baby bok choy is a smaller variety, with heads 3 to 4 inches in length. It is also called pak choy or pak choi. Find it at most supermarkets, or substitute spinach.

Cardamom 小豆蔻籽 (*xiǎo dòu kòu zǐ*): A spice native to Asia that is related to ginger, it has a warm, pungent taste. The spice is sold as pods as well as ground. The pods can range in color from light green to dark brown and are the size of raisins. Each pod contains about 20 small seeds that hold the spice's flavor. When cooking with cardamom pods, lightly crush the pods and then throw them whole into what you are cooking, or remove the seeds and grind them into a powder using a mortar and pestle.

Chili bean sauce 豆瓣酱 (*dòu bàn jiàng*): This savory sauce made from fermented soybeans and hot chiles is sometimes referred to as chili bean paste, hot bean paste, spicy black bean sauce, or Sichuan hot bean paste. It is sold in jars in the Asian food aisle of most supermarkets. Substitute a four-to-one ratio of Chinese black bean sauce and chili sauce.

Chili oil 辣椒油 (*là jiāo yóu*): This is a condiment made from vegetable oil or peanut oil and sometimes sesame oil that has been infused with dried red chiles, turning it a red color. You can buy it in a jar or bottle at an Asian grocery store or easily make your own (see page 257).

Chinese black bean sauce 豆豉酱 (*dòu chǐ jiàng*): A lumpy brown sauce made from fermented soybeans, it has a savory flavor and can be found in jars at most Asian grocery stores. When cooking with it, it is usually wise to omit salt from the recipe, because the sauce can taste very salty. It is sometimes referred to as black bean paste. You may substitute Chinese whole fermented black beans or chili bean sauce.

Chinese dried black mushrooms 干香菇 (*gān xiāng gū*): These are dried shiitake mushrooms and can be black, light brown, or speckled. They have thick caps, curled edges, and a meaty flavor. Although shiitake mushrooms are also available fresh and can be substituted, dried mushrooms are sometimes preferred because the drying process intensifies their flavor. Soak them in warm water for 20 minutes to rehydrate them before cooking. According to traditional Chinese medicine, these mushrooms boost the immune system and act as an aphrodisiac.

Chinese five-spice powder 五香粉 (*wǔ xiāng fěn*): This reddish brown spice made of ground star anise, fennel seeds, cloves, Sichuan peppercorns, and cinnamon can be obtained at the spice section of any supermarket.

Chinese pickled mustard greens 酸菜 (*suān cài*): These are mustard leaves that have been pickled in brine, sometimes with chile. The leaves have a slightly sour, salty taste and are used as a condiment or flavoring agent. Make sure to rinse them well before using to remove extra salt. Don't worry if you can't find these exact pickled greens at an Asian grocery store. There is a seemingly endless variety of Chinese pickled greens sold in packages, and most vary only slightly in taste and will work just fine in most dishes. These are also called preserved mustard cabbage, and preserved vegetables.

Chinese sweet noodle sauce 甜面酱 (*tián miàn jiàng*): This thick, dark brown sauce has a rich, savory flavor and is often used in marinades for meats or as a condiment. It is made from sweetened fermented soybeans. This is the sauce normally eaten with Peking duck, not hoisin sauce, which is sweeter. It is sometimes referred to as sweet bean sauce, sweet soybean paste, or sweet flour sauce. It is sold in jars at Asian grocery stores.

Cilantro 香菜 (*xiāng cài*): This annual herb looks similar to parsley and the leaves have a sharp citrusy taste. It is not only popular in Asia but also is an important ingredient in Mexican and South American cuisine. It is sometimes referred to as coriander or Chinese parsley.

Cinnamon 肉桂 (*ròu guì*): This brown spice comes from the bark of a type of evergreen tree. Chinese cooks usually use a type of cinnamon known as cassia. Cassia has a thicker bark and less delicate flavor than Ceylon cinnamon. Cinnamon is sold whole as quills of bark or in powdered form. You may use either variety in these recipes.

Clear rice vinegar 白米醋 (*bái mǐ cù*): Clear rice vinegar is made from fermented white rice and has a milder flavor than Western white vinegar. Find it bottled at any Asian grocery store or most supermarkets. You may substitute cider vinegar.

Coconut milk 椰子汁 (*yē zi zhī*): Not to be confused with the water drained from the inside of a coconut, coconut milk is a sweet, milky white liquid made from blending the white flesh of a coconut with water in a blender and then straining the liquid. You can buy it canned at any Indian or Asian grocery store and at larger supermarkets.

Coriander seeds 香菜籽 (*xiāng cài zǐ*): These are the dried light brown seeds of the coriander (cilantro) plant. The seeds have a light, lemony flavor and are used in Xinjiang cuisine. Find them in the spice section of the supermarket.

Crushed red chile flakes 干辣椒碎 (*gān là jiāo suì*): These are made from finely chopped dried red chiles, including their seeds. These are the same flakes often sprinkled on pizza in the West.

Cumin 孜然 (*zī rán*): This yellowish brown spice is sold as whole seeds or ground into a powder. It has an aromatic, nutty flavor and is used in Tibetan and Xinjiang cuisine.

Curry powder 咖喱粉 (*gā lí fěn*): A bright yellow powdered spice made from a blend of more than a dozen spices such as fennel seed, fenugreek, saffron, coriander, and turmeric (which gives the spice its distinctive yellow color). Common in Indian cuisine, it is used in Tibet, Xinjiang, and also Macau, where it was introduced by Portuguese traders who brought it from India.

Daikon radish 白萝卜 (*bái luó bo*): Sometimes referred to as Japanese radish or Chinese radish, these roots resemble a very large white carrot. Eaten raw, they taste like a mild red radish, but they lose their spiciness and taste more like a turnip after being cooked. Store them for weeks without their leaves in a cool, dry place. Substitute white turnip if you can't find daikon radish.

Dried red chiles 干辣椒 (*gān là jiāo*): Whole Asian dried red chile peppers are 2 to 3 inches long. You can buy inexpensive bags of them at Asian grocery stores or pricier jars of Asian chiles at most Western supermarkets in the spice section. Their spicy seeds are usually removed before cooking.

Dried tangerine peel 陈皮 (*chén pí*): When cooked in a dish, these dried brownish orange pieces of peel add a nutty, faintly orangy flavor; they are usually discarded before serving the dish. When the peels are simmered in a soup, they can be added directly, but otherwise they should be rehydrated in warm water before using. According to traditional Chinese medicine, dried tangerine peel can be used to treat indigestion problems, and eating it plain can cure a hangover. It is sold in bags at Asian grocery stores, but you can easily dry your own. The next time you eat a tangerine, save the skin and use a spoon to scrape off most of the white pith. Leave the peels in a dry place until they are hard and dry. Store in a tightly covered container for up to 1 year. These are also called dried mandarin orange peel.

Dumpling wrappers 饺子皮 (*jiǎo zi pí*): These round dough wrappers form the skin around a variety of Chinese dumplings, such as Jiaozi Dumplings (page 12), Guotie Pot Stickers (page 42), and Shanghai Soup Dumplings (page 51). They are usually made with only wheat flour. Making them from scratch can be quite time-consuming, so if you are short on time, we recommend buying them premade from an Asian grocery store. If you want to make them yourself, follow the recipe on page 258. They are also known as dumpling skins.

Edamame beans 毛豆 (*máo dòu*): Edamame is the Japanese name for fresh soybeans, and they can be bought fresh or frozen at most supermarkets. They should be blanched or steamed before eating. If they come in pods, they must first be shelled. The beans are extremely healthy and are rich in protein and vitamins A, B, and C.

Fenugreek seeds 胡芦巴籽 (*hú lú bā zǐ*): These tan-colored seeds are used as a spice in Tibetan and Indian cooking. The aromatic seeds have a sweet, slightly bitter flavor that is somewhat similar to maple syrup. The seeds are very hard and should be first dry-roasted in a pan and then crushed before using. Find them in the spice sections of specialty grocery stores or at an Indian grocery store.

Fish sauce 鱼露 (*yú lù*): Popular throughout Southeast Asia, fish sauce is a thin, amber-colored liquid made from salt and fermented fish. It is typically used as a flavor enhancer in soups and sauces. At first whiff it smells like dirty socks, but when it is combined with other ingredients its unpleasant smell disappears and it brings out a dish's natural umami flavor. We like to add a dash of fish sauce to non-Asian dishes, like spaghetti Bolognese, to increase their flavor. It is sold bottled at Asian grocery stores.

Ginger 生姜 (*shēng jiāng*): Fresh gingerroot is a spice added to many Chinese dishes. The tan-colored roots are knobby and look kind of like stubby fingered hands. Gingerroot has a refreshing lemony flavor and a light spiciness. It should usually be peeled before cooking. In addition to its culinary use, traditional Chinese medicine hails ginger as a cure for everything from the common cold to poison ingestion to nausea. Ground ginger is not a substitute because it has a completely different flavor.

Glutinous rice flour 糯米粉 (*nuò mǐ fěn*): Contrary to its name, glutinous rice flour does not contain gluten and is fine for gluten-free diets. It is made from a type of short-grain rice that becomes very sticky and gluey when cooked. You can find this flour at Asian grocery stores. Sometimes it is called sticky rice flour.

Green onions 小葱 (*xiǎo cōng*): These onions have small white bulbs and long green stalks. To prepare them for cooking, slice off the bottom 1 inch of the root and discard. Some recipes call for the white parts and green parts to be added at separate times during cooking because they cook at different rates. They are very similar to scallions and can be used interchangeably.

Hoisin sauce 海鲜酱 (*hǎi xiān jiàng*): A Chinese condiment similar to barbeque sauce, it has a sweet, tangy, mildly fruity flavor and is made with fermented soybeans, garlic, vinegar, and sugar. While it is often thought to be the sauce eaten with Peking duck, Beijingers actually eat that dish with sweet noodle sauce. Hoisin sauce is readily available in the Asian food aisle of the supermarket.

Jujubes 干枣 (*gān zǎo*): These fruits are sometimes called Chinese dates or red dates. Fresh jujubes resemble small red apples and are often eaten as a snack with tea or added to soups for flavor. They have a sweet and tangy flavor and are sometimes used medicinally to reduce stress and soothe a sore throat. Dried jujubes are sold in bags and can be found at most Asian grocery stores. If you can't find them, substitute dried dates.

Leek flower sauce 韭菜花酱 (*jiǔ cài huā jiàng*): A dark green condiment made from the Chinese leek flower plant (Chinese chives), this sauce has a strong garlicky flavor and should be used in small quantities so that it doesn't overpower a dish. You can find it in jars at Asian grocery stores.

Lemongrass 香茅草 (*xiāng máo cǎo*): The long, thin green stalks of the lemongrass plant are used to flavor Yunnanese and Southeast Asian cuisine. True to its name, it has a lemony fresh flavor. Most of the stalk is rough and woody, so only the tender lower 4 inches are used in cooking. Lemongrass stalks can be found fresh at most specialty grocery stores next to other fresh herbs.

Lily buds 金针菜 (*jīn zhēn cài*) or 黄花菜 (*huáng huā cài*): These yellow day lily flower buds are sometimes called tiger lily buds or golden needles. They have a delicate, musky flavor. The buds are sold dried and packaged in bags at Asian grocery stores. Before cooking with lily buds, soak them in warm water for 20 minutes and remove any hard stem tips. There is no substitute; however, it is often okay to omit lily buds from a recipe because they are added mostly for texture rather than flavor.

Lotus root 藕 (*ǒu*): The large pink lotus flowers that float on the top of lakes in China grow from roots anchored in the mud below the surface. The roots resemble large white potatoes strung together like sausage links, and they are a common vegetable eaten in China. When sliced, the inside of a lotus root has holes that make a lacy pattern. You can buy them fresh or canned at Asian grocery stores. Substitute potatoes or jicama if you can't find lotus root.

Lychee 荔枝 (*lì zhī*): A fruit native to Southeast Asia that grows in grape-like bunches, they have a distinctive flavor—floral, sweet, and tart. They have rough purple skins and white translucent flesh with a large seed in the center. Peel and remove the seed before eating the flesh. Buy them fresh or canned in syrup at Asian grocery stores.

Mandarin pancakes 北京烤鸭面饼 (*běi jīng kǎo yā miàn bǐng*): Thin wheat crêpes that look similar to Mexican tortillas, they are used to roll up duck meat and other fillings when eating Peking duck. You can make them yourself with the recipe on page 260, or go the easy route and buy them frozen from an Asian grocery store. If using frozen ones, they should be warmed individually in a dry skillet just before serving. They are also called Mandarin crêpes or duck pancakes.

Matcha green tea powder 抹茶 (*mǒ chá*): A type of finely ground green tea powder used to color and flavor drinks and baked goods, matcha is actually a Japanese variety of green tea powder, but it is the most readily available tea powder in the West and the best quality for baking. Matcha may seem expensive, but a little goes a long way. You can substitute Chinese green tea powder or grind your own from loose green tea leaves in a coffee grinder or spice grinder. Find matcha at specialty tea shops or online.

MSG 味精 (*wèi jīng*): Also known as monosodium glutamate, this seasoning has gained a bad reputation in the West. It is a naturally occurring amino acid that is found in many vegetables, especially in seaweed. It doesn't really have a flavor of its own, but when it is added to a dish it brings out a dish's umami flavor. Umami is sometimes referred to as the "fifth taste" and is a cross between a salty and a sweet flavor. In China, MSG is sometimes added with a heavy hand, which can make dishes tend to taste all the same, but when used sparingly, it does wonders for flavor. We don't cook with MSG, but if you want to, you can find it at any Asian grocery store. It is a white powder that looks similar to salt and is usually sold in bags. Chances are you already eat MSG every day. It is a flavoring ingredient in most salad dressings, bagged chips, canned broths, and fast food.

Mung bean flour 绿豆粉 (*lǜ dòu fěn*): This is a very fine flour made from ground mung beans. Dough made with the flour turns translucent when cooked. It is used in making glass noodles and various pastries. Find the flour at Asian grocery stores.

Mung bean sprouts 绿豆芽 (*lǜ dòu yá*): The crunchy sprouts of germinated mung beans have the green buds still attached. Choose sprouts that are crisp and dry; avoid wet or slimy-looking ones. Fresh mung bean sprouts are available at most grocery stores, but you can also easily grow your own. Soak 1 cup of mung bean seeds overnight in water, then drain and place them in a large bowl covered by a damp towel. Rinse the seeds twice a day for 4 to 5 days, or until the sprouts grow to 3 inches long. Fresh bean sprouts will keep for up to 2 weeks in a sealed container. Soybean sprouts are a good substitute. Find them at Asian grocery stores or health food stores.

Napa cabbage 大白菜 (*dà bái cài*): This hearty cabbage originating in northern China has long white, tightly packed leaves with pale green tips. It is an excellent source of potassium, folic acid, and vitamin A. It is also known as Chinese cabbage. You may substitute savoy cabbage.

Noodles 面条 (*miàn tiáo*): Chinese cooks use a variety of noodles. The chewy texture of fresh round noodles is great in soups in which you want the noodles to soak up flavor; fresh noodles can be purchased at Asian grocery stores. Japanese udon noodles are a good substitute for fresh noodles. Dried Asian egg and rice noodles can be bought at most supermarkets and stored unopened for up to 1 year.

Oyster sauce 蚝油 (*háo yóu*): This thick brown sauce made from oysters, brine, and sugar has a light, salty taste and is used as a condiment and frequently added to stir-fries to enhance flavor. It is sold in bottles in the Asian food aisle of the supermarket.

Paprika: This is a spice made from ground red peppers that is used to add color and sometimes heat to dishes. There are two main varieties: sweet paprika 甜椒粉 (*tián jiāo fěn*) and hot paprika 红辣椒粉 (*hóng là jiāo fěn*).

Peanut oil 花生油 (*huā shēng yóu*): Made from peanuts, this cooking oil is sometimes called groundnut oil. It has a slight peanut taste and a high smoking point, which makes it excellent for deep-frying. It should not be used when someone has a peanut food allergy. Canola oil is a good substitute.

Pine nuts 松仁 (*sōng rén*): These ivory-colored teardrop-shaped nuts come from the pinecones that grow on certain varieties of evergreen trees. These nuts are high in fat and can be stored in the refrigerator for up to 3 months. There are two types of pine nuts available, Italian pine nuts and Chinese pine nuts. We recommend cooking with Italian pine nuts, as the Chinese variety can have a lingering bitter taste. Italian pine nuts are sometimes referred to as pignoli nuts.

Pork belly 五花肉 (*wǔ huā ròu*): This is meat from the belly of a pig and is the same cut of meat used to make bacon. It is very fatty and flavorful. You may substitute fatty pork loin.

Red fermented bean curd 红腐乳 (*hóng fǔ rǔ*): This mixture is made of small cubes of tofu that have been fermented with soybeans, salt, vinegar, and oil. It is used as a condiment and flavoring in Chinese cooking and has a strong savory flavor. The cubes are sold in jars in a red liquid and should be mashed into a paste before using. It is sometimes called tofu cheese and can be bought at any Asian grocery store.

Sesame oil 香油 (*xiāng yóu*): Made from sesame seeds, there are two kinds, light (untoasted) and toasted. The light variety can be used for cooking. The toasted variety is an amber-colored oil made from roasted and pressed sesame seeds. It is very fragrant and has a slight peanut flavor. It is generally not used for frying but is added at the end of cooking or as a condiment to add flavor.

Sesame seeds 芝麻 (*zhī ma*): These are small white or black seeds used to add crunch and decoration to dishes. They have a nutty, buttery taste. They are sold in jars in the spice section of supermarkets or in bags at Asian grocery stores.

Sha cha sauce 沙茶酱 (*shā chá jiàng*): Not to be confused with Thai satay peanut sauce, Chinese sha cha sauce is made with ground soybeans, garlic, and brill fish. The sauce is used by Fujianese and Taiwanese cooks to infuse soup broth with a sweet and savory flavor. Make sure you stir the sha cha sauce in the jar well before spooning it out, as the ingredients have a tendency to separate between uses. It is also called sa cha sauce, and you can find it at any Asian grocery store.

Shaoxing rice wine 绍兴酒 (*Shào xīng jiǔ*) or 黄酒 (*huáng jiǔ*): This is a variety of rice wine that comes from the Chinese city of Shaoxing in Zhejiang Province and that has a sweet, dry flavor similar to Japanese sake. It gets its amber color from the red yeast rice used during fermentation and it is commonly aged for ten or more years before selling. You can find bottles of Shaoxing rice wine in the Asian food aisle of most supermarkets.

Shiitake mushrooms (*see Chinese dried black mushrooms*) 鲜香菇 (*xiān xiāng gū*): Shiitake is the Japanese name for fresh Chinese black mushrooms and is the name they are most often given in Western supermarkets. They have thick dark brown caps, curled edges, and a meaty flavor. Their flavor is not as intense as the dried variety, and they are best suited for use in salads and stir-fries.

Shrimp paste 虾酱 (*xiā jiàng*): A pinkish-grayish sauce made from fermented shrimp ground with salt, it has a very strong, fishy, pungent odor and flavor. When used sparingly in Chinese cooking, the smell and flavor disappear and the paste enhances the flavor of the dish. It is referred to as *balichāo* in Macanese cuisine. Shrimp paste is sold in jars at Asian grocery stores.

Sichuan peppercorns 花椒 (*huā jiāo*): Actually not peppercorns but the dried outer hulls of a tiny fruit grown in Sichuan Province, these have a spicy, citrusy taste, and when eaten they create a slight tingly numbness in the mouth. They are an extremely popular flavoring in Sichuan cooking. The peppercorns are sometimes called Chinese prickly ash or Szechuan pepper. Find whole Sichuan peppercorns and ground Sichuan peppercorns (花椒 粉, *huā jiāo fěn*) at Asian grocery stores or at online spice retailers.

SOY SAUCE

Light soy sauce 生抽 (*shēng chōu*): This is the most commonly used version of the ubiquitous Chinese condiment and is sometimes just labeled as soy sauce in Western supermarkets. It is made with fermented soybeans and has a light, salty taste. Its name literally means "fresh soy sauce" because it is made from the first pressing of the soybeans after fermenting.

Dark soy sauce 老抽 (*lǎo chōu*): This is used primarily in cooking to add a brownish red coloring to a dish. It gets its distinctive color and viscosity from fermented soybeans and dark molasses. It is sometimes called superior soy sauce and can be found at specialty grocery stores or Asian grocery stores.

Spring roll wrappers 春卷皮 (*chūn juǎn pí*): These thin, square sheets of dough are used to wrap egg rolls, spring rolls, and popiah rolls. They are sometimes referred to as spring roll skins. Find them frozen at any Asian grocery store and most supermarkets.

Star anise 八角 (*bā jiǎo*): This small star-shaped spice (the Chinese name literally means "eight corners") has a flavor similar to fennel seed. It is sometimes called whole star anise and should not be confused with aniseed. Find it in its whole star form or ground into a powder in the spice section at most supermarkets or at Asian grocery stores.

Steamed bread 馒头 (*mán tou*): Chinese kitchens do not traditionally have ovens. Instead, bread dough is cooked by steaming it in stacked bamboo steamers. There are a variety of sizes available of steamed bread buns. Small buns are often fried and dipped in condensed milk, and clamshell-shaped buns can be filled with meat. You can find steamed bread buns frozen at Asian grocery stores.

Sweet red bean paste 红豆沙 (*hóng dòu shā*): This paste is made from red azuki beans boiled with sugar. It is commonly added to desserts as a filling and a flavoring. It is sold canned at Asian grocery stores. You may substitute sweet lotus paste.

Tamarind concentrate 罗望子酱 (*luó wàng zǐ jiàng*): A thick, dark brown sauce made from the fruit of a tree native to Asia, it has a sweet and sour flavor and is used in Southeast Asian, Indian, and Macanese cooking. If you cannot find the concentrate form of the fruit at a specialty grocery store or Indian market, you can buy tamarind pulp at an Indian or Spanish market, soak it in warm water, and then strain the juice and discard any bit of shell and fibers.

Tofu 豆腐 (*dòu fu*): White blocks of soybean curd made from soybeans, water, and a curdling agent, tofu is chock-full of protein and calcium and absorbs spices and flavorings well when you cook with it. There are two main types of tofu: soft/silken (also called Japanese-style) and firm/extra-firm/regular (also called Chinese-style). It is sometimes called bean curd and is sold fresh or packaged at most supermarkets.

Turmeric 姜黄粉 (*jiāng huáng fěn*): A bright yellow powder used in Chinese and Indian cooking, ground turmeric is made from grinding up a root that is related to gingerroot. It is the main ingredient in curry powder, has a slightly pungent flavor, and is primarily used as a coloring agent. We recommend wearing rubber kitchen gloves when touching it, because it will stain your hands.

Water chestnuts 荸荠 (*bí qí*): These are the tubers of a plant that grows in water. When fresh, they are small balls with a thin, dark brown skin. They have a bland flavor but are often added to stir-fries for their crunchy texture. They are sold peeled (whole or sliced) in cans or jars at supermarkets.

Winter melon 冬瓜 (*dōng guā*): A large gourd, about the size of a watermelon, with a dark green skin and white flesh, it has a light flavor similar to zucchini and is often sliced and added to soups and stir-fries. The outside of the melons can accumulate a white wax-like coating, which gives them their alternate name: wax gourd. They can be bought year-round at Asian grocery stores.

Wonton wrappers 馄饨皮 (*hún tún pí*): These square dumpling wrappers are used to wrap wonton dumplings, and they are different from the round dumpling wrappers used to wrap *jiaozi* dumplings. They are made with flour and egg and are slightly yellow in color. They are sometimes referred to as wonton skins and can be bought in packages at some supermarkets and any Asian grocery store.

ONLINE INGREDIENT RESOURCES

If you don't live near a Chinatown or an Asian grocery store, don't worry: There are many online retailers that sell hard-to-find ingredients and cooking equipment. Here are a few that we recommend.

The Wok Shop
www.wokshop.com
This shop has a great selection of Chinese cooking equipment at good prices.

Amazon.com
www.amazon.com
This site has everything from equipment to spices. If Amazon doesn't have what you're looking for, chances are one of the sellers in their network does.

Kalustyan's
www.kalustyans.com
The Web site is a little difficult to navigate, but they have a huge selection of Chinese sauces and spices for sale.

Asian Food Grocer
www.asianfoodgrocer.com
This site carries predominately Japanese food products, but they have a nice selection of Chinese sauces and dried noodles.

Ethnic Foods Co.
www.ethnicfoodsco.com
This store has a huge selection of Asian spices and ingredients, with many organic options.

WAYS TO LEARN MORE ABOUT CHINA

www.feedingthedragon.com
Our Web site is a resource of how-to videos, pictures of ingredients, and stories and news about China.

www.lonelyplanet.com
This online extension of the excellent Lonely Planet travel books is a must-see for anyone considering a visit to China.

www.nciku.com
This site features a free online Chinese-English dictionary along with many other useful language tools.

www.chinesepod.com
This is an excellent comprehensive language site for learning Chinese.

www.pleco.com
Pleco Software makes Chinese language and dictionary applications for iPhones and other smart phones.

China: A Century of Revolution
Documentary film directed by Sue Williams; Zeitgeist Films, DVD released 2007. An amazing six-hour documentary series chronicling the history of modern China, it includes rare archival footage and eyewitness interviews.

China: A Portrait of a Country
Written by James Kynge, Karen Smith, Liu Heung Shing; Taschen America LLC, 2008. A photography book documenting the development of the People's Republic of China since 1949, it includes the work of Pulitzer Prize–winning photojournalist Liu Heung Shing.

SIMPLE LANGUAGE GUIDE

Mandarin (pǔtōnghuà, 普通话, or "common language") is the official standard language of mainland China. Its pronunciation is based on the Beijing dialect, and the Chinese government mandates that it must be spoken in all schools and in all media (TV, radio, movies, and so on) throughout mainland China. However, there are hundreds of distinct and mutually incomprehensible dialects spoken locally in provinces and cities across the country. For example, Cantonese is widely spoken in Guangdong Province, Hong Kong, and Macau, while Shanghainese is commonly spoken in Shanghai. Despite the many different pronunciations of Chinese, the written word is universally understood. Written Chinese is made up of more than 50,000 Chinese characters, or ideograms, that each individually represent one syllable and one word. Many characters were originally created as recognizable pictorial representations of words or phrases, but over thousands of years they have evolved into what have become modern Chinese characters. Now there is no way to look at a character and know for sure its meaning or pronunciation other than by first memorizing it. It is estimated that a person should know 3,000 to 4,000 characters to be able to read a Chinese newspaper.

PINYIN

Pinyin is a system for phonetically transliterating Chinese using the Roman alphabet. Without such a system there would be no way to spell Chinese words or names and no way to phonetically sound out their pronunciation. It would also be even more difficult to learn Chinese as a foreigner. Before pinyin became the international standard (it was officially adopted by the People's Republic of China in 1979), the less accurate Wade-Giles system of transliteration was widely used around the world. With the switch in systems came changes in the spellings of Chinese dignitary names, cities, and other words in official documents. For example, Chairman Mao Tse-tung became Chairman Mao Zedong, the city of Nanking became Nanjing, and on menus, Peking Duck became Beijing Duck.

PRONUNCIATION AND TONES

Characters are discerned in Mandarin by assigning them one of four tones. Pronouncing these tones correctly is the most difficult part about learning to speak Chinese. If you just sound out syllables willy-nilly in Chinese like you can when speaking English, the meaning in Chinese will be unintelligible or incorrect. For example, in English you might raise your voice at the end of a sentence to indicate a question, but in Chinese doing this would completely change the meaning of the words in the sentence. As you can see below, it is very easy to say something with a different meaning than intended . . . like calling your mother a horse!

First Tone
Example: mā (mother)
Pronounced by keeping your voice at one constant pitch.

Second Tone
Example: má (numb)
Pronounced by sliding your voice from a lower pitch to a higher pitch.

Third Tone
Example: mǎ (horse)
Pronounced by sliding your voice from a higher pitch to a lower pitch and then back to a higher pitch.

Fourth Tone
Example: mà (swear)
Pronounced by sliding your voice from a higher pitch to a lower pitch.

In addition to the four tones, there is actually a fifth neutral tone that appears without a tone mark. It is normally pronounced softly and briefly, and the pitch of your voice can vary depending on what you are saying. For example, when speaking the word for mother, you pronounce the first syllable mā and leave the second toneless and unstressed: māma.

Greetings

Hello.	你好。	Nǐ hǎo.
How are you?	你好吗?	Nǐ hǎo ma?
I'm very good, and you?	我很好，你呢?	Wǒ hěn hǎo, nǐ ne?
I'm doing well. Long time no see.	我也很好。好久不见。	Wǒ yě hěn hǎo. Hǎojiǔ bujiàn.
My name is _____.	我叫_____。	Wǒ jiào _____.
Goodbye.	再见。	Zàijiàn.
Have you eaten yet?	你吃了吗?	Nǐ chī le ma?

Food Phrases

You have a big appetite!	你的胃口太好了!	Nǐ de wèikǒu tài hǎo le!
Tastes delicious!	好吃!	Hǎochī!
I would like a glass of Coca-Cola.	我要一杯可口可乐。	Wǒ yào yì bēi kěkǒukělè.
I would like an order of kung pao chicken.	我要一份宫保鸡丁。	Wǒ yào yífèn gōng bǎo jī dīng.
I'm a vegetarian. I can eat vegetables, tofu, and eggs.	我吃素。我能吃蔬菜，豆腐，和鸡蛋。	Wǒ chīsù. Wǒ néng chī shūcài, dòufu, hé jīdàn.
He can't eat spicy food.	他不能吃辣的。	Tā bùnéng chī là de.
Why hasn't my food arrived yet? I am starving!	我的菜怎么还不来? 我饿死了!	Wǒ de cài zěnme hái bùlái? Wǒ èsǐ le.
The tea is cold.	茶凉了。	Chá liáng le.
I want three bottles of beer.	来三瓶啤酒。	Lái sānpíng píjiǔ.
You sure can hold your liquor. Have another glass.	你是海量，再来一杯。	Nǐ shì hǎiliàng. Zài lái yì bēi.
Cheers!	干杯!	Gānbēi!
Oy! I am stuffed. I love Chinese food.	啊，我吃撑了。我爱死中餐了。	Ā! Wǒ chīchēng le. Wǒ àisǐ zhōngcān le.
Waiter, the bill.	服务员，买单。	Fúwùyuán, mǎidān.
The meal is my treat.	我请客。	Wǒ qǐngkè.

Helpful Words and Phrases

1 2 3 4 5 6 7 8 9 10	一 二 三 四 五 六 七 八 九 十	yī èr sān sì wǔ liù qī bā jiǔ shí
Thank you.	谢谢。	Xièxie.
Don't mention it.	不客气。	Bù kèqi.
I'm sorry.	对不起。	Duì bu qǐ.
Where is the bathroom?	厕所在哪儿?	Cèsuǒ zài nǎr?
This is my first visit to China.	这是我第一次来中国。	Zhè shì wǒ dìyīcì lái zhōngguó.
Driver, can you take me to this address?	师傅，你能把我送到这个地方吗?	Shīfu, nǐ néng bǎ wǒ sòngdào zhège dìfāng ma?
Can I get your phone number?	能给我你的电话号码吗?	Néng gěi wǒ nǐde diànhuàhàomǎ ma?
How much does it cost?	多少钱?	Duōshǎo qián?
Too expensive! We are old friends. Can't you give me a discount?	太贵了! 我们是老朋友。能便宜吗?	Tài guì le. Wǒmen shì lǎopéngyou. Néng piányi ma?
No way!	不行!	Bù xíng!
Let's dance!	我们去跳舞吧!	Wǒmen qù tiàowǔ ba!
Eh, what are you gonna do?	没办法。	Méi bànfǎ.

ACKNOWLEDGMENTS

We have so many people to thank for making this book a reality that it is hard to know where to begin. Mom and Dad, you showed us that life can and should be an adventure and passed on to us your passion for food. Thank you for always encouraging us to pursue our dreams and to achieve great things, and thank you for all the sacrifices you made to allow us to do so. We wrote this book for you.

To the most amazing literary agent any writer could possibly have, JL Stermer, we owe the publication of this book. Thank you for understanding our vision, and sculpting our awesome proposal, and pairing us with Andrews McMeel, where we could not have been in better hands. To our publisher, Kirsty Melville, thank you for your encouragement and for taking a chance on first-time authors. To our editor, Jean Lucas, thank you for your patience and guidance all along the way, and to our designer, Kate Basart, thank you for making a most beautiful book. Thanks to Qu Xiu and Tian Sanwen—you were both invaluable in editing the Chinese in this book. To our friend and brilliant photographer, Jonathan Leijonhufvud, thanks for taking an amazing photo of us in an alley south of Tiananmen Square. Every time we see the cover of the book we are reminded of your incredible generosity and talent. Also a big thanks to our copyeditor, Valerie Cimino: you amazed us with your precision and expertise.

We could not have written this book without our many amazing friends who have always been there to encourage us and taste our recipes. A special thanks to Laurel McGovern for supporting us from the very beginning and being a wonderful friend. Thanks to Lauren Thompson and Ben Hazelwood for your invaluable and insightful suggestions early on in our writing process, and to Laura Berry for joining us on part of our adventure.

A special thanks goes to all of our family. In particular we'd like to thank our grandmothers. Mary Jo Curtis (Jomom), thank you for showing us the joy that can be found in cooking meals for family. Janet Tate (Mammaw), thank you for always encouraging us to follow our dreams—no matter where they take us. Thanks to Martha Elvebak and Kelly McCormick (who might as well both be family), and also our cousin Gina Webb.

It is not possible for us to express our gratitude to all the wonderful people in China who over the years have generously shared with us their knowledge and helped us in our culinary pursuits in the making of this book. We have interviewed people from all walks of life and professions, and we specifically owe a world of gratitude to the many cooks across the country who gave us their time and guidance. A special thanks to Du Linglong, Gao Linnan, Li Bijia, Lin Yuanyuan and her family, Tess Johnson, Amelia Kallman and everyone at Gosney and Kallman's Chinatown Shanghai, Ben Miao, David Wong of the Macau Culinary Association, and Ken Wong and Mee Chun Canning Co., Ltd (Kowloon Soy).

INDIVIDUAL THANKS

Mary Kate: To Krista Anderson, thank you for helping me get through my first year of Chinese class and everything since. To Juliana Torres, thank you for inspiring me with your brilliant writing. To Paige Gregory (a.k.a. C3PG), thank you for your unconditional friendship and being so awesome. Thank you to H. Shawn Brown for believing in me, inspiring me, and for joining me on the other side of the world for a crazy biking adventure. Jen Chi Tsou, Jennifer Soo Kim and David Hertog, and Liz Entin— thank you for your priceless support and encouragement. Also thanks to Professor Wen-Hua Teng and the Asian Studies Department at the University of Texas at Austin.

Nate: To Brian Malik, thank you for your friendship— your creativity in the kitchen is inspiring. Thanks to Adam and Renée Hammonds for being fellow schemers and dreamers and encouraging me to finish this book. To Jen Dunlap, thank you for championing this project long before it was anything. Thank you to Ben Hazelwood (孔子) for your friendship and believing in this book from early on. Thanks to Siri Betts for visiting me and braving the jungles and graves in Yunnan. Thank you to Peter Buchanan-Smith, Debbie Millman, and Graham Elliott for your mentorship and encouragement. Thanks to Li Xuanxuan for all your help and kindness. Thank you to Yoje Ho and Sergio Reynoso for your positivity and friendship. Thanks to Gaia Puleston for gallivanting around China with me— your enthusiasm for Chinese culture was infectious.

SELECTED BIBLIOGRAPHY

Over the years while writing this book, we have consulted numerous publications, including books, periodicals, and cookbooks, some of which are written in Chinese. Here is a brief list of the titles that proved invaluable in our study of history, our exploration of food in Chinese culture, and our research of ingredients.

Anderson, E. N. *The Food of China*. New Haven: Yale University Press, 1988.

Chang, K. C., ed. *Food in Chinese Culture: Anthropological and Historical Perspectives*. New Haven: Yale University Press, 1977.

Chang, Leslie T. *Factory Girls*. New York: Spiegel & Grau / Random House, Inc., 2008.

Dunlop, Fuchsia. *Land of Plenty: A Treasury of Authentic Sichuan Cooking*. New York: W. W. Norton & Company, Inc., 2003.

Fairbank, John King, and Merle Goldman. *China: A New History, Second Enlarged Edition*. London: Belknap, 2006.

Farquhar, Judith. *Appetites: Food and Sex in Post-Socialist China*. Duke University Press, 2002.

Goldstein, Melvyn C. *The Snow Lion and the Dragon: China, Tibet, and the Dalai Lama*. Berkeley: University of California Press, 1999.

Lee, Calvin B. T. *Chinese Cooking for American Kitchens*. New York: Putnam, 1959.

Liu, Junru. *Chinese Food*. Beijing: China Intercontinental Press, 2009.

Maze, Laura G., and Dorothy Bowden. *Bon Appétit: Secrets from Shanghai Kitchens*. Privately printed, 1940.

So, Yan-Kit. *Yan-Kit's Classic Chinese Cookbook*. Dorling Kindersley Limited, 1984.

Spence, Jonathan D. *The Search for Modern China, Second Edition*. New York: W. W. Norton & Company, Inc., 1999.

Wang, Ling. *Tea and Chinese Culture*. San Francisco: Long River Press, 2005.

Young, Grace, and Alan Richardson. *The Breath of a Wok*. New York: Simon & Schuster, 2004.

METRIC CONVERSIONS AND EQUIVALENTS

Metric Conversion Formulas

To Convert	Multiply
Ounces to grams	Ounces by 28.35
Pounds to kilograms	Pounds by .454
Teaspoons to milliliters	Teaspoons by 4.93
Tablespoons to milliliters	Tablespoons by 14.79
Fluid ounces to milliliters	Fluid ounces by 29.57
Cups to milliliters	Cups by 236.59
Cups to liters	Cups by .236
Pints to liters	Pints by .473
Quarts to liters	Quarts by .946
Gallons to liters	Gallons by 3.785
Inches to centimeters	Inches by 2.54

Approximate Metric Equivalents

Volume

¼ teaspoon	1 milliliter
½ teaspoon	2.5 milliliters
¾ teaspoon	4 milliliters
1 teaspoon	5 milliliters
1¼ teaspoons	6 milliliters
1½ teaspoons	7.5 milliliters
1¾ teaspoons	8.5 milliliters
2 teaspoons	10 milliliters
1 tablespoon (½ fluid ounce)	15 milliliters
2 tablespoons (1 fluid ounce)	30 milliliters
¼ cup	60 milliliters
⅓ cup	80 milliliters
½ cup (4 fluid ounces)	120 milliliters
⅔ cup	160 milliliters
¾ cup	180 milliliters
1 cup (8 fluid ounces)	240 milliliters
1¼ cups	300 milliliters
1½ cups (12 fluid ounces)	360 milliliters
1⅔ cups	400 milliliters
2 cups (1 pint)	460 milliliters
3 cups	700 milliliters
4 cups (1 quart)	0.95 liter
1 quart plus ¼ cup	1 liter
4 quarts (1 gallon)	3.8 liters

Weight

¼ ounce	7 grams
½ ounce	14 grams
¾ ounce	21 grams
1 ounce	28 grams
1¼ ounces	35 grams
1½ ounces	42.5 grams
1⅔ ounces	45 grams
2 ounces	57 grams
3 ounces	85 grams
4 ounces (¼ pound)	113 grams
5 ounces	142 grams
6 ounces	170 grams
7 ounces	198 grams
8 ounces (½ pound)	227 grams
16 ounces (1 pound)	454 grams
35.25 ounces (2.2 pounds)	1 kilogram

Length

⅛ inch	3 millimeters
¼ inch	6 millimeters
½ inch	1¼ centimeters
1 inch	2½ centimeters
2 inches	5 centimeters
2½ inches	6 centimeters
4 inches	10 centimeters
5 inches	13 centimeters
6 inches	15¼ centimeters
12 inches (1 foot)	30 centimeters

Oven Temperatures

To convert Fahrenheit to Celsius, subtract 32 from Fahrenheit, multiply the result by 5, then divide by 9.

Description	Fahrenheit	Celsius	British Gas Mark
Very cool	200°	95°	0
Very cool	225°	110°	¼
Very cool	250°	120°	½
Cool	275°	135°	1
Cool	300°	150°	2
Warm	325°	165°	3
Moderate	350°	175°	4
Moderately hot	375°	190°	5
Fairly hot	400°	200°	6
Hot	425°	220°	7
Very hot	450°	230°	8
Very hot	475°	245°	9

Common Ingredients and Their Approximate Equivalents

1 cup uncooked white rice = 185 grams

1 cup all-purpose flour = 140 grams

1 stick butter (4 ounces • ½ cup • 8 tablespoons) = 110 grams

1 cup butter (8 ounces • 2 sticks • 16 tablespoons) = 220 grams

1 cup brown sugar, firmly packed = 225 grams

1 cup granulated sugar = 200 grams

Information compiled from a variety of sources, including *Recipes into Type* by Joan Whitman and Dolores Simon (Newton, MA: Biscuit Books, 2000); *The New Food Lover's Companion* by Sharon Tyler Herbst (Hauppauge, NY: Barron's, 1995); and *Rosemary Brown's Big Kitchen Instruction Book* (Kansas City, MO: Andrews McMeel, 1998).

PHOTOGRAPHY NOTES

ii: A dumpling restaurant in Menkuang Hutong, one of the narrowest alleys in Beijing.

ix: Carved stone tiger guarding a temple in the jungles of Xishuangbanna.

x: *Top*: Mary Kate rides on the back of a motorcycle, wearing a wicker helmet, in the Hakka village of Yongding in Fujian Province. *Bottom*: Nate holds a lamb he just purchased at the Kashgar Bazaar in Xinjiang Province.

xii: *Left*: Two brothers in Kashgar, Xinjiang Province, look at a digital picture Nate took of them. *Right*: Ten-year-old Guoyi Zhongshu (with his father) gives Nate and Mary Kate a Chinese calligraphy lesson at his European colonial-era mansion on Gulangyu Island located just off the coast of Xiamen, Fujian Province.

xv: Mary Kate learns to make soup dumplings in a Shanghai kitchen.

BEIJING

xvi: A construction worker in front of a construction site hidden by a canvas painted with a Chinese poem describing a beautiful village scene.

3: Buddhist monks walk across an incense smoke–clouded courtyard inside the Lama Temple.

4: A punk rock band relaxes after their concert in an abandoned roller skating rink in Wudaokou.

5: A shirtless man reads the *People's Daily* on a hot summer day in a *hutong* alley near Houhai Lake.

6: Crowds of tourists inside the Forbidden City funnel through an ancient doorway and toward the Gate of Heavenly Peace (Tiananmen).

13: One of the thousands of red lanterns hanging from the trees above Ghost Street is a blur as Mary Kate rides by on her bike.

14: A group of women play mah-jongg in a *hutong* alley.

19: A street peddler holds up a pet cricket for my inspection. Hundreds of other caged crickets are tied together and draped over the back of his bike in a giant chirping heap.

22: A soldier stands guard at Tiananmen Square below Chairman Mao's iconic portrait.

23: Typical in Beijing, men crowd a Chinese chessboard in an alley south of Tiananmen Square.

26: A lone camel and his master cross the sand dunes of the Gobi Desert in Baotou, Inner Mongolia.

28: Two horses and their riders stop for a rest on the grasslands of Inner Mongolia.

29: A horse race below towering windmills on the grasslands of Inner Mongolia.

SHANGHAI

32: In the early morning, a martial artist practices *wushu* on the Huangpu waterfront.

35: Shanghai Lil, a burlesque dancer at Gosney & Kallman's Chinatown, strikes a pose in her feathered costume.

36: *Left*: Art Deco buildings along the Bund at night. *Top*: Bikes taking a drive around the People's Square. *Bottom*: A friendly restaurant cook in the 50 Moganshan art district.

37: Local police officers break for tea.

38: *Left*: Carved lacquer boxes and opium pipes at the Dongtai Lu Antique Market. *Right*: New and antique copies of Chairman Mao's *Little Red Book* for sale.

39: *Left*: Round and flat dried noodles. *Right*: A collection of Chairman Mao pins from the days of the Cultural Revolution.

40: Famous foreign celebrities (such as Leonardo DiCaprio) as well as Chinese celebrities cover magazines for sale at a roadside newsstand.

45: An old man unleashes his homemade patriotic-themed kite into the morning sky along the Huangpu waterfront.

46: "The Bird Man," as locals in the French Concession area know him, looks on from his apartment doorway while kids play with the dozens of magpies, finches, and budgies that he hangs above the sidewalk every day.

47: A cook serves *sheng jian bao* pork dumplings to students from nearby Nanjing Normal University.

53: A local retiree and his dog exit a restaurant with a doggie-to-go bag in hand.

59: Du Linglong poses next to the communal telephone in her university dorm lobby.

60: A commuter on a scooter and cell phone whizzes past a graffiti mural at the 50 Moganshan art district.

FUJIAN

64: A couple transports impossibly huge bags of used plastic bottles and cans down Highway 324, bound for a recycling plant.

66: A fisherman aboard his colorful junk boat anchored in the South China Sea.

67: Steaming bowls of noodle soup at a roadside restaurant outside of Fuzhou.

68: The interior of a traditional *tu lou* building in the mountain village of Yongding, where the Hakka minority people have lived for centuries in clans. They live in rooms along the circular walls while all cooking and eating is done in the central courtyard.

70: *Left*: Lychee fruit for sale at Xiamen's Bashi outdoor market. *Right*: This lady left Nate and Mary Kate in her dust as she climbed a remote steep mountain pass with a tethered water buffalo trotting alongside her.

71: A fisherman displays his fresh fish at Xiamen's Bashi outdoor market.

76: An ancient hand-carved wooden door screen in a traditional courtyard home in Jiangxi Province.

80: A Chinese tourist on Gulangyu Island. When we told him that the word on his shirt, "Chimerica," is a mixture of the words "China" and "America," he said he thought it was "cool."

81: A woman holds a bowl of food close to her mouth so as not to drop any pieces with her chopsticks. Contrary to Western table manners, this practice is completely acceptable.

82: A farmer carries just-harvested napa cabbage through a rice paddy in a remote mountain valley.

83: An orange sunset shines through bamboo leaves.

87: Floating on a bamboo raft, our guide grabs a fish out of the water with his bare hands, and scales and cleans it.

88: A potter at a ceramics factory in Jingdezhen uses a potter's wheel to form a bowl.

89: A hand-painted dragon motif on a traditional blue-and-white ceramic vase in Jingdezhen.

HONG KONG

94: Restaurant and business signs jut out from buildings over the street.

97: At one of the many busy night markets on Hong Kong Island, a produce vender tries to stay cool.

98: Hong Kong and its surrounding territories viewed from atop Victoria's Peak.

99: A blur of neon signs outside of Nate's taxi window on Nathan Road.

100: A Hong Kong fashionista near Times Square in Causeway Bay.

106: Sauces and condiments for noodles at a booth at the Temple Street Night Market.

107: In the small fishing village of Tai O, a woman brings in the morning's catch of crabs, fish, eels, and shrimp to be sold at the market.

108: The Cheung Po Tsai, a Chinese junk boat, sets sail in Hong Kong Harbor.

109: A fisherman in Tai O wears a woven bamboo hat to block the sun while fishing.

115: Three generations of Hong Kong people protest "the wrath of the Communist Party" at the 7-1 March, a yearly prodemocracy protest. Their shirts bear the logo of the *Epoch Times*, an independent Hong Kong newspaper that was forced to halt printing due to being critical of the communist government.

121: Ken Wong, the third-generation owner of the soy sauce factory Kowloon Soy, uncovers a clay pot filled with fermenting soybeans.

MACAU

122: Once Macau's red-light district, the Rua da Felicidade (Happiness Street) is now a row of shops, and was once used as a stand-in for Shanghai in the movie *Indiana Jones and the Temple of Doom*.

125: A diner with a dragon tattoo and jade necklace enjoys milk tea and a Macanese pork bun at the Café Tai Lei Loi Kei.

126: *Top*: Typically colorful plastic chopsticks in Macau. *Bottom*:

Blinking neon lights on the Casino Lisboa, Macau's oldest casino.

127: A classic Macanese apartment building on the Calçada do Monte.

128: A restaurant cook in Taipa Village sorts through spinach leaves.

129: Typical noodle joint in Macau.

136: Palm tree branches at Hac Sa Beach.

139: A lion dancer performs at the grand opening of a new Dairy Queen restaurant.

140: *Left*: An old-timer in Coloane Village shows his local pride. *Right*: Hibiscus flowers on Coloane Island from a bike in motion.

141: Greyhounds at the Canidrome, Asia's only greyhound racing track.

146: Mela, a Portuguese baker in Macau, shows off the Mediterranean-style bread his bakery makes every day.

YUNNAN

148: A Dai minority man trekking through the jungles of Xishuangbanna (his water buffalo is walking just out of frame).

151: A man living on a remote tea plantation in Xishuangbanna takes a smoke break.

152: A husband and wife who graciously let us stay the night in their village home near the Sanchahe Nature Reserve. The wife is wearing her clan's traditional formal dress.

153: A tea plantation owner in Xishuangbanna brings a kettle to refill our teacups.

154: Morning light streams through cracks between the floorboards of a home on stilts as the man of the house prepares breakfast.

156: Buddhist monks on motorbikes in Xishuangbanna.

157: A pig farmer walks by a Buddhist temple in Xishuangbanna.

160: A rice paddy worker who helped us cut a path through the jungle with a machete shows us a crab he found crawling on the jungle floor.

161: Tea farmers in the Sanchahe Nature Reserve survey their tea shrubs.

167: Pumpkin seeds set out to dry in the sun.

166: A boy and girl guide their water buffalo home after a day working in a rice paddy.

170: *Left*: A Naxi minority woman in Lijiang wearing traditional Naxi dress. *Right*: A farmer in Xishuangbanna.

171: Lijiang's man-made Black Dragon Lake dates back to the Ming Dynasty. Its water is so clear that thousands of koi fish are visible below the surface.

TIBET

174: Monks at rest outside Lhasa's Jokhang Temple.

177: A Tibetan woman wearing her traditional headdress of coral, gold, and turquoise that has been passed down from her grandmother to her mother to her.

178: Monks show Nate how to make *tsampa* at a monastery in the mountains.

179: Young monks at a remote monastery line up in anticipation of getting their photo taken.

183: Yaks pull timber through mountains on the Tibetan Plateau.

186: The altitude is so high in Tibet that it feels as if you could reach up and touch the clouds in the clear sky.

188: Children in a village line up for a photo. The kid in the middle is the clear ringleader.

189: Tibetans gather in a field to drink barley beer called *chhaang*.

191: A Tibetan woman turns a row of prayer wheels with her hand and says a prayer. The surfaces of the wheels are inscribed with Buddhist prayers.

192: The Potala Palace in Lhasa was once the home of the Dalai Lama.

193: A fresco painting on a temple wall.

197: A girl sits pensively next to a spire of prayer flags in Lhasa.

SICHUAN

198: Fresh red chiles for sale at an outdoor produce market in Chengdu.

201: Our two guides on a horseback riding trek to Ice Mountain in Songpan.

202: A busy Saturday produce market in Chengdu.

203: A golden squash is carved and weighed at a market.

208: Dried red chiles are snipped with scissors and their seeds shaken out.

214: *Top*: A horseback trekking guide in Songpan. *Bottom*: Our guides cook hand-torn noodles in a pot over a campfire in Songpan.

215: Green terraced mountains near Songpan.

218: A young panda eats bamboo at the Chengdu Panda Breeding and Research Center.

219: A panda stands on his hind legs to reach the tender leaves of a bamboo stalk.

224: A Tibetan woman riding home at night in the mountains of Sichuan.

225: *Top*: Nate taking a photo near Ice Mountain. *Bottom*: Mary Kate's horse eats a dinner of oats out of a basketball feedbag.

XINJIANG

226: A devout Muslim woman sells naan bread to passersby.

228: A Uighur cook fans kebabs on a sidewalk grill.

230: Two Uighur men herd unhappy sheep through the Kashgar Bazaar.

231: A Uighur boy balances a huge bowl of fried dough twists on his head at a bazaar.

235: A baker removes naan bread from the walls of a *tandoor* oven using long steel rods.

236: A menu painted on a restaurant wall, written in both Chinese and Uighur.

237: *Top*: A potter steals a midday nap in Kashgar. *Bottom*: A wealthy Uighur family in Kashgar's Old Town sit at a table with sweets and pastries. Nate was told that the woman on the left was the family's slave. She was permitted to change into an attractive dress for this photo.

240: A cook serves hand-pulled noodles to a diner at the Kashgar Bazaar.

241: Uighur men drink cinnamon tea and eat *laghman* noodles with tomato sauce.

246: *Top*: A farmer and his wife drive a donkey cart in from the countryside loaded with goods to be sold at the Kashgar Bazaar. *Bottom*: A Uighur dancer at a vineyard in the oasis town of Turpan.

247: An ancient narrow alley in Kashgar's Old Town. Since writing this book, Old Town has been torn down by the Chinese government.

251: A spice seller in Urumqi sells his wares.

INDEX